Murderous Derbyshire

Sentenced to Death in the Twentieth Century

Murderous Derbyshire

John J. Eddleston

The Breedon Books
Publishing Company
Derby

First published in Great Britain by
The Breedon Books Publishing Company Limited
Breedon House, 44 Friar Gate, Derby, DE1 1DA.
1997

ISBN 1 85983 111 7

Printed and bound by Butler & Tanner Ltd., Selwood Printing Works, Caxton Road,
Frome, Somerset.

Colour separations by RPS Ltd, Leicester.

Jackets printing by Lawrence-Allen Colour Printers, Weston-super-Mare, Avon.

Contents

Dedication

I would like to dedicate this book to Yvonne Berger,
whose assistance in the production of this and all my
other volumes has proved so invaluable.

Acknowledgements

I would like to thank a number of people without whom
writing this book would have been much more difficult.

My greatest thanks must go to my long-suffering and
very patient partner and researcher, Yvonne Berger. She
has spent many hours with me both at the Public Record
Office and at the British Newspaper Library, poring over
documents, making copious notes and finding
illustrations suitable for inclusion in the final volume.
She has also proof-read every chapter, and her
suggestions for alterations have only ever been an
improvement.

Turning to the research side, I would like to express my
gratitude to the staff of the British Newspaper Library at
Colindale in London, and the excellent and highly
efficient staff at the Public Record Office, Kew. My
especial thanks here must go to Edward Tilley and
Josephine Matthews of the image library, who have done
a first-rate job in providing illustrations, and to Brian
Carter who copied so many original photographs for me.

Finally I would like to thank my publishers, Breedon
Books Ltd, for the faith they have shown in me, and must
make particular mention of Mr Anton Rippon who has
given me every support and encouragement.

Thank you one and all.

Introduction

THE people whose stories are told in this volume all had one thing in common. All of them were accused of taking the life of at least one other person, faced a trial for that crime, and were sentenced to hang by the neck until they were dead.

Some, such as John Silk, who beat his mother to death, Percy Atkin, who buried his wife alive, or Albert Burrows, who claimed four lives and threw the bodies down a disused mine shaft, did pay that ultimate penalty. All the others, with one exception, had their death sentences commuted to one of life imprisonment, the exception being Ernest Prince whose murder conviction was quashed on appeal and a manslaughter verdict substituted.

The killers in this book have claimed the lives of spouses, parents, friends and strangers, for motives ranging from anger to jealousy, and old-fashioned greed. Read their stories for yourself and decide if those who died at the end of a rope all deserved that fate, and equally, if all those who escaped that terrible fate, should have done so.

One final point. I would like to explain the chronology of some of the stories. In most cases, the chapters are simply in year order, starting with the earliest. Where there are two chapters in the same year, such as with 1901, the chapters are in date order of the death sentence. That is why Hobbs comes before Harrison since he was sentenced to death just two days earlier.

John J. Eddleston
Sussex
Summer 1997

Chapter One

King of the Castle

ALTHOUGH he was only 20 years old, George Edward Hobbs had already endured something of a difficult life. Living at home with his parents and a family of eight, Hobbs, as the oldest male child, had a duty to bring money into the house at 140 High Street, Eckington, just as soon as he was able. Like many others of his generation, he left school as soon as he could, and went into the mines. Unfortunately, on October 27th, 1898, when Hobbs was only 17, a fall of coal struck him on the foot and the resulting injuries rendered him unable to work again.

It was not until the summer of 1901 that he finally received some financial compensation for his injury. The sum of £100 was paid over to Hobbs, who by now had to walk with the aid of a stick. It was a considerable amount of money but much as the family might have needed it, they asked Hobbs only for enough to cover his board and lodgings. As for the rest of the cash, that appeared to be largely spent in the local pubs, for by now George Hobbs had become rather fond of drink. Indeed, so much did he consume that by the middle of July there was only £5 5s left.

Wednesday, July 17th, 1901, was a glorious summer's day. Hobbs' mother, Johanna, was at home with seven of her brood: Annie Marie, who was 24, Joseph 19, Agnes 17, Albert 14, Cecilia 11, Maggie, who was nine, and the youngest child, Edmund who was only three. The father of this large family, 48-year-old John William Hobbs, had gone to watch a cricket match and George was also out of the house.

It was 4.45pm when George Hobbs returned to the house and immediately demanded his tea. Johanna, his mother, said that it would be ready in about five minutes but Hobbs ignored this and shouted, "Where's my father and who's boss of this house?" It was then that Johanna, rather than try to cool the situation, made what was to be a fatal error of judgment. Instead of trying to humour her son, she replied that his father was the boss and would remain so until he died. Infuriated, Hobbs rose from his chair, went out into the yard as fast as his injured foot would allow, and shouted that he would fight anyone, including his father. Only now did Johanna go into the yard and try to calm her son, but he would have none of it, screaming, "I'll be the boss of the house and will show you something before night." Seeing that she was not getting through to her son, Johanna told him that she would not speak to him again until he cooled down, and then she closed the door on him.

Ten minutes later Hobbs came back into the house, but he had certainly not cooled down. He demanded to know if his father had come in yet, and when told that he hadn't, rushed upstairs. Within a few minutes, Hobbs came back downstairs, went out into the yard again and shouted further threats about being willing to fight any man. Then, finally, all fell quiet.

Johanna Hobbs might well have thought that the trouble was finally over, but 15 minutes later she saw her son standing in front of the house, holding a revolver in his hand. Muttering that it was he who 'kept the house', Hobbs walked off up High Street, towards the Bird in Hand inn. Johanna rushed to her front door while Annie Maria followed her brother to see what he might do.

By this time 14-year-old Albert Hobbs, who worked as a colliery pony driver, as his brother once had, but was now off work with an injury of his own, was in the High Street. He had spent the early part of that day watching some men fishing in the canal. Later he had been at home when his eldest brother began shouting threats from the back yard and at one stage had heard George shout, "Either me or my father will have to die tonight!" Once the situation had apparently calmed down, young Albert had gone outside, but as he stood in the street he suddenly saw his brother, a revolver gripped in his hand, go into the Bird in Hand. The youngster wasted no time in dashing back towards his home, meeting Annie Maria on the way, and telling her where their brother had gone.

While Annie Maria went towards the pub, Albert ran over the fields towards the cricket match his father was watching. Again he had not gone very far when he met John Hobbs at the end of School Board Lane. Albert quickly told his father of the trouble George had caused and the threats he had made, and then both walked on towards the pub. It was close by the Bird in Hand that John and Albert Hobbs ran into George. It was now almost 6.00pm.

George Hobbs saw his father and stopped in his tracks. Still holding the revolver he shouted, "I've been an infidel all my life, and I'll be one while I die. Either I'll put a bullet into you, or me." John Hobbs did not believe that his son would hurt him and thought that once again, the drink was talking. This was all a bluff, a stupid game of King of the Castle. John smiled and said softly, "The pistol's not loaded."

George Hobbs did not speak but pointed the revolver towards the sky and pulled the trigger. A shot rang out and he shouted, "That will show you whether it's loaded or not." Seeing now that the situation needed to be defused, John Hobbs walked forward and tried to take the revolver from his son. A struggle followed and both men fell to the ground. Albert, meanwhile, was watching from a distance and by now, Annie Maria had also come upon the scene.

Another shot rang out and John Hobbs cried, "Oh, I'm shot." Both men climbed to their feet but it was obvious that John was injured. He staggered off towards the Bird in Hand but had not gone very far when he fell to his knees and groaned, "For Heaven's sake Geordie [his son's nickname] don't shoot again for I'm half dead now." This plea did not move George Hobbs, though, for he slowly raised the revolver, aimed it at his father and fired again, the bullet striking John in the thigh. Even as John fell forward, George Hobbs muttered, "I'll finish you in less than five minutes."

Seeing his father shot for a second time, young Albert bravely rushed forward and struck his brother over the head with a small parasol he was carrying. George Hobbs was knocked over and Albert, too, rolled on the ground, the momentum of his run carrying him too far. As Albert tried to rise, George Hobbs got to his knees, pointed the weapon at his younger brother and fired again. Albert felt a searing pain as the bullet struck the fingers of his left hand.

It was now that some of the regulars came out of the Bird in Hand and, seeing the carnage in front of them, ran forward to carry John and Albert into the relative safety of the inn. As all this was happening, Annie Maria turned to her brother and begged, "George, don't do any more." Hobbs, though, had still not finished. He climbed to his feet, turned towards his sister and with a shout of "Take that," fired a bullet at her. The shot struck Annie in her arm near the right elbow and even as she cried out, a second shot was fired. Luckily this missed and she, too, now ran into the Bird in Hand as George Hobbs walked back down High Street.

Leonard Gregory, who ran a butcher's shop in High Street, Eckington, heard the shots that Hobbs had fired. Going out into High Street, Gregory saw Hobbs coming down the street shouting, "I've done it!" Hobbs stopped and faced Gregory, but within seconds another man, Benjamin Jones, crept up behind Hobbs and snatched the weapon from him. Hobbs was then escorted to the police station where he was handed over to Constable James Hicks, who charged him with attempted murder.

Three members of the Hobbs family had been rushed to hospital in Chesterfield. Annie Maria was not badly wounded and allowed home that same day after she had been treated. Albert needed an operation on his hand and ended up losing one of his fingers. John Hobbs, though, was in a serious condition, suffering from two wounds, one on the right side of his chest below the fourth rib and one in his left thigh. Fortunately, though, he began to respond to treatment and started to make a good recovery.

George Hobbs appeared before the magistrates on July 19th when only evidence of arrest was given. His second appearance, before Mr John Borough, took place on July 22nd when he was remanded to the 29th. On that same day, John Hobbs was allowed out of bed and spent some time pottering about his hospital ward.

It might be thought that the wound which would cause most concern would be the chest wound John Hobbs had suffered, but in fact that was healing nicely. The same could not be said for the thigh wound, however, and no sooner had John started to walk about the ward than his leg began to swell. A second operation was needed on September 5th, when it was discovered that the bullet had travelled upwards and lodged in the muscles of the abdominal wall. Yet more surgery was needed on September 13th, when the bullet was removed, but John Hobbs slipped into unconsciousness soon afterwards and at 3.55am on Saturday, September 14th, he died. George Hobbs was now charged with wilful murder of his own father.

The inquest took place at the hospital on September 17th before the Scarsdale coroner, Mr C.G. Busby. George Hobbs, who was present in court, was represented by Mr J.T. Jones. All the witnesses were heard and the jury, after consulting for just ten minutes, returned their verdict, that John William Hobbs had been murdered by his son who was then sent for trial on the coroner's warrant.

The police court proceedings continued, though, and only concluded on October 2nd when again Hobbs was committed to the next Assizes. They opened at Derby on Monday, December 2nd 1901, and it was on that first day that Hobbs appeared before Mr Justice Bigham. The case for the prosecution was led by Mr J.H. Etherington Smith, who was assisted by Mr Lawrance while Hobbs was defended by Mr Hole.

The first witness was the prisoner's mother, Johanna Hobbs. She explained that her husband had been a joiner and that her son had, until his accident, been a pony driver at the Hornesthorpe Colliery. She went on to tell the court that when George Hobbs had home in on the afternoon of July 17th, he had been argumentative and used foul language to her. After seeing him walk off with the revolver, Johanna stood at the front door until she heard the first shot fired.

Rushing off up High Street, she saw her son seven or eight yards away from the Bird in Hand, with the gun still in his hand. Going into the pub, Johanna saw her husband lying in the arms of Mr Rotherham, the landlord. Albert was also in the same room, bleeding badly from a hand wound.

Albert Hobbs explained what he had seen in the lane outside the Bird in Hand. Later, after he, too, had been shot, he was taken into the tap room of the inn from where he heard two more shots fired and soon afterwards, Annie Maria came in saying that she had also been shot.

In addition to relating how she was injured, Annie Maria Hobbs told the court that when her brother had first come home, he smelled strongly of drink although she would not describe him as drunk. She also testified that she had once before heard Hobbs threaten his father saying, "Some time I shall be doing something to you that you won't get over."

Annie Hobbs was seeing a young man named Alfred Edward Reeves and he had arrived at 140 High Street at 5.00pm on July 17th. At the time, George Hobbs was complaining bitterly about his tea not being ready, and soon launched into a vicious verbal attack upon his mother. Some time later Reeves saw George standing at the front of the house with a revolver in his hand. Once Annie had run after her brother, Reeves had followed and saw the shot being fired into the air. Later he saw George Hobbs wound his father and brother. He was unable to see Annie shot as there was a wall in the way but he did hear her cry out and ran forward to help her.

The butcher, Leonard Gregory, who had seen Hobbs disarmed, was a close friend of the family and had spent much of the early part of that day with the prisoner. That morning he and George Hobbs had gone to Broughton Lane and then on to Sheffield where they had a repair done to the four-wheeled carriage which Gregory was driving. They called into a couple of public houses where they had a total of three pints each and got back to Eckington a few minutes before 4.45pm. At 5.15pm, Gregory saw Hobbs in his backyard, that house being six doors away from his own. Gregory could clearly hear the foul language and threats that Hobbs was shouting and he could also see, at 5.30pm, that Hobbs was carrying a revolver which he loaded. Hobbs was having some difficulty with this and dropped a couple of cartridges on the floor. Later still, after Hobbs had been disarmed and was being taken to the lock-up, Gregory asked him what he had done and Hobbs replied, "I've done it for a bit of fun."

Benjamin Jones also lived in High Street, next door to the Hobbs family. He also heard the shouting and saw George Hobbs emerge with the revolver and a number of cartridges. At the time of the shooting, Jones was in the Bird in Hand and witnessed the events there. After

Annie Maria had been shot, Jones saw Hobbs go down the High Street towards his house and followed him. As Hobbs stopped to face Leonard Gregory, Jones walked up behind him and took the gun from him. Hobbs offered no resistance and did not struggle as he was taken to the police station. Jones broke open the revolver and saw that there was still a live bullet in one of the chambers. He then took the weapon into his own yard and discharged this last bullet into the soil before taking the gun to the police.

Samuel Lloyd lived in Pit Street but he was talking to some friends in High Street when Hobbs came up and asked them if they had seen his father. Lloyd told him that John had gone to a cricket match and Hobbs walked off without comment. Lloyd was still in High Street when the shooting took place an hour later and he, too, followed Hobbs back down High Street. He saw Benjamin Jones disarm Hobbs and then helped to take him to the police station where he was handed over to Constable Hicks. Another of the men who took Hobbs into custody was Alexander Fanshawe and on the way he asked Hobbs why he had done this terrible thing. Hobbs smiled and replied, "I hope the old bugger is dead." A minute or so later he added that it was 'all over some money troubles'.

Constable James Carberry was on duty in Eckington when he heard of the trouble and went to the Bird in Hand. By the time he arrived, at about 6.20pm, George Hobbs had been taken into custody but John Hobbs was sitting in a chair in the back yard of the inn. He looked very pale and Carberry believed that he was in imminent danger of dying.

Constable Hicks had been in Church Street when he saw a crowd of people bringing George Hobbs to the lock-up. Hicks took Hobbs into custody and charged him with intent to murder. Soon afterwards, Constable Carberry arrived at the station and told him that John Hobbs' condition was serious. Hicks then interviewed the prisoner again and told him that there was a possibility of a more serious charge. Hobbs retorted, "Is that all? That's all right." Two months later, on September 14th, Constable Hicks went to Derby prison to tell Hobbs that his father had died and he would now be charged with murder. Hobbs made no reply.

Dr George Henry West Jones had been called to the Bird in Hand and arrived at 6.30pm on July 17th. He ordered all three of the wounded to be taken to hospital and it was he who had to amputate the third finger of Albert's left hand. Annie Maria was X-rayed and a bullet removed from her arm on July 26th. On the day of the shooting, Dr Jones had also examined George Hobbs in the lock-up. He still appeared to be very excited but he was certainly not drunk.

The house surgeon at Chesterfield Hospital was Dr Bernard Newmarch Molineux. He had treated John Hobbs from his admission until the time he died and had operated on him a number of times. After John had died, Dr Molineux performed a post-mortem. The bullet which had entered the chest was found free in the pleural cavity and had done no more damage than breaking a rib. The second bullet had entered the very top of the left thigh and travelled up into the muscles of the abdomen, causing a large abscess which in turn had led to peritonitis, although the direct cause of death was shock following the last operation.

When John Hobbs had first been injured it was thought that he might not live very long and so John Kitching Denny, a magistrate's clerk, attended the hospital and took the man's deposition. This document began, "I, John William Hobbs of Eckington in the county of Derbyshire, joiner, being perfectly aware of my danger and entertaining no hope of recovery ..." It went on to detail how he had attended the cricket match and later met his son at the bottom of School Street *(sic)*. It continued, "He said. 'Have you a bloody bobby with you to have me locked up because I'm going to shoot you?' He said that either him or me would have to die. I asked him what for. He said he would show me when I got home. When we got about 30 yards nearer home he said some bugger would have to die. He pulled out a pistol and fired one shot in the air. I pushed him to disarm him. He fell to the ground. He fired two shots at me when I was on the ground. One shot hit me in the breast, the other shot struck me in the hip.

"I have had no quarrel with him. He had had some drink. I do not know of any reason why he should have shot me. We were fairly good friends. He had some money given to him from a club. What money I had from him was to buy things for him and to pay for his keep and lodgings. I do not know the amount. I was with him when he bought the revolver. I advised him not to do so as it might get him into trouble. It is five or six weeks since he bought it. He bought it in Nottingham."

George Hobbs was called to the stand to explain his actions on July 17th but said that he had no memory of the events. All he could recall was arguing with his mother, as he believed she had been telling untrue stories about him to his father. This, he said 'got his temper up'. He also claimed that he had bought the revolver with no particular intention and certainly not to commit the crime with which he was now charged.

Having heard all the evidence, the jury took just 30 minutes to decide that George Hobbs was guilty as charged, although they added a recommendation to mercy on account of his youth. The law, though, prescribed only one possible penalty for murder and George Hobbs was then sentenced to death and removed to Derby prison to await his fate.

In addition to the jury's recommendation, a petition, begging for a reprieve and signed by many local people, was forwarded to the Home Office. After due consideration, the Home Secretary announced, on December 20th 1901, that he had advised the King to commute the sentence to one of life imprisonment.

Chapter Two

The
Boatman

WALTER Ancliff had worked for Thomas Campion, on and off, for ten years. Both men worked the canals on their own boats, but from time to time Ancliff would assist Campion who owned a number of boats and was quite a successful entrepreneur. Just such an arrangement was made for Wednesday, July 31st, 1901.

It was very early on that day that Ancliff left his home at 19 Chaucer Street, Ilkeston, and strolled down to the canal where he met Campion on his boat. By the time they pulled away, it was still only 6.00am and the destination was the Blacking factory at Borrowash which they hoped to reach by early afternoon.

It was around 2.00pm that Campion and Ancliff were overtaken by another boat operated by a man they had both known for many years, and indeed to whom Campion had also given employment – one Joseph Henry Harrison. He shouted a greeting and Ancliff asked him where he was headed. Harrison said that he was just enjoying a run round and having determined where Campion was going, said he would meet him there and help him to moor his boat. Just half an hour later, at 2.30pm, both boats were safely tied up at Borrowash and the three friends were enjoying tea together.

At 6.00pm, Thomas Campion announced that he was going to a pub in the village to have a pint. Ancliff and Harrison were left on Campion's boat together until, at around 8.00pm, Harrison said, "I am going up to the public to Tom." Ancliff was invited to join him but as he had no money on him, and did not want to ask for charity, he politely turned Harrison down. The last Ancliff saw of Harrison he was strolling purposefully up the canal towpath.

The landlord of the Nag's Head at Borrowash was Henry Foster but he was absent from the pub for most of July 31st, having gone to Derby for the day. When he returned home, at 7.30pm, he saw among the customers his old friend Thomas Campion. They fell into conversation and Foster remarked to Campion that he was looking particularly happy with himself. Campion replied, "I've sold my boat and I've got the sack. I've drawn a quid on it and I've sold it for £15." Campion was, of course, a self-employed man and Foster realised that he was saying he had decided to retire and had already sold his boat.

At some time between 8.00pm and 9.00pm, Henry Foster served a man who he did not recognise. The man bought himself a pint and asked, "Is my boss in?" Foster asked to whom he was referring and the man replied, "Tom Campion." Foster watched as the stranger, a man he subsequently identified as Joseph Harrison, went over to Campion and asked to borrow a shilling. A still cheerful Campion had no hesitation in reaching into his pocket and handing a coin over to Harrison. The two men then stayed drinking together until Foster saw them leave at closing time, 10.00pm.

Thomas Smith also knew Campion very well and had met him as he strolled up the lane which led to the Nag's Head, at some time around 6.30pm. The two walked towards the pub together and Campion mentioned that he had sold his boat and that he had received £1 on account to fasten the deal. Smith had a drink with Campion and was still in the pub when Harrison entered and joined Campion. By the time these two left, Smith had already returned to his home in Brook Road, and was in bed well before 10.00pm. It was at that time that his rest was disturbed by loud voices outside.

Smith instantly recognised one of the voices as that of Thomas

Campion. The other voice was a strange one to him but they were both speaking so loudly that every word was audible. The man with Campion shouted, "I am gaffer of you anywhere and I'll cut your bloody head off." This was repeated several times until Campion replied, "You can't. Let it be till the morning and we will see who is the bloody gaffer then." This shouted conversation went on for perhaps half an hour before finally, the noise stopped abruptly and Smith tried once more to get some sleep.

Although Thomas Smith had not actually seen the man who was with Campion in Brook Road, Samuel Stevens certainly had. Stevens was the village blacksmith and he, too, had known Campion for years. At 8.15pm on July 31st, Stevens had gone for a well-earned drink at the Nag's Head, after a hard day at the forge, and saw Campion sitting in the corner by himself. Some time later, Harrison came in and Stevens heard him ask Campion for a shilling. Stevens also left the pub at closing time and he saw Campion and Harrison, who were in front of him, walking off arm in arm. They had gone perhaps 30 or 40 yards when Campion told Harrison to let go of him, and pulled away. The last time Stevens saw the two men was at the corner of Brook Road. They turned into the lane and Stevens continued on to his smithy.

Harrison and Campion were also seen together by Stephen Sims who ran a florist's shop not far from the Nag's Head. He was at his front door at 10.00pm and saw them walking along the lane, arm in arm. Sims saw Harrison release his hold on Campion, who promptly fell down as they entered Brook Road, giving Sims the impression that the man was very drunk. Harrison helped Campion to his feet, but he was very unsteady and fell over again almost immediately. Harrison helped him up a second time and as he did so, Sims heard him remark, "You know Tom, I am your bloody gaffer." It was a bright moonlit night and Sims watched them stagger down the lane. Before he went back inside his house, he saw both men fall down together in a heap.

It was at about the time of this last fall that Walter Skertchley was returning to the house he shared with his parents near Brook Road. As he cycled down the lane he saw two men lying together in the hedge. Although he could not distinguish the features of either man, they were talking and Skertchley recognised Thomas Campion's voice. Campion, who did not seem best pleased, cried, "You bloody swine, are you going to leave me here?" Skertchley continued on his way but looking back, he saw one of the men get up and walk down the middle of the road, only to fall back down again seconds later. He stayed where he was for a while, then pulled himself to his feet and went back to where the other man still lay and got down next to him. Skertchley left them to it and went home.

It was 10.45pm when John Samuel Cook, who lived at Mill Cottage in Brook Road, was disturbed by the sound of his dog barking out in the lane. Going outside, Cook found his dog standing near a hedge and upon investigating further, saw that there was a man lying on his left side with his head on the road and his feet and legs in the bushes. Thinking that the man was merely drunk, Cook tried to pull him to his feet and it was then that he noticed a large gash on the right side of the man's face. Cook called out, "Look sharp Sam!" This remark was addressed to his brother-in-law, Sam Thompson, who was visiting at the time. Sam heard the summons and rushed outside to see Cook bending over the injured man.

Cook knew the victim, Thomas Campion, and asked who had done this to him. Campion managed to gasp out the words, "That boatman," three times before Cook placed him gently back on to the road and ran to Walter Skertchley's house for assistance. Skertchley went back out with Cook and saw that Campion was in almost exactly the same position as the two men he had earlier seen lying in the hedge together. Skertchley told Cook and Thompson to stay with the injured man while he ran for the doctor and a policeman.

It was 11.15pm by the time Dr John Aspinall Hunt arrived at Brook Road. Campion was still alive although he was breathing heavily and there was blood and air escaping from a wound in his throat. Dr Hunt immediately noted four wounds in all: two superficial skin wounds over the windpipe, one on the lower jaw on the right side which extended from near the corner of Campion's mouth up to his right ear, and one from the windpipe up to below his ear. This was by far the deepest and most dangerous wound but even as Dr Hunt was attending to it, Thomas Campion gave a shudder and died.

At 11.35pm, Skertchley returned with Sergeant David Davies. By now, Campion was dead and so Sergeant Davies made an examination of the area. He noted two large pools of blood by Campion's side and there was evidence of a struggle having taken place 18 yards away, for here Davies found disturbed soil and a cap and tobacco box. Looking at the body, the sergeant saw that the left side of Campion's trousers were torn down to the knee, exposing his thigh. This had probably been caused when the assailant tore at Campion's clothes in order to steal items from his pockets. Campion was searched and Sergeant Davies found a pocket knife, a sovereign, sixpence and a key. The knife was certainly not the murder weapon, though, for the blade was closed and upon opening it, Davies saw no traces of blood.

Back at Campion's boat, Sam Thompson had told Walter Ancliff what had happened and he, too, was now at the scene of the crime. Indeed, Ancliff had arrived before Campion breathed his last. Ancliff was able to tell Sergeant Davies that when Campion left the boat, he had had his silver watch and chain with him. Since this was no longer on the body, it seemed reasonable to assume that the killer had taken it. Ancliff was also able to give the police the name of Joseph Harrison as the man who had set out to join Campion for a drink. A cordon of plain-clothes police was thrown around the immediate vicinity, in an attempt to apprehend the man.

Harrison was certainly a cool customer, though, for not only did he manage to evade that cordon but he also returned to Campion's boat to collect the jacket he had left there. When Ancliff left with Sam Thompson, Harrison's coat had been hanging on a hook inside the cabin, but when he returned at 6.30am on August 1st, the jacket had gone.

A full description of the wanted man was circulated, pointing out that among his nicknames were 'Peggy' and 'Redhead'. The description continued: "Age about 19 years, height five feet five inches, reddish brown hair, pale face, small ferrety eyes (grey), set deep; full forehead, slim build, shuffling gait, and bends in the knees when walking ...Is believed to have with him a silver English lever watch, number 5461, medium size, gold hands, rusty inside." The police notice went on to give details of the clothes Harrison had last been wearing.

Since it was accepted that Harrison would need to earn money to keep himself, and would almost certainly stay away from the canals where he was well known, the description was also given to business-men in the area and beyond, and they were asked to keep an eye out, especially for people seeking casual labour. One such man who read that description was Mr Hughes, a farmer from Car Colston, three miles from Bingham in Nottinghamshire. He had taken on a labourer on the afternoon of Thursday, August 1st, and he fitted that detailed description perfectly. Mr Hughes called the police and at 8.00pm on August 3rd, Sergeant Overston Would called at the farm and had this new employee pointed out to him. Would also thought that the man could be Harrison, so he identified himself as a police officer and demanded the man's name.

The labourer was sitting outside the farm kitchen and replied that his name was Burton and he had come from Nottingham. Sergeant Would informed him that he fitted the description of a man wanted for a serious matter at Borrowash and asked 'Burton' to stand. Noticing blood on the man's clothing, Would cautioned him and said that he wished to search him. No resistance was offered and Would then found a knife and a silver watch, bearing the serial number 5461. Harrison now admitted his true identity and was taken to Bingham police station. On the way, Harrison asked, "Is the man dead?" and Would replied that he believed he was. The next day, at 1.00pm, Sergeant Davies travelled over from Derbyshire and charged Harrison with murder. In reply, Harrison said, "He struck me first. He was going to strike me again. I had my knife in my hand, cutting tobacco. I was going to save the blow and my knife just touched him. He should not have given me so much to drink."

On Monday, August 5th, Harrison appeared before Mr S.R. Cox in the offices of the clerk to the county magistrates. Only evidence of the discovery of the body and the arrest was given before Harrison was remanded to the following Thursday. Meanwhile, the inquest had already been formally opened, on August 2nd, before Mr William Harvey Whiston, at the Nag's Head inn. Evidence of identification was given by the dead man's son, James Campion, who said that his father was 58 years old. He also produced a receipt for a watch repair which showed that his father's silver watch bore the number 5461. Matters were then adjourned, also until Thursday, August 8th.

On the Thursday, the police court proceedings opened first but were immediately adjourned until the following Wednesday, pending the outcome of the resumed inquest. That opened in the afternoon when, all the witnesses having given their testimony, the jury returned a verdict that Campion had been murdered by Harrison. On Wednesday, August 14th, this procedure was repeated in the police court, now held at the County Hall at Derby, and Harrison was sent for trial.

On December 4th, just two days after he had sentenced George Edward Hobbs, the subject of the previous chapter, to death, Mr Justice Bigham also presided over the trial of Joseph Harrison, at Derby.

In addition to repeating the testimony he gave at both the police court and the inquest, Walter Ancliff stated that he had positively identified both the knife used to kill Campion, and the cap found at the crime scene. The knife belonged to Harrison, and Ancliff had seen him use it to cut tobacco for his pipe. The cap belonged to Thomas Campion and he had been wearing it when he left the boat on the evening of July 31st.

John Samuel Cook, in addition to describing the finding of the body, also reported that he had seen Harrison walking up the lane towards the Nag's Head some time between 8.00pm and 9.00pm. Later he called in for a drink and saw Harrison and Campion sitting together. Cook also said that when he left, he would have described both men as under the influence of drink, but not actually drunk.

Mary Jane Smith lived at 5 Belle Vue Cottages on Draycott Lane and she testified that at 10.45pm, she was returning home after running an errand for her mother. A man she had since identified as Harrison approached her, staggering. He was in his shirt sleeves and asked her which was the quickest way to the canal side. Frightened, Mary Jane had not answered him, whereupon Harrison, noticing a woman standing near her front door, slurred, "Well, if you won't tell me, this missus here will." Mrs Swinscue, the woman he referred to, then pointed Harrison in the right direction. All this took place at almost the exact same time as John Cook was finding Campion lying on the roadway.

One of the final witnesses was Dr Sidney Barwise from the University of London. He had made a scientific examination of Harrison's clothing and confirmed that although there was no blood on his boots, there was extensive staining on the sleeves of his shirt and the left cuff was soaked through with blood. Faced with all this evidence, the jury had little difficulty in finding Harrison guilty as charged.

Prison officials at Derby were now in the throes of preparing for a double execution, that of Harrison and George Hobbs, on December 27th.

Various petitions were organised to save Harrison's life, most of them concentrating on the fact that he was only 19 years old. Finally they paid off and on December 15th, 12 days before Harrison was due to die, the Home Office announced, in a letter received by the Under Sheriff for Derbyshire, Mr B.S. Currie, that the sentence had been commuted to one of life imprisonment. It was speculated at the time that Harrison might be released in 15 to 20 years, if he proved to be a model prisoner.

Chapter Three

A Killer's Handiwork

I N 1902, Nancy Price lived in a beautiful old cottage in Parker's Lane, Duckmanton, with her husband, Joseph. Their home was only just inside the parish since the nearby White Hart Inn was situated in Calow.

Joseph Price, who was much older than his 48-year-old wife, had once earned his living as a miner until he met with a serious accident at the Hartington Colliery, which necessitated him finding alternative employment. Unfortunately, a second accident, some years later on the Great Central Railway, meant that he was now a cripple, as well as being extremely deaf, and had not worked for some considerable time. Nancy was now the breadwinner and in order to bring money into the house, eked out a living selling fried fish from a small shop at the Arkwright Town Bridge.

It was in 1892 that Nancy Price first encountered a man named John Bedford, known as Tommy to his friends, a miner from Calow Green who worked for the Grassmore Colliery Company. He was seven years her junior but they were attracted to each other from the very beginning and soon became lovers. For the best part of ten years, the couple shared what time they could, and grew even closer together until soon it appeared that everyone knew what was going on, except that was for old Mr Price himself. Then, towards the late spring of 1902, John Bedford began to believe that someone else was trying to replace him in Nancy's affections. She tried her best to reassure him, but Bedford, a very jealous man, brooded to himself and determined to sort the matter out, once and for all.

It was noon on Wednesday, June 25th, 1902 when Joseph Price went to Chesterfield to visit his brother-in-law, Samuel Hadley, who lived at 30 Church Lane. The trip was rather a difficult one for Joseph, so he decided to stay overnight, something he had done many times before. He had no concerns over leaving his wife alone at Duckmanton.

William Storey was the barman at the White Hart and he was on duty at 9.00pm on June 25th when Bedford came into the public bar. Seeing that Nancy was already there, Bedford bought a couple of glasses of hop bitter and went over to sit with her. They seemed to be quite friendly towards each other and stayed together until 9.45pm, when Alice Round came into the pub, looking for Nancy.

Alice needed to borrow a skirt and her mother had told her to ask Nancy, who would probably be in the White Hart. After explaining what she wanted, Alice was asked to come back to the cottage so that Nancy could find something suitable for her. It was just before 10.00pm when Nancy and Alice strolled slowly down the winding lane to Duckmanton, leaving Bedford behind at the pub.

Alice Round had been in Nancy's house about 20 minutes when there was a knock on the front door. Nancy answered it and John Bedford entered. He then went into the kitchen while the two women spent a few more minutes in the living room talking about clothes. When the time came for Alice to leave, Nancy said she would walk her part of the way back and explained to Bedford that she wouldn't be long. It was now just after 10.30pm.

John Bedford lived with his parents at Calow Green and it was midnight when his father, James Bedford, had to get out of bed to let him into the house.

As Bedford entered he remarked to his father, "I didn't think of telling you, but I will tell you, I have done the job." Totally baffled as to what this cryptic message might mean, James returned to his bed but minutes later, Bedford came into his bedroom and asked if he might have a smoke of his father's pipe, adding that it would be for the last time.

This strange behaviour continued the next day, June 26th. James rose at 4.30am, as he did most days, and was having breakfast when his son came downstairs, announced that he would have no breakfast himself and left the house with the comment, "I will bid you goodbye."

Bedford was next seen at 6.40am when he walked into the White Hart and was served with a pint by William Storey. Bedford went to sit with three or four men from the village and stayed, in all, for about 45 minutes. He then left the pub, only to return within half an hour when he ordered another pint. He was still sitting in the bar at 9.00am when Storey went out.

Just 15 minutes after William Storey had left the White Hart, a close friend of Bedford's, Frederick Wagstaff, a coal miner who lived at 38 Arkwright Lane, entered the public bar and was invited by Bedford to have a drink. The two men sat together for a few minutes until Bedford asked his friend to step outside as he had something he wished to tell him in private. Wagstaff followed Bedford into the yard and there heard him say, "I have done it." Wagstaff asked what he meant and Bedford replied, "I have killed her."

Wagstaff knew immediately to whom Bedford was referring. He, like almost everyone else in the village, was aware of the relationship between Bedford and Nancy Price, and of the fact that Bedford had been jealous of late. Indeed, just a few days before, Bedford had been talking to Wagstaff about the matter and had suggested that he would 'swing for her'. Despite this knowledge, Wagstaff made it plain to his friend that he did not take him seriously. At this, Bedford pointed downwards and said, "Look at my trousers and boots." Wagstaff did so and noticed a number of stains that looked very much like blood. The two men then went back inside the pub and rejoined the others, only for Bedford to repeat the same story to them.

Still no one seemed to be taking Bedford seriously, so as the group left the pub he shouted, "None of you believes it. Come with me. I have got the key and will show it to you." Even so, only Wagstaff said he would go with him and he followed Bedford towards Nancy Price's house. On the way they met Robert Davison, another friend of Bedford's, and he, too, was invited along to view the scene of the supposed crime.

By the time the three men reached Nancy's house it was 11.00am. Bedford unlocked the door and they trooped in. The house was in darkness as the blinds were still down, but Bedford crossed the room and opened them. Immediately Wagstaff and Davison could see that Bedford had not been lying. There on the settee sat Nancy Price, looking almost as if she were asleep, but the mass of blood on her face and the splashes up the wall showed clearly that she was not enjoying a pleasant nap. She had been brutally battered about the head.

Tentatively, Frederick Wagstaff moved forward to check if Nancy was dead. Even as he did so, Bedford said, "Yes, she is cold enough. I did it last night." Both men had seen enough and left the house, Wagstaff giving the key back to Bedford, believing that it may represent evidence. Davison then went for the police while Wagstaff returned to the White Hart with Bedford.

It was 11.45am when Constable Frank Outram arrived at the White Hart. As soon as he approached, Bedford said, "I have done it. It is a bloody fact. I ought to have done it three years ago." He was immediately charged with murder and taken into custody. Outside, Outram met Sergeant James William Hudson and together they escorted Bedford back to the murder scene. Once again Bedford produced his door key and as they entered the house he repeated, "I have bloody well done it."

The two police officers made a careful examination of the premises. Nancy Price was sitting on the sofa with her feet on the floor. She had a stocking in one hand and a darning needle pushed into her dress implying that she had been busying herself with sewing when she had been suddenly attacked. Lying on the floor nearby was a bloodstained poker and as Sergeant Hudson carefully picked it up, Bedford exclaimed, "That is what I have bloody well done it with." The house was once again locked up and Bedford taken to the police station. On the way he remarked, "I have killed one of the best women that ever lived. I ought to have been married and it would not have happened."

While all this was taking place, Joseph Price was on his way back from Chesterfield. Arriving back in Calow at 2.30pm, he cheerily greeted Frederick Wagstaff, only to be given the shattering news that his wife was dead. Going back to his house as quickly as he could, Price found that the door was locked and since he had left his key inside when he went out the night before, he was unable to gain access. The old man stood on his own front step for half an hour until Sergeant Hudson arrived with the key and let him in. Nancy had still not been moved to the mortuary and poor Joseph saw for himself just what had been done to her.

The inquest opened at the White Hart, before Dr Albert Green, on June 27th when evidence of identification was given by the distraught husband. Matters were then adjourned until July 3rd. Bedford appeared at the police court the same day when, evidence of arrest was given, Constable Outram explaining that when he first went into the White Hart he had told Bedford he was being arrested for the murder of his wife. Bedford told Outram that it was not his wife he had killed but once the matter was cleared up, he was handcuffed. At the time Bedford was laughing and joked to his friends that this was better than any coronation (referring to the forthcoming crowning of King Edward VII) and as he was taken from the pub sang, "Goodbye Dolly, I must leave you," very loudly. The proceedings were then adjourned until July 4th.

On Sunday, June 29th, the body of Nancy Price was laid to rest in the parish churchyard at Duckmanton. There were large crowds both around the dead woman's house, from where the cortege started, and the church itself but it was noted that many people, in addition to paying their respects, were also expressing sympathy for Bedford, believing that his actions had been totally out of character.

The inquest reopened on July 3rd, again at the White Hart, and Bedford was present under police escort. Joseph Price was recalled and stated that he had never heard Bedford issue threats to Nancy. Hearing this, Bedford called out, "You are a liar, sir," and an event which took place in April was then recalled. Bedford had visited Nancy at home, while Joseph was there and his language had become rather abusive. Joseph had ordered Bedford from his house and he had retaliated by breaking some panes of glass in the window. All the other witnesses were then called and the jury deliberated for 20 minutes before returning a verdict of wilful murder.

Bedford was told that he would be sent to the next Derbyshire assizes but as he was escorted back to prison, many of those who had been in court listening to the evidence, pushed themselves forward and shook Bedford warmly by the hand, many of them in tears. The next day, he was back before the magistrates, who again sent him to Derby to face his trial.

The case against John Bedford was heard on July 11th before Mr Justice Lawrance. Mr Appleton and Mr Lawrance appeared for the prosecution and Bedford was defended by Mr B. Stephen Foster.

Frederick Wagstaff repeated his story of the events at the White Hart on June 26th. After Bedford had told him that he had killed Nancy, Wagstaff had expressed disbelief but Bedford had said that he hoped he may die if he wasn't telling the truth and then pointed out what looked like bloodstains on his dark blue trousers. For the first time Wagstaff began to believe that there might be something in what Bedford was saying after all, but the prisoner begged him to say nothing just yet as he wished to spend a little more time with his friends before the police came for him. Back inside the inn, Bedford had told his friends that he had only three more Sundays to live, referring to the normal time span between a sentence of death and an execution, but they didn't seem to understand so he elaborated and told them, too, that he had killed Mrs Price. None of them believed him, laughed in his face and told him to be quiet.

Eventually, Wagstaff had agreed to accompany Bedford to the house to see for himself. They met Mr Davison on the way and he, too, came along. As they stepped inside the doorway Bedford said, "You'll find her there, in the corner, on the sofa." After looking at the body for a few moments, Bedford had said, "God bless thee old darling. I loved thee but thou hast not been true."

The doctor who had been called to examine Nancy was Dr Sidney Worthington. He saw that the walls and ceiling around the sofa were sprinkled with blood and Nancy bore a vertical wound on her forehead which had caused rivulets of blood to run down her face. Dr Worthington also performed the post-mortem which revealed a fractured skull beneath the forehead wound. There were other fractures behind both ears, and fragments of the skull had been driven deep into the brain. There were no defence wounds and nothing to show that any struggle had taken place. In Dr Worthington's opinion, the attack had come from in front and had been totally unexpected.

Bedford had made a statement after his arrest and this was now read out. According to this, he had been cohabiting with Nancy for the past ten years and since her husband was often away from home, sometimes spent as many as three or four nights a week sleeping with her. Things had been fine between them until the last couple of months when he had discovered that she was seeing another man, although he had no idea of his rival's identity. This was the cause of all the trouble between them and this was why he had taken her life.

Not surprisingly, it took the jury just a few minutes to determine that Bedford was guilty of murder and he was sentenced to death. No reprieve was forthcoming and at 8.00am on Wednesday, July 30th, 1902, just over a month after he had killed Nancy Price, John Bedford was hanged at Derby by William Billington and Henry Pierrepoint who gave him a drop of exactly seven feet.

Chapter Four

Madly in Love

J UST off the Mansfield road, some four miles from Chesterfield, on the lane which led from Bond's Main to Calow and Duckmanton, lay a farm run by Abraham and Rebecca Redfern. The Redferns had three sons and two daughters, all of whom were unmarried and helped the family run the business. One of those sons was 25-year-old Samuel, who although he supported his parents with whatever work he could, also earned his living as a wagoner for another farmer, Samuel Renshaw Parker, who owned Hill Farm at Temple Normanton and served as the vice-chairman of the Chesterfield Board of Guardians. Among the other people employed by the Parkers was 16-year-old Frances Rawson, a domestic servant.

At 5.30pm on Tuesday, October 6th, 1903, Samuel Redfern walked into the kitchen at Hill Farm to get some matches so that he could light the fire under the copper. At the time, Frances Rawson was out of the house, having gone to the Post Office to buy some stamps. When she returned shortly before 6.00pm, Samuel Parker's wife, Emma, handed her a bucket and asked her to fill it with sticks which would be used to light the fire in the morning.

The sticks were kept in the cart house, out in the yard, and as Frances went out to carry out this task, Emma and Samuel Parker relaxed in their parlour. The parlour door, which led to the kitchen, was open and so there was a clear view of the back door. It was with utter horror that the Parkers saw young Frances stagger back into the kitchen, blood pouring from a wound underneath her chin. She managed to gasp out, "Oh, Mrs Parker …sticks …Sam," before she fainted and fell to the floor.

Samuel and Emma rushed forward to offer what help they could. Samuel Parker brought some water and whisky but it did no good. Frances was in need of urgent medical attention, so Samuel ran across to the wash house where he found James Laude and William Levin, two of his other workers, and told Laude to run for the police and Levin to fetch a doctor.

Laude ran to the lodgings of Constable William Allblaster and the two men returned to the farm, but by the time they arrived it was clear that Frances Rawson was already dead. Constable Allblaster and James Laude now went in search of Samuel Redfern. They found him lying face down on the floor of the cattle shed, his throat cut and a widening pool of blood underneath his head.

Allblaster got some water and as he was tending to Redfern, the injured man muttered, "Is she dead Jim?" Laude replied that he did not know, whereupon Redfern continued, "Is she cut much?" Laude told him that she was, and Redfern asked him to send a telegram to his family, explaining what had happened. Laude asked why he had done this thing and Redfern whispered it was because she had been deceiving him.

Dr John Buckley was soon on the scene. He first examined Frances and confirmed that she was dead, before going to the wash house and attending to Redfern. The doctor noted two parallel wounds, both of which were superficial, but he stitched them anyway. Redfern was then taken to hospital in Chesterfield where he was detained until his wounds healed.

Constable Thomas Lavin was in charge of Redfern at the hospital. On October 7th, Redfern told him, "I'll tell you all about it, will you write it down?" Lavin cautioned Redfern and told him that anything he did say might be used in evidence against him. Redfern said that he understood, but believed that he was dying and wanted to tell the truth. He then made a full statement which Constable Lavin took down in his notebook and which Redfern subsequently signed.

The inquest on Frances Rawson opened on October 8th before Dr Albert Green. It was held in the kitchen where the young girl had died and the jury began by viewing the body which had now been moved to one of the bedrooms upstairs. The coroner explained that he was only willing to hear evidence of identification and that the proceedings would then be adjourned until Redfern was fit enough to attend. John Brooker, the dead girl's uncle, then testified that he had identified the body and that he had last seen his neice alive on October 4th. Before the inquest had concluded its business for the day, though, Superintendent Faulkner arrived to explain that Redfern was making an excellent recovery and should be able to attend on the following Monday. Dr Green decided to leave matters a little longer, however, and adjourned until October 13th at the Lord's Arms, Temple Normanton.

On October 13th, all the witnesses were heard and a verdict of wilful murder returned. The following day, October 14th, Redfern appeared before the stipendiary magistrate, Mr J.M. Clayton, at the Chesterfield police court. In addition to all the witnesses who had testified at the inquest, Constable Lavin was also heard, and read out the statement Redfern had made in the hospital. The prisoner was then sent for trial at the next assizes.

Samuel Redfern appeared at Derby before Mr Justice Channell on Thursday, December 3rd, 1903. Mr Smith appeared to prosecute and Redfern was defended by Mr White. The trial lasted all day and a verdict was not returned until 9.00pm that evening.

Emma Parker described Frances Rawson as one of the best servants she had ever had, adding that she was obliging and of a bright and sunny disposition with a kind word for everyone. On the day of the attack, Redfern had left the kitchen after collecting some matches. Frances came back from her errand soon afterwards and had her tea before going out to fetch the sticks for the next morning. When the poor girl returned and fell to the floor, Mr Parker had rushed to support her head and blood had spurted all over him and Emma. The doctor was sent for and a message sent to Frances' mother, telling her what had taken place. Mrs Parker also stated that she had seen Redfern following Frances about and doing odd jobs for her, but was sure there was no emotional involvement between them.

Samuel Parker, too, had heard that Redfern was 'sweet' on Frances. He had also heard that there was another young man interested in Frances and that this man had threatened to thrash Redfern if he didn't leave Frances alone. There was no proof of this, though.

Turning to the day of the attack, Samuel Parker told the court that Frances had returned to the kitchen five minutes after she had gone out with the bucket. She staggered, lent on a dresser and then fell to the ground. As he helped his wife to support her, he heard Frances give two heavy sighs before she fell still and died. Samuel Parker ended his evidence by describing Redfern as a quiet, harmless man and a good worker.

James Laude said he had seen Redfern doing jobs for Frances, and Redfern had once asked him if he had ever seen Frances with anyone. Although Redfern was obviously interested in Frances, Laude did not believe that these feelings were reciprocated. On October 6th, Laude had been in the wash house and Redfern was with him. Redfern had finished work for the day and was just talking casually with him and Levin until he left and walked over to the shed where the sticks were kept. A few minutes later, Mr Parker had come across and told him that Frances' throat had been cut and asked him to run for the police. When he returned with Constable Allblaster, they had searched for Redfern and found him in the cattle shed. Laude then told of the conversation that had passed between him and Redfern as the latter was being treated. He was also able to say that the razor used had belonged to Redfern and was normally kept on a shelf in the wash house.

The other man in the wash house when Mr Parker had told Laude that Frances had been hurt was William Levin, who now confirmed some of the testimony of James Laude. As Laude had run for the police, Levin had gone for the doctor and when they returned he helped to carry Redfern from the cattle shed to the wash house where he was treated.

In addition to examining Frances at the scene, and stitching Redfern's wounds, Dr Buckley had also performed the post-mortem. Frances' throat was cut on the right side, the jugular vein being severed by the four-inch long wound which was two inches deep at the right. There were also two fresh cuts on the left side of her chin and three deep wounds on the fingers of her right hand. The wounds must have been inflicted from in front and so Redfern would have faced Frances when he attacked her. The wounds on the hand were caused when Frances tried to defend herself.

Constable Allblaster had examined the scene meticulously and found bloodstained wooden sticks scattered around the floor of the shed where the attack had taken place, but there were no signs of blood anywhere else, until some hay was moved and a large pool of blood found, with a few sticks lying in it. From this evidence, it appeared that Frances had been lying on the ground when her injuries were inflicted.

Redfern was found in the cattle shed which was 40 yards away and in a manger near him Allblaster found the open razor and a bloodstained muffler which had been shown to belong to Redfern. The next morning, Allblaster and Sergeant Moorcroft followed a trail of blood from the upturned bucket in the shed, all the way to the farm kitchen, 50 yards away. On October 8th, he and Sergeant Thomas Moorcroft went to Chesterfield where they interviewed Redfern in the infirmary and charged him with murder. In reply, Redfern had said, "I did it with neither with malice or *(sic)* jealousy." Initially, Redfern had said that he wanted to see Frances' mother as he would only tell the truth of what had happened to her, but the shock of what had happened had made Mrs Rawson ill and she was now confined to bed.

Charlotte Rawson was Frances' mother and she told the court that she had last seen her daughter alive on October 4th, when she visited her at Hasland. Redfern had come up in conversation, as he had on an earlier visit which took place on August 26th. Frances had explained that Redfern had asked her to walk out with him but she had told him that he ought to be ashamed of himself as he was old enough to be her father, even though he was actually only nine years her senior. Charlotte had told Frances at the time that if Redfern continued to bother her, she should report him to Mr and Mrs Parker. On September 24th, Frances had visited again and she, Charlotte and another daughter had gone to visit Chesterfield. On the way, Frances mentioned that Redfern had offered her a silver chain but she had told him that she wanted nothing from him.

Redfern's statement was then read out in court. This began with the words "It's deceit that brought it on." He went on to explain that he had already been in the shed when Frances came in to fetch some sticks. It was she who brought the razor out of her pocket and confessed that she had been carrying it since the previous Sunday when he had last used it. Frances then said that she had been leading him on, just for a bit of fun. This annoyed him and he told her that he 'had a good mind to finish her'. At this, Frances put her arm around his neck and they kissed before he took the razor from her and cut her throat. Redfern then told her that he would kill himself and she muttered, "Goodbye," and left the shed.

Redfern said that he believed Frances was involved with a man in Hasland, and although she had never encouraged him, Redfern was jealous of this other man. This was the deceit of which he spoke.

Evidence was now called to show that Frances was, however, a church-going girl who did not have a boyfriend. Redfern had been frequently seen following Frances when she went out and he had indeed observed her with another man, but this was only her uncle who wished to make sure that she arrived home safely after visiting her mother. It was this act of kindness which led directly to her death.

In his summing up for the defence, Mr White suggested that Redfern was not responsible for his actions when he took Frances' life. He referred to Redfern's claim that the girl had brought the razor to the scene, and provoked him in to using it. In reply, Mr Smith said that there was no evidence of any insanity when Redfern killed Frances and stated that he believed it highly unlikely that Frances had carried the razor with her since the Sunday. Mr Justice Channell, in his own summation, stated that he believed the crime to be premeditated. The burden of proof as far as insanity was concerned rested with the defence and this had not been demonstrated in this case, even though it had been shown that there was a good deal of insanity in the family.

It took the jury 55 minutes to decide that Redfern was guilty as charged, although they did add a recommendation to mercy on account of his weak intellect. Redfern made no comment as the death sentence was passed, although he looked quite weak as the warders escorted him back to the cells below.

Samuel Redfern did not suffer death at the end of a rope. On December 14th, the Home Office announced that the sentence had been commuted to one of life imprisonment. Others in 1903 were not so fortunate, a total of 24 men and three women dying on the gallows of England and Wales in what was a record year for executions.

Chapter Five

Mother Love

IN 1903, John Silk was discharged from the Army having served his country well in both India and South Africa. Returning to his home town of Chesterfield, Silk took up residence with his mother, Mary Fallon, at 3 Spa Lane. Mary Fallon was a cripple and got about only with difficulty, using a crutch. Her son usually treated her well and with affection, but on the occasions that he took too much to drink, he became abusive and violent towards her.

Towards the end of the summer in 1904, Mary Fallon decided to bring a few extra shillings into the house by letting out a room to a lodger. This led to Thomas Meakin moving into 3 Spa Lane and for the best part of a year, Meakin, Silk and Mary, lived with varying degrees of harmony, under the same roof. More than once, though, Meakin was a witness to Silk's drunken outbursts and saw him even go so far as to strike his mother with his open hand.

On the evening of Saturday, August 5th, 1905, Thomas Meakin, who had already had a couple of drinks during the day, decided to go out for a pint of beer and went to the Hour Glass public house. He had only the one drink but since he had gone out quite late, it was almost closing time when he returned to Spa Lane. Letting himself into the house, Meakin found that only 51-year-old Mary Fallon was at home.

Meakin later claimed that it was around 11.00pm when John Silk finally came home. Mary was sitting on the sofa in front of the fire in the living room and she and Silk exchanged a few words. Silk had obviously been drinking but for ten minutes or so he behaved reasonably enough towards his mother until, at about 11.15pm, he remarked that the paraffin lamp which stood on a small round table, was not giving out enough light. Silk tried to turn the wick up but Mary did not want him to interfere with the lamp and told him to leave it alone. Without another word, Silk struck his mother across the face, with his open hand. The blow was fairly gentle but Mary, determined to have her way, pushed the lamp a little further back so that her son would not be able to reach it.

Meakin saw that this action infuriated Silk, who took hold of his mother and a brief scuffle took place. The small table was knocked over and the lamp fell to the floor, just as Mary was knocked from the sofa on to the carpet. The lamp broke and the room was plunged into darkness but Meakin heard Mary scream, "Don't John!" as the sound of wood cracking filled the air.

Silk was calling his mother an 'old bitch' and an 'old bugger', and as Mary cried, "Police! Murder!" Meakin said he had seen enough and was going to summon the police. As he left the house, he met Emma Watson who lived nearby, told her what was going on and asked her to fetch a policeman. Mrs Watson, wanting nothing to do with the affair, told Meakin that if he wanted a policeman he had better fetch one himself and then went on her way.

Thomas Meakin did not immediately run off to find a constable, though, for he now knocked on the door of 10 Spa Lane where James Kelly lived. Kelly opened the door and listened as Meakin explained that there was a bit of bother across the road. Meakin explained, "Johnnie is ill-using his mother very badly. He is kicking her. He has kicked her right under the sofa." Kelly, too, did not want to interfere, for he also told Meakin to get a policeman and Meakin left his house.

Going to the top of Spa Lane, Meakin found Sergeant Prince and explained to him what was taking place at number three. Prince listened carefully to Meakin's story before telling him, "It's only a family affair. It'll be alright in a few minutes." Astounded at this lack of interest from an officer of the law, Meakin reluctantly walked off saying, "Well, don't forget that I reported it to you." James Kelly was still standing at his front door and he saw Meakin return down Spa Lane, go to the front door of number three and try to gain access. The door was apparently locked, for Meakin could not get in. It was very quiet inside the house now, so Meakin went back across to Kelly's, explained that he was locked out and was invited to spend the night there. By the time Thomas Meakin finally got to bed, it was 1.00am on August 6th.

Henry Dye earned his living as a labourer for a local brewery but on Sunday mornings he also delivered newspapers to earn a few extra coppers. It was 9.50am on Sunday, August 6th, when he arrived at 3 Spa Lane to deliver Mary Fallon's paper. Dye knocked on the door but got no answer. This was highly unusual so Dye tried the door and found that it was unlocked. Going into the house, he had only to look into the living room to see that something terrible had taken place. Mary Fallon lay on the floor, her head near the fireplace. She was on her back, and there was a great deal of blood around her face and head. Dye left the house immediately and noticed Mrs Canavan standing at her front door at 1 Spa Lane, next door to Mary's house. Dye knew that John Canavan was Mary Fallon's brother, making Mrs Canavan her sister-in-law, and so he told her that she had better go next door as there was something 'not right'. Dye then dashed off to find a policeman.

The first officer Dye found was Constable Frank Sykes. He arrived at 3 Spa Lane at 10.10am, entered the house and confirmed Dye's story before closing the door behind him while he went to call for Dr Symes. Sykes then returned to the house and made an initial examination of the scene. There was a broken chair four or five feet away from the body. Off to one side was a small round table on which stood a broken paraffin lamp. Glass from this lamp, together with a broken brown pot, a broken glass tumbler and a broken cruet, lay scattered around the floor. Going upstairs, Constable Sykes found John Silk in bed, his face turned to the far wall and his back towards the bedroom door. Sykes touched him gently and Silk immediately turned around.

"Do you know what has happened?" demanded Constable Sykes. Silk replied that he didn't and Sykes then informed him that there was a woman lying dead downstairs. Silk said that he could give no account of what had taken place and as he sat up in his bed, Sykes noticed that there was dried blood on his hands and face. Silk was told to dress and as he did so, Sykes asked if anyone else lived in the house. Silk told him of Meakin but when asked where he was, Silk replied, "He did not sleep here last night. I don't know where he is." Taken downstairs, Sykes then watched as Silk carefully washed all the blood and, of course, the evidence it represented, off his skin. He was then taken to the police station where he was charged with his mother's murder.

Silk appeared at the police court on Monday, August 7th. Here it was explained that he was a labourer for the council but until a few years ago, had served in the 5th Irish Lancers. The details of the argument witnessed by Meakin were then outlined, as was the scene discovered by Constable Sykes the next morning. The only witness called was Thomas Meakin and then matters were adjourned until the next morning.

It was also on August 7th that the inquest opened at Chesterfield cemetery before Dr Albert Green. Evidence of identification was given by John Canavan, who said that his sister would have been 52 on August 19th. She was not in good health, suffering from heart disease, and was also crippled by sciatica and rheumatics, which had lately got so bad that she sometimes had to be carried around. She had been married three times, the first being to a man named Silk who died of scarlet fever. She had then married a man named Corbett but he too had died. Her third husband, Edward Fallon, had been a collier but he left her two years ago.

Turning to Silk's drinking habits, John Canavan swore that Silk was a most dutiful son except when he had taken too much drink, although the only occasion Canavan knew of where Silk ill-treated his mother was about four months ago when the lodger called him in. Silk was being difficult and although he had tried to lash out, Canavan 'mastered' him and calmed the situation down. On August 5th, the night this tragedy had taken place, Canavan had seen Silk at about 8.00pm. At the time Silk was at the top of Spa Lane and it was obvious that he had taken a good deal of drink already. Canavan saw him again at 9.35pm and at that time Silk was walking as if he were very drunk. After this evidence had been heard, the inquest was adjourned until Thursday, August 10th.

On August 8th, Silk was back before the magistrates but a remand was granted until August 10th. On that date it was pointed out that the inquest was to take place that same afternoon so Silk was again remanded, this time for a week. That same day, the reconvened inquest ruled that Mary Fallon had been murdered by her son.

There were further appearances at the police court, Silk being brought before the magistrates on August 17th, August 24th, and August 31st when Mr J. Middleton for the prosecution and Mr Bertram Mather for the defence were both willing to proceed. Unfortunately, one of the prosecution witnesses, Dr Symes, was away and could not attend until the next day and on that day, Mr Mather himself had another case so could not appear. As a result, a further remand was ordered, this time until September 1st. On that date the last police court hearing took place and it was now that all the witnesses were finally heard and Silk sent for trial.

The trial of John Silk took place at Derby on December 5th, 1905, before Mr Justice Bucknill. Silk was represented by Mr Dominic Daly while the prosecution case was led by Mr J.H. Etherington Smith who was assisted by Mr Magee.

The most important prosecution witness was, of course, the lodger, Thomas Meakin, but some of his testimony was at odds with that given by other witnesses. Before he gave evidence, though, some of Silk's movements earlier on that fateful night were outlined.

Ruth Allsopp, who was only 16 years old, lived at 5 Spa Lane. She often went to Mary Fallon's house and sometimes ran errands for her. On August 5th, Ruth had gone to number three at 10.15pm and at that time, Mary and Silk were both in the house. Silk had already been drinking but was on his way out to get more. Mary handed him a bottle and asked him to fetch her some whisky. Silk smashed this against his mother's crutch which she held underneath her arm. Glass fell on to the floor and Silk bent down, picked up some of the larger pieces and threw them into his mother's face. He then left the house and Ruth ran next door to Mr Canavan and told him what she had seen. John Canavan, like so many other people involved in this case, seemed unconcerned and told Ruth, "Never mind, they'll be alright soon."

Thomas Meakin told the court what he had seen on August 5th and swore that at no time had he seen anyone else in the house that night. This testimony did not agree with that of Michael O'Brian or Henry Goodwin. O'Brian lived at 56 Chester Road, Chesterfield, and Mary Fallon was his wife's sister. He had visited Mary on August 5th, at 7.00pm, when Meakin said he was still at home, stayed about an hour and was there when John Silk came in. He described Silk as being in a playful mood, rather than a temper. O'Brian also said that he had seen nothing of Thomas Meakin.

Henry Goodwin lived at 30 Eyre Street and he had seen Silk at the top of Spa Lane at 11.15pm on August 5th. Silk was very much the worse for drink, so Goodwin escorted him home and went inside with him. Although Goodwin was only there for two or three minutes, during that time Silk was jovial and laughing and said he was going straight up to bed. Goodwin, too, saw no sign of Meakin. The next morning, at around 10.00am, Goodwin was walking up Spa Lane when he passed number three. The door was open and Mrs Canavan was sitting on a chair just inside the doorway, crying. Looking inside the house, Goodwin could plainly see the body of Mary Fallon and he, too, not knowing that Constable Sykes had already attended, went to fetch a doctor.

Emma Watson of 1 Hall's Court, off Spa Lane, said that she had seen Silk standing at his mother's front door, around 11.00pm. He was in his shirt sleeves at the time. Less than an hour later, she saw Meakin come out of the house and ask her to bring a policeman as Silk was hitting his mother. As she was telling him to go himself, Silk came to the door. He had heard the earlier conversation for he shouted, "Oh, you will fetch a policeman will you?" went back inside and bolted the door behind him. Emma Watson then heard Mary Fallon groaning inside the house but took no action since Meakin had already gone off to find a constable.

Dr William Johnstone Symes had arrived at the house at 10.45am on August 6th. Mary Fallon was lying on her back in the front room, her head, face and neck covered in blood and her hair matted over her mouth and nose. There were bruises on her forehead and on the right side of her face. Her nose was fractured and she had bled copiously from the nose and mouth, leaving a large pool of blood on the floor by her head. Dr Symes also performed the post-mortem, during which he saw that the right hemisphere of the brain was bruised. Mary had also suffered a number of broken ribs consistent with someone jumping on her, or kneeling on her. One of these ribs had torn through the right lung and death was due to shock and loss of blood due to the severity of the injuries she received.

Continuing his testimony, Dr Symes stated that the victim would have been sitting or standing when she received the blow which caused the bruises to the right side of her head. Either the broken chair leg or the end of the crutch could have inflicted this injury. It was a severe blow which probably caused immediate unconsciousness. Dr Symes had also examined Silk's clothing after his arrest. There was blood on the front of his shirt and on the left shoulder. Other stains were seen on both trouser legs and there were also some grey hairs which matched the deceased woman's.

In his summing up for the defence, Mr Daly said that it had never entered into his mind to ask for an acquittal but suggested that there were points in this case which suggested a verdict of manslaughter. There was no malice aforethought and Silk was mad with drink at the time of the attack. The jury, though, took only 15 minutes to decide that Silk was guilty of wilful murder and he was sentenced to death, Mr Justice Bucknill telling him that he should make his peace with his Maker and hold out no hope in this world.

There was indeed no hope for Silk. On December 27th, the Home Office announced that despite a petition which had many signatures, there would be no reprieve. That same day Silk received his last visit from his relatives. He was composed throughout the meeting saying, "My mind is a blank, but I shall meet my fate like a soldier." However, he broke down completely as they bade him farewell for the last time.

At 8.00am on Friday, December 29th, 1905, John Silk was hanged at Derby by Henry Pierrepoint who was assisted by John Ellis. It was a cold, wet, miserable day but nevertheless, about 100 people gathered outside the prison to read the notices of execution as they were posted on the gates.

Chapter Six

A Cry For Help

AT some time after 6.20pm on the evening of Friday, November 10th, 1905, Joseph Pickup, a mill worker, was enjoying a meal at his home, 5 Mount Street, Glossop, when he heard a scream, followed by a cry for help. Pickup recognised the voice as that of his next door neighbour, 72-year-old Ann Smith, who ran a general shop from number seven. He jumped to his feet and ran to Ann Smith's house.

As Pickup reached number seven he heard another cry of, "Oh, do come in," but as he tried the door he found it locked against him. Satisfied that old Mrs Smith was in need of help, Pickup gave one good lunge at the door and broke it open. As he entered the living room, Pickup saw that Ann Smith was kneeling on the floor, with her left forearm on the edge of a table, supporting her. She had obviously been injured in some way for there was a good deal of blood flowing down her face and even as Pickup surveyed this scene, the injured woman's nephew, 23-year-old George Alfort Smith, came running in from the kitchen shouting, "My aunt's fell *(sic)* on the fender and cut her head."

Ann Smith was badly injured but she still managed to gasp, "Nay, you've done it." To this, George Smith replied, "No I haven't aunt," and then added, "I'm going now," and made for the front door. Joseph Pickup, satisfied that Smith was responsible for his aunt's injuries shouted, "Nay, you are not," and tried to grab Smith as he passed. Smith did make it out of the front door but Pickup dashed after him, grabbed him by the collar and both men fell to the footpath, with Pickup on top. Smith was soon subdued and Pickup said that he would hold him until the police arrived to take him in charge.

Other neighbours had also heard Ann's screams and cries for help, and they too had run to the house to see what they could do. Sarah Jackson had some nursing experience, so she was able to render basic first-aid until a doctor arrived. Another neighbour was Eliza Bentley, who saw Smith being held as she arrived. Once she had left the house, a man she had never seen before handed her a blood-stained rolling pin which she in turn handed to another woman, Mary Ann Hurst.

The man Eliza Bentley referred to was Samuel Doodson, who was on Princess Street when he heard the sounds of a commotion in Mount Street. Going to investigate he saw a crowd holding a man, the prisoner, in the street. The door to number seven was open but a throng of people were jammed in there. Doodson, going closer, saw something in the channel at the edge of the pavement. He picked it up and saw that it was a bloodstained rolling pin. He handed this over to a woman standing nearby and then left, before the police arrived.

The first policeman on the scene was Constable Thomas Henry White, who timed his arrival at 6.30pm. By now there were about ten people milling about the house and the street outside. By this time, Dr Nicol had also arrived and was tending to Ann in her living room. After speaking briefly to the doctor, Constable White took Smith into custody and escorted him to the police station where he was charged with unlawful wounding. Smith made no reply and when the Chief Constable, John Gregory Hodgson, asked Smith if he understood the charge he replied, "Yes, I know, I am saying nothing."

Ann Smith was too ill to be moved and so received constant treatment at her own home. So serious was her condition that it was thought she might perish at any time, so the following day, November 11th, a dying deposition was taken from her. That same day, Smith, whose home address of 13 Fitzalan Street was given, appeared before the stipendiary magistrate, Mr J. Merry. Only the briefest details of what Ann Smith had said were read out. She had claimed that her nephew had arrived soon after 5.00pm and had spent some time reading a newspaper. She was sitting at the end of the table when suddenly she received a severe blow to the top of her head which knocked her to the floor. Later, Smith took a cushion and put it over her face to smother her and when this did not work, he tried the same thing with his cap. Details were also given of the bloodstained rolling pin being found on a shelf near the fireplace and the fact that when the police arrived, the front door lock was hanging off. This evidence having been heard, Smith was remanded in custody until the following Monday in the hope that by then, a date for Ann's appearance in court might be determined.

Smith was back before the same magistrate on Monday, November 13th, Detective Sergeant William Scott said that he had visited Ann at her home that morning and she was still much too ill to attend court. Smith was consequently remanded for a further week and taken back to Knutsford jail. A further appearance followed on November 20th, when Smith's father and brother offered to put up bail, which was refused. Smith was back in court on November 27th, by which time Mr F.G. Knowles had taken on Smith's defence. Dr Arthur Walker told the court that he had now visited Ann at her home and she was very weak. Allied to her injuries, which were not healing, she also had bronchitis and heart disease, conditions which had been aggravated by the shock of this attack upon her. However, Dr Walker believed that Mrs Smith would recover in due course and would eventually be able to appear in court to give her own version of events. A further remand was ordered.

Other appearances followed on December 4th and December 11th, when Smith was remanded for a further week. At each appearance, details were given of Ann's condition and confirmation given that she was still much too ill to attend. Then, before Smith was due to make his next appointment with the magistrates, Ann Smith died at 2.15pm on Thursday, December 14th. Two days later, the inquest opened before Mr Sydney Taylor, the High Peak coroner, at the Glossop Town Hall. The first witness was Joseph Pickup who described what he had heard on November 10th, and what he had found when he burst through the door of Ann Smith's house. The next witness was Sarah Jackson who lived at 40 Mount Street. She testified that while she was helping the injured woman she had said that her nephew had hit her on top of the head but she could give no reason for why he should have done such a thing. Sarah said she continued to treat Ann until Dr Nichol arrived a few minutes later.

Dr Arthur Walker, who ran his practice from 16 High Street West, Glossop, told the court that he had been attending Ann Smith for some time prior to this attack upon her. He described her as a feeble old lady who was subject to attacks of bronchitis and had a history of heart disease. On November 10th, Dr Walker had also visited Ann at her home to find Dr Nichol already there. Ann's head was covered in blood and there were at least two wounds on the scalp, which was still bleeding. Both wounds were two and a half inches long and were parallel. There was also a large bruise on the forehead and while this wound might well have been caused by a fall, the ones on top of the head certainly were not. Since November 10th, Dr Walker had visited Ann at last twice a day and although she was very weak, she did respond to treatment until a day or two before her death.

Medical evidence would obviously be crucial in this case. Ann Smith was a frail old woman with a weak heart and for a case of murder to stand, it had to be shown that her nephew's attack upon her had either caused her death directly, or was a major contributory factor. Dr Walker now testified that he had also performed the post-mortem on Ann. He noted no signs of inflammation around the head wounds which, by the time of Ann's death, had merged into one large wound. The skull bone was not bruised or fractured and the brain appeared to be quite normal. Turning to his examination of the heart, Dr Walker said that it was surrounded by a large amount of fat and the walls of the blood vessels were hardened but no other signs of disease were noted. The rest of the internal organs appeared to be healthy and in Dr Walker's opinion, the cause of death was that the blows to the head had set up a mild form of meningitis and this, together with shock, had caused the woman to die from exhaustion. He also stated that had a younger and fitter woman sustained the injuries which George Smith was accused of inflicting, she would almost certainly have survived.

Another doctor had been present at the post-mortem and he was now called to give his own opinion as to Ann Smith's death. Dr Alexander Campbell Nicol had attended Ann at her home on November 10th. He reported the initial injuries he had treated and then testified that he largely agreed with the statements made by Dr Walker, although he added that he did not see sufficient evidence in the nature of the head wound to account for Ann's death. He believed that Ann's heart was not a normal one and that this had caused her death. As for the mild meningitis, he agreed that the membrane around the brain was slightly inflamed but this was a condition from which Ann Smith was recovering. In other words, George Smith was not directly responsible for his aunt's death.

Further evidence was given by James Walton, a weaver of Station Road, Hadfield, and the brother of the dead woman. He said that Ann had been married to James Smith who had died 14 months before. On February 10th, he was in a shop run by another of his sisters, Deborah Higginbottom, in Victoria Street, Glossop, when he heard that there had been an incident in Mount Street. He arrived there at 6.35pm and saw Ann being treated by Sarah Jackson. There was a pool of blood on the hearth but this was 16 to 18 inches away from the fender which Smith claimed Ann had hit her head upon.

At this point, the proceedings were adjourned for lunch and the first witness afterwards was the Chief Constable, Mr Hodgson, who told of Smith being brought into the police station and charged with wounding. Once this had been done, Mr Hodgson, along with Sergeant Scott, went to Mount Street and saw for himself the extent of the injuries Ann had received. A statement was taken from the woman and this was now read out in court. It began, "At about 5.00pm tonight, George Alfort Smith, my nephew, came to my house, 7 Mount Street. He began asking me about a bill, and then stood reading the newspaper, leaning against the table in the house place, and I was at one end of the table, sitting on a chair. He put the newspaper down and then something hit me on the head, knocking me senseless. I don't know what he hit me with, but I fell down, and then he got a pillow, put it over my mouth, and also got his cap and put that over my mouth. He never said anything to me. I struggled and screamed and someone came in. The rolling pin produced is not mine. I was saturated with blood. No one else came until after I was struck."

Mr Hodgson also explained that no traces of blood had been found on the fender Smith referred to and this, along with the rest of his evidence, was corroborated by Sergeant Scott. The next day, when it seemed that there was no improvement in Ann's condition, Mr Theodore Walter Ellison, the magistrate's clerk for the Borough of Glossop, had visited her and taken her deposition. In this, Ann Smith again referred to her nephew asking for a bill which he had paid a few weeks before but she did not know where it was. Smith seemed to be satisfied with this and started to read a newspaper before standing up and going to look out of the window. He then asked her if he might buy a pair of mohair laces from the shop and she sold him some for 1d. She now had her back towards him and suddenly he struck out at her with something. Ann said she did not know what it was her nephew used but that 'it were a savage blow'. She added, "It were enough to kill me dead."

One of the final witnesses was Mary Jane Smith, the prisoner's mother who was very emotional while she gave her evidence. She stated that the rolling pin produced in court belonged to her. She had last seen it in the pantry at Fitzalan Street on the night of Thursday, February 9th.

The jury deliberated for half an hour before returning a verdict that the deceased had died as a result of violence and that such violence was inflicted by George Alfort Smith. The coroner pointed out that this was tantamount to a verdict of murder and Smith was returned to Knutsford jail. On December 28th, all of this evidence was repeated in the police court and Smith sent for trial.

The trial of George Smith opened at Derby on Monday, March 5th, 1906, before Mr Justice Jelf. The proceedings lasted for two days during which Smith was defended by Mr T. Hollis Walker while the Crown's case was led by Mr H.Y. Stanger who was assisted by Mr Leadam.

Most of the two days were again taken up with conflicting medical evidence. Dr Walker still maintained that the blows to the head had brought on mild meningitis which led directly to Ann Smith's death, while Dr Nicol persisted in his belief that Ann was suffering from angina and this was what had killed her. Dr Walker also gave evidence of the prisoner's history when it was revealed that he was suffering from a form of epilepsy and had even had an attack while held in Knutsford awaiting trial.

In an attempt to solve the medical conflicts, Dr William Henry

Wilcox, the Registrar of St Mary's Hospital in London, was called. He had read the findings of both doctors and had come to the conclusion that Dr Walker was right but was of the opinion that only one heavy blow had been struck. Dr Wilcox stated categorically that death was not due to heart disease, bronchitis or angina pectoris. Dr Wilcox had also examined the rolling pin, cushion and Smith's cap. He found extensive bloodstaining on the pin including one five and a half inches long extending almost halfway around it. There were also human hairs adhering to the rolling pin and these matched Ann Smith's. There were also stains on the cushion which were human blood and some on the lining of the cap, although these were too small to test.

Further medical testimony was given by Dr Fennell, the medical officer of Knutsford jail. Although Smith had now been moved to Derby jail, Dr Fennell had examined the prisoner a number of times and reported that on November 27th, he had suffered an epileptic fit.

The first witness for the defence was Mr Alfort Smith, the prisoner's father. As he stepped into the witness box, Smith broke down and sobbed, "Father, forgive me." Mr Smith stated that his son was 23 years old on November 24th last. He had, when she had become widowed, lived with the aunt he was now accused of murdering, and she had treated him like a son. Lately, though, Smith had lived in Fitzalan Street, with his parents. Referring to his son's epilepsy, Mr Smith said he had seen him have six fits and knew of another five which had taken place when he was not around.

Samuel Thomas Ashton said he had known the prisoner all his life and had once seen him have a fit while he was playing football on Christmas Day, 1902. Ashton had to carry him home afterwards. He also stated that Smith was prone to mood swings. One moment he would be morose and depressed and the next, happy and cheerful as if he hadn't a care in the world.

In his lengthy summing up, Mr Justice Jelf told the jury that, bearing in mind the medical testimony, there were three verdicts open to them: guilty, not guilty, or guilty but insane. In the event, the jury took 20 minutes to decide that Smith was guilty of wilful murder, although they did add a strong recommendation to mercy. The black cap was placed on the judge's head and the death sentence given, after which Smith said, "I shall die happy. I shall go to that home above, where the sun never sets." He then fainted and had to be supported by the warders who guarded him. The execution was set for Wednesday, March 28th, at Derby, but no sooner had the trial ended than a petition for a reprieve was set up. This listed a number of points to be brought to the attention of the Home Secretary, including that Smith was delicate, that the dead woman was very frail, her skull was not fractured and that since she remained conscious when the blow was struck, it could not have been one of such severity as to intend murder. By March 16th, over 3,000 signatures had been received, including those of five members of the jury which had found Smith guilty. By the time the petition was closed, there were precisely 7,724 names on it, of which 3,238 came from Glossop.

On the Friday before he was due to die, March 23rd, Smith's solicitor was informed that a commutation of the death sentence had been granted, although he requested that this not be made public until Saturday the 24th, by which time official written confirmation would be sent by the Home Office. That same day, Smith wrote to his parents to give them the good news.

Chapter Seven

An Old Soldier

WALTER Marsh had certainly led a most distinguished military life. By the early part of this century, he had served a total of 17 years in the Army and had even fought at the Battle of Omdurman. In November, 1901, Marsh had married Eliza Gascoyne but the following month he was sent to South Africa to fight in the Boer War and he did not return to England until June, 1902. It was not, however, until August 1903 that he was finally discharged from military service having served his country well around the globe, and reaching the rank of colour sergeant.

Returned to civilian life, Marsh obviously had to find a new way to earn a living, so he and Eliza took the lease on a public house at Sheffield. Unfortunately this did not prove to be a commercial success and in 1904, Marsh and his wife left the pub and moved to Chesterfield where they rented 6 Goyt Terrace, Brampton, a house which, along with others in the same row, was owned by Edward Silcock. This gentleman was also Marsh's new employer since he acted as rent collector for his landlord.

By 1906, the relationship between 39-year-old Marsh and Eliza, who was 17 years his junior, had soured appreciably, so much so that by May 31st, Eliza had left the marital home and moved in with her father, George Gascoyne, who lived at 20 Shipley Street. Just seven days later, on June 7th, Eliza went to the magistrates and asked for a summons against her husband, seeking a separation order on the grounds of his cruelty. The magistrates threw out the claim, saying that there was not enough corroborative evidence and mentioning Marsh's distinguished army record. It seemed, though, that this course of action had done some good because after receiving the summons, Marsh expressed his regrets for his past behaviour, promised that things would be different from now on and asked Eliza to return to him. Eliza, believing that Marsh was trying hard to make up for the past, agreed to go back to Goyt Terrace. For the next few weeks, Marsh and Eliza appeared to live happily enough together and it seemed that at long last they might have sorted out their problems. However, all this was to change on Wednesday, July 4th, 1906.

It was on that day that Marsh's landlord and employer, Edward Silcock, called at 6 Goyt Terrace to examine the rent books in order to complete a government return. Walter Marsh was out of the house at the time so Mr Silcock only stayed for a few minutes. Before he left, though, he handed a shilling to Eliza, asking her to buy some beer for his tenants on his behalf, as the local Wakes were in progress. When Marsh did finally return home and heard what had happened, he immediately accused Eliza of performing sexual favours for Edward Silcock and shouted that this was why she had been given the shilling. Eliza's protestations could do nothing to persuade Marsh that he was wrong and he even went to Mr Silcock's home at the Bold Rodney public house on Wheatbridge Road to tell him what he thought. As a result of that outburst, Marsh was dismissed on the spot and told to vacate his house. This, of course, did nothing to cool Marsh's temper and, as before, his anger was taken out on his long-suffering wife, Eliza.

Alice Julia Wootton lived at 5 Goyt Terrace, next door to Eliza Marsh. Alice knew of the troubles Eliza had been having. Occasionally, Alice had heard arguments coming from next door and seen Eliza sporting fresh bruises the next day. More than once, Marsh had locked his wife out of the house and Eliza had sought refuge with Alice until he cooled down. Twice this had necessitated Eliza staying at number five all night.

On the afternoon of July 5th, the day after Marsh had lost his job, Alice Wootton heard him calling Eliza a 'dirty cow' when they were in the yard shared by the houses in Goyt Terrace. Later that day, Alice heard the sounds of a scuffle coming from the yard and upon going to investigate, found Eliza lying on the doorstep, half in and half out of number six, while Marsh was lying on top of her, holding both her wrists and attempting to pin her arms down. Alice called out to Marsh, whereupon he released his grip and allowed Eliza to get up.

Things did not improve the next day, for on July 6th Eliza came out of her house dripping wet and told Alice Wootton that Marsh had thrown some water over her. The situation was now so bad that Alice suggested that it might be better if Eliza stayed at her house for the night. In fact, Eliza slept at the Woottons' house on the nights of July 6th and 7th, but on July 8th, at around noon, she once more returned to her husband.

Rose Bunting was the married daughter of Alice Wootton, but since October 1905, she had lived with her parents at 5 Goyt Terrace and she, too, knew all about the troubles at number six. It was around 9.00pm on July 8th, well after Eliza had returned home, that Rose saw her, sitting at her back door with her youngest child on her knee. Suddenly, even as Rose watched, Marsh appeared, bolted the back door and pulled down the blind. Eliza, obviously fearful of what might happen, immediately unbolted the door and ran out into the yard. Walter Marsh did not follow, but to be on the safe side, Eliza stayed in the yard for a full hour, after which Marsh threw open the door and called her back in. A timorous Eliza cried, "You threaten so Walter, I'm frightened," and held back whereupon Marsh said that if she didn't come back inside, he would go and fetch a policeman. Eliza still did not move, so Marsh put on his hat and coat and left the house. Seeing all this, Rose Bunting advised Eliza to go back inside while she knew her husband was out of the way, but even as they spoke, Marsh returned to say he hadn't seen a policeman but had noticed Ted Silcock waiting at the top of the street for Eliza.

Denying once again that there was anything between her and Edward Silcock, Eliza told Marsh to go inside and get to bed, but to this he retorted that it was obvious she wanted him to be out of the way so that she could get up to fresh improprieties with Silcock. At this point, Rose Bunting went back inside her own house and did not see anything else that took place between Marsh and his wife. The situation must have calmed down, though, for the next day, Monday, July 9th, Alice Wootton saw Marsh and Eliza between 2.00pm and 3.00pm and they appeared to be friendly enough towards each other.

It was closer to 3.00pm when Rose Bunting saw her neighbours in the common yard. Eliza was holding the baby, Gladys, in her arms and Marsh suggested that she should go upstairs, put the child to bed and have a lie down herself while he slept on the couch downstairs. As Rose watched, Marsh then took some money out of his pocket and handed it to Eliza, who looked down at it and then announced to Rose that he had given her a half sovereign. Rose Bunting thought this was kind of Marsh and said as much to him, to which he replied that he would give Eliza anything if only she would stop telling people what passed between them when they quarrelled. Eliza said she would be quite happy to do as Marsh asked, if only he would stop accusing her of things that were simply not true. Satisfied that the couple were happy enough with each other again, Rose went back inside number five.

Two hours later, at about 5.00pm, Rose Bunting went into the yard again and saw Walter Marsh standing at his back door. Rose did not speak to Marsh but as soon as he saw her, he called out, "She's too bloody idle to wash the dinner pots up." Rose ignored the comment and went back inside, only to go into the yard for a second time, five minutes later. Marsh was still at the back door with his son, Harold, to whom he said, "Go upstairs to your bloody mother." Rose Bunting did not see Walter Marsh again until 5.20pm when she noticed him walking up towards Factory Street. Going back inside her house, Rose heard the factory hooter sound which meant that it was now 5.30pm. Moments later, there was a knock on the back door and Rose opened it to find Marsh, who wanted to speak to her mother, Alice Wootton. Rose told Marsh that Alice was not at home to which he said, "Rose, fetch a bobby will you?" Asked to explain why he should want a policeman, Marsh told a horrified Rose that he had killed Eliza and only then did she see that Marsh was holding a razor in his right hand and that there was a good deal of blood on his fingers.

Without waiting to see if Rose Bunting would do as he asked, Marsh went back to his own house but left the back door open after he had gone inside. Gingerly, Rose walked across to number six but did not go in. There was a door at the bottom of the stairs and Rose could see that this was also bloodstained. She dashed back towards her own house and told her father, William Wootton, what she had seen and what Marsh had said.

Wootton had been in his kitchen reading when he heard Marsh tell Rose that he had killed his wife. Now he went across to number six and once inside, saw Marsh who greeted him with, "Mr Wootton, I've done it for her this time. Go upstairs and see her and then fetch a policeman." As Marsh walked into his front room, Wootton went upstairs as he had been asked and in the back bedroom he found Eliza Marsh with her throat cut and her head almost severed from her shoulders. Wootton fled back downstairs, left the house and ran to West Ward police station where he reported what he had just seen to Inspector John Fennemore.

Even as William Wootton was speaking to the police, reports of what Marsh had done had begun to circulate and these had reached the ears of George Gascoyne, Eliza's father. George and his son, John Gascoyne, rushed to Goyt Terrace to see if the story they had heard was true and upon arrival, John went to the back door while George positioned himself at the front. Even as George Gascoyne turned into Goyt Terrace, he saw Walter Marsh leaving his house without bothering to close his front door behind him. As George walked into the hallway, calling for Eliza, his son came through the house from the back and ran out after Marsh. George Gascoyne did not give chase but went upstairs where he found Eliza and waited with her until the police arrived.

John Gascoyne finally caught up with Marsh in Factory Street where a brief scuffle took place. John Ashmore, a coal agent who lived in Factory Street, was standing at his front door, saw this altercation and helped Gascoyne subdue Marsh. Then, together with another man who had also seen the fight, Ashmore walked Marsh towards the police station. On the way, Marsh was heard to remark, "I've killed my wife, will you look after me till I give myself up to the police?" Ashmore then told Marsh that this was exactly where he was being taken, to which Marsh replied, "What should you do? She's never got me a meal ready since last Wednesday." The party never reached the police station, though, for at the junction of Chatsworth Street and Factory Street they met Inspector Fennemore and William Wootton who were on their way back to Goyt Terrace. Marsh was taken into custody by Fennemore and, told that he was being arrested, Marsh remarked, "I shall go all right. I've done it. I was just coming to give myself up." Inspector Fennemore advised his prisoner to say no more just yet but Marsh continued, "I've killed my wife. I have cut her throat with a razor. The razor is in a cupboard in the front room. There are two razors in one box. My wife has been drinking with a man named Silcock last week and I meant to do it."

The inquest on the dead woman opened on July 11th and there was little difficulty in returning a verdict of wilful murder against Marsh. The following day, the police court proceedings opened before Councillor W. Jacques. Marsh was represented by Mr A.W. Foster who made no objection to a remand until the following day.

On July 13th, Marsh was back at the police court but another remand was requested so that the Treasury could be contacted. For Marsh, Mr Foster again made no objection but told the court that his client wished to make arrangements with relatives for his two children to be looked after. He also wished to give them the money he had in his possession when he was arrested. Marsh made two more appearances before the magistrates, one on July 19th and the last on July 20th when he was sent for trial at the next assizes.

It was December 5th when the murder trial took place at Derby before Mr Justice Ridley. Sir W. Ryland Adkins MP appeared for the Crown and was assisted by Mr Tangye while Marsh was defended by Mr Hole. Marsh pleaded not guilty and put forward the argument that he had acted in self-defence.

The prosecution began by outlining some of the apparently turbulent history of Walter and Eliza Marsh. George Gascoyne explained to the court that he was Eliza's father and lived at 20 Shipley Street. After Marsh had returned to Chesterfield from Sheffield, George and his family had lived with him and Eliza at Goyt Terrace for the first year they were there, not moving out until Christmas 1905. George Gascoyne stated that in his opinion, Marsh treated Eliza badly and he had often seen his daughter with bruises and black eyes. Under cross examination, though, George had to admit that he had never actually seen Marsh strike Eliza, although he had heard him threaten to 'do a John Silk' on his wife, a reference to the subject of a previous chapter.

Sophia Gascoyne was Eliza's sister and she, too, had once lived at 6

Goyt Terrace. One night, a couple of weeks before Christmas 1905, Sophia saw Marsh strike his wife while they were in the yard at the back of the house. At the time, Marsh was shouting something about Eliza being with another man and the next morning the argument started anew, for Sophia heard sounds from inside Marsh's bedroom which sounded like him striking Eliza. Sophia had tried to gain access to the bedroom to stop this attack, but the door had been bolted against her. Later that same morning, Sophia saw Marsh hit Eliza again and it was then that he made another reference to John Silk who at the time was under sentence of death and awaiting execution.

Rose Bunting and Alice Wootton also testified that there were constant arguments between Marsh and Eliza but again neither woman had seen any blows struck. Finally, John Gascoyne said that he knew that Eliza was being badly mistreated by Marsh, even though this information only came from stories he had heard.

Turning to the day of Eliza's death, John Gascoyne also gave details of what he had found when he went to Goyt Terrace with his father. Going to the back door he had found it locked but broke it down in time to see Marsh disappearing out of the front door. Rushing out, Gascoyne gave chase, caught Marsh and struck him. Marsh had cried out, "Don't strike me. I've done it. If you strike me you're not a man."

Dr James Anderson Goodfellow had been called to Goyt Terrace by Inspector Fennemore. Dr Goodfellow found Eliza lying on the back bedroom floor, her head away from the window and lying in a pool of blood. There were two distinct wounds on Eliza's throat, one of which was on the left and one and a half inches long. This was only superficial and the cut which had caused death was six and a half inches long and extended down to the spine. Eliza was only partially dressed and there was evidence that the bed had recently been slept in. This, together with bloodstains on the pillows and blankets, led Dr Goodfellow to suggest that Eliza had been attacked while she lay in bed. The first wound had been inflicted and she had then possibly been carried to where she was found and there the second, fatal wound was administered.

Inspector Fennemore said that after Marsh had been taken to the police station, he went to Goyt Terrace to examine the scene for himself. There were splashes of blood on the dressing table, a towel rail, a chair and the wall, but there was no sign of any struggle, apart from a single broken glass ornament. Looking in the cupboard in the front room, Inspector Fennemore found a box of razors, one of which had blood on the handle and blade.

For the defence, Mr Hole asked the jury to ignore all statements relating to quarrels which had allegedly taken place between Marsh and his wife. These were not borne out by independent witnesses and only Sophia Gascoyne had ever seen any blows being struck. Marsh had a 17-year good conduct certificate from the Army and had received a Silver Star and the Khedive's Medal for the action at Omdurman and the Queen's Medal with clasps for his service in South Africa. Mr Hole then called a number of witnesses who confirmed that Eliza had been lazy, intemperate and quarrelsome.

Eliza Bennett was Marsh's niece and she said that Eliza had been idle and rather fond of drink. Sarah Elizabeth Berresford from Stafford said that Marsh and Eliza had once lived near her and she had got to know them quite well. She too said that Eliza was lazy and always nagging Marsh. Finally, Charles Marsh, the prisoner's brother, explained how in his presence, Eliza had once struck Marsh with a poker and threatened him with a knife.

Telling his own story, Marsh said that on the day of Eliza's death, he was preparing to shave himself and mentioned to Eliza that he had been trying to get another house for them so that they might make a fresh start. She ignored this comment and he then remarked that she was only good for lying in bed, reading cheap novels and drinking beer. Eliza then picked up a glass ornament and threw it at him and then struck out at him with a roller blind. He then turned to defend himself and the only reason Eliza was injured was because he happened to have the razor in his hand at the time. This seemed to be at least partially corroborated by medical evidence for after his arrest, Marsh had been examined by Dr Edmunds who did find fresh bruises on his head.

Despite this testimony, the jury deliberated for only 20 minutes before deciding that Marsh was guilty of murder and he was duly sentenced to death. There was no appeal court at this time so Marsh's only hope now lay in a petition for a reprieve. The condemned man, though, refused to allow any such efforts to be made on his behalf, saying that life-long imprisonment held more fear for him than death.

Just 22 days after the trial, at 8.00am, on Thursday, December 27th,

1906, Walter Marsh was hanged at Derby by Thomas Pierrepoint who was assisted by John Ellis. It was almost exactly a year since the execution of John Silk whom Marsh had threatened to emulate.

Chapter Eight

A Moment of Madness

AT 5.00pm on Monday, March 18th, 1907, James Gordon Bennett, a postman, was delivering mail to houses in Highfield Road, Chesterfield. As he approached Mr Isaac Eyre's house, which was on a bend in the road, Bennett saw a man and a woman talking together. They were on the pavement and the woman had a large perambulator with her, necessitating Bennett walking into the road to pass them. As he did so, he heard no raised voices and no argument. They seemed to be an ordinary couple engaged in an ordinary conversation.

James Bennett continued on his round and had walked perhaps a further 20 yards when he heard what sounded like the chopping of wood. Puzzled as to who might be carrying out this task in the middle of the street, Bennett turned around and saw a sight that would remain with him to the end of his days. The woman he had just passed was now lying on the ground, face downwards, and the man with her was standing over her with a hatchet in his raised right hand. Bennett watched, frozen to the spot as the man brought the hatchet crashing down on to the back of the woman's head. The chopping sound he had heard was now all too horribly identified. The man was trying his very best to decapitate his victim.

Looking around for someone to help him, Bennett saw Tom Wright, the coachman for Dr Worthington who was working in the doctor's stable yard. He called out to Wright and both men slowly approached the man with the hatchet. Only now could they see that there was a large quantity of blood all around the woman's head. The assailant, meanwhile, had apparently completed his task to his own satisfaction for, seeing Bennett and Wright coming towards him, he threw the hatchet into an adjoining garden, pointed a finger after it and shouted, "There's the hatchet. I'm going to give myself up. She's fetched me from work this afternoon."

All three men now started to walk up Highfield Road, towards the nearest police station. Seeing that the attacker was now quite subdued and unlikely to offer any resistance, Bennett asked Wright if he thought he might manage alone, since he still had his round to complete. Wright replied in the affirmative and, perhaps surprisingly considering what he had just witnessed, Bennett went off to deliver the rest of his letters.

Wright and his prisoner had not gone very far when the man turned around and began to walk back towards where the woman lay, saying, "I'll go and get the hatchet." Wright advised him to leave it where it was, which the man agreed to do, and carried on walking, but when Wright remembered that there had been a pram, and therefore presumably a child inside it, and remarked "What are you going to do with the child?" the man replied, "It's my wife and my child. I'll bring it." He went to get the pram and as he reached the scene, bent down and kissed the woman he had attacked only minutes before.

Once again Wright and the attacker walked up Highfield Road, the stranger pushing the pram in front of him. As they walked down Newbold Road, Wright saw two men in a trap, signalled for them to stop, told them what had happened and asked them to find a constable. They rode off and as they disappeared, the man with Wright remarked, "She has been and brought me from work this afternoon and wanted some money. She has been the ruination of my life."

Sergeant Samuel Fisher was on duty in the police station when he received a telephone message stating that there had been an incident in Highfield Road. He paused only to inform a senior officer what had happened and then made his way towards the scene. On the way he met Wright, who was with the attacker and a constable they had met en route. Instantly, Fisher recognised the prisoner as a man he had known for at least 15 years. The man in custody for the brutal attack in High-field Road was 47-year-old William Edward Slack, a married man who lived in Shipley Yard, Chesterfield.

Fisher also knew that Slack was a painter by trade and indeed was now dressed in a white jacket and apron over a brown coat. In addition to the usual splashes and smears of various colours of paint, Fisher could plainly see blood upon the apron, Slack's hands and wrists. Even the pram, which Slack still pushed before him, was splashed with blood and what looked like brain tissue. Sergeant Fisher ordered the constable to continue on to the police station with the prisoner, while he went to the scene of the attack, but before they parted, Slack commented, "It's Mrs Wilson, her that caused that other trouble when my wife went away." Fisher now knew that despite what he had said before, Slack had not used the hatchet on his wife, but on a woman named Lucy Wilson.

Arriving at Highfield Road at about the same time as the police horse-drawn ambulance, Sergeant Fisher helped to place Lucy's body on to the vehicle, just as Dr Sidney Worthington arrived. By now it was around 5.40pm and Dr Worthington made a quick examination, noting several deep, incised wounds about the head and neck. He confirmed that Lucy Wilson was already dead and ordered that the body be removed to the mortuary.

Even as the body was being moved, Sergeant Fisher was searching the garden where Tom Wright said the weapon had been thrown. He found the heavily bloodstained hatchet in a gooseberry bush. The blade still had long black hairs adhering to it and appeared to have been recently ground, for it was still quite sharp. Fisher took the hatchet back to the police station where he interviewed Slack, and that evening charged him with murder. In reply, Slack said, "That's right. I did not think of it before till I got to my work. A man who kills a woman is not fit to live. I told her at dinner time today, against the theatre, that if she came up I should cut her head off and that I should have no more to do with her. I found the hatchet in the market a while ago and had it ground at Topliss."

On the day after the attack, March 19th, Slack was brought before the magistrates. Normally only evidence of arrest would have been given at this first appearance, but Slack was more than eager to talk. As soon as the charge had been read out, Slack said, "We've been going together several months." He was immediately warned by the magistrates to reserve what he had to say but Slack ignored this and continued his speech, "I didn't go with the forethought of killing her. I tried to frighten her. I told her that if she followed me to my work I ..." At this point the assistant clerk to the court interrupted and cautioned Slack that anything he said would be taken down. Again this was ignored and Slack said, "I struck her. She said 'There's your bloody bastard,' and I didn't deny it. Of course, everyone knows it's my child."

Satisfied that he had got what he wanted to say off his chest, Slack then fell quiet and was remanded. The inquest, before Dr Albert Green, soon concluded that Lucy Wilson was the victim of murder and on April 3rd, Slack made his last appearance before the magistrates, when he was sent for trial.

William Slack faced his trial at Derby on June 25th, 1907, before Lord Coleridge. Sir W. Ryland Adkins and Mr McCardie appeared for the prosecution and Slack was defended by Mr Harold Wright.

George Wilson was the dead woman's husband and he stated that they had lived together at 38 Spa Lane. Wilson worked nights as a ticket checker at the Chesterfield Theatre and Lucy had also served there, during the day, as a cleaner. They had been married for 15 years.

On March 18th, the day that Lucy died, Wilson had been at the theatre until 12.30pm when he left to go home to Spa Lane. Lucy was still at the theatre when Wilson left and she did not get home until 1.30pm when they had their dinner together. At 4.40pm, Wilson went back to the theatre. At the time, Lucy was in the front room of their house and the baby was dressed, in its pram and ready to go out. Wilson said that he had never seen his wife alive again. He confirmed that he did not know the prisoner and had never set eyes on him until he saw him at the police court in March. Finally, Wilson swore that he believed Lucy's child was his and she had never said anything to the contrary.

When this evidence had been given at the police court, Slack had immediately jumped to his feet and claimed that he was lying. Slack not only claimed that Wilson had seen him with his wife in the theatre bar that very day, but that he had also been to Wilson's house while he was there. Wilson was now pressed on this point by Mr Wright for the defence but he persisted in stating that Slack was the one telling lies, he had never seen him before, Slack had never been to his house and the child which had born in June 1906 was not Slack's. George Wilson also maintained that he had enjoyed a very happy marriage.

The next witness was William Henry Madin, a joiner, who said that on March 18th, he had been working on the same house as Slack, at 37 Avondale Road. They had been working on this property for several weeks and on the day in question, Madin started work at 6.30am, although the first time he actually saw Slack, since he was working at the back of the house, was 7.00am.

The two men worked together until 11.45am, when Slack asked Madin if he might take a little time off and go to Eastwood to see a man who owed him 15s. Madin gave his permission and he watched as Slack walked off towards the town. Just after 1.00pm Slack returned and Madin asked him if he had got his money. Slack replied, "No, but a woman is bringing it up to me this afternoon." Slack went on to say that the woman would be wearing dark clothing and a big black hat and would have a 'cart' with a baby in it. He explained that he would be working at the back of the house again and as Madin might see her first, he should give him a shout.

At 3.30pm, Slack had come around to the front of the house and walked off down Avondale Road. Madin watched as he met a woman who fitted the earlier description precisely. He recognised her as the same woman he had seen the previous day. She and Slack spoke together for about 20 minutes, during which Slack turned away from the woman two or three times as if to walk away but was always called back by the woman. Finally, Slack returned to work and the woman walked off towards Highfield Road. About 15 minutes after she had gone, Slack appeared again from the back of the house, asked another of the workmen to finish a window off for him and walked off down Avondale Road, in the same direction the woman had taken.

The pram Lucy Wilson had with her was now produced in court, and Madin said that it was the same as the one the woman he had seen was pushing. Shown the hatchet, he confirmed that such a tool would not be needed by a painter but added that when they had all been working on a previous job, at the Park Hotel, Slack had seen him sharpening an axe on a whetstone and remarked that he had a hatchet that needed sharpening. Madin invited him to use any of the whetstones they had lying about but had no idea whether Slack took him up on the offer or not.

Elizabeth Osborne was another of the cleaners at the Chesterfield Theatre and she knew Lucy Wilson and her husband very well. On March 18th, Elizabeth was working with Lucy when, at some time between noon and 1.00pm, Lucy went outside into Corporation Street. Later, Elizabeth was also outside and she saw Lucy talking to a man near one of the theatre doors. She had positively identified that man as Slack.

James Bennett and Tom Wright then told the court what they had seen and heard in Highfield Road. Both said that Slack's demeanour was very calm after the attack, and that he was not drunk and appeared to be perfectly normal.

Medical testimony was given by Dr Worthington, who in addition to attending at the scene, had also performed the post-mortem. All the injuries except one were limited to the head and neck. The wound which had been the direct cause of death was in fact two cuts which combined to a depth of four inches in the neck. All the muscles and both carotid arteries on the right side had been divided. Another wound on the left side had penetrated the spinal canal and there were four other wounds on the skull, all of which caused fractures and the exposure of the underlying brain tissue. The single wound which was not on the head or neck was in all probability a defence wound for Lucy's little finger on her left hand had been severed. Dr Worthington believed that all the injuries had been inflicted from behind, probably while Lucy was lying face down on the floor.

When Sergeant Fisher detailed his evidence, he added that he knew that Slack had been in the Army and had served in India. His discharge papers were marked 'good' but Sergeant Fisher was also able to say that Slack might be the kind of man who lost his temper easily and was therefore prone to violence, since he had been convicted of an assault upon a police officer which appeared to be totally unprovoked.

Two of the final prosecution witnesses were called to show that this crime might well have been planned months in advance. Bartholomew Murphy was a close friend of the prisoner and had been with him in Market Place when he bought a hatchet some eight or nine months before the attack. While that might not be significant in itself, Arthur Butler, who worked at Allen and Orr's wood yard, which had until recently been called Topliss' wood yard, testified that he had seen Slack carefully sharpening a hatchet three months before Lucy Wilson died.

The time came for the defence to put its case. Mr Wright said they were not disputing that Lucy Wilson met her death at the hands of Slack but that she had provoked him into it and this should reduce the crime to one of manslaughter. The first witness Mr Wright called, was Slack himself. Slack began by explaining that before he had been a painter, he had served as a carpenter and he had bought the hatchet, for 3d, with the intention of using it to make handles for hammers and other tools. He then referred to his Army career, stating that he had served more than five years, being discharged on June 16th, 1897.

Turning to his relationship with Lucy Wilson, Slack claimed that he first met her two years ago and they had sex on that very first meeting. Further, this affair had continued ever since and he had even made love to Lucy in her own home while her husband was downstairs. Lucy had told him that her husband hadn't given her any money in seven years and since he went with other women, she would go with other men. She had even asked Slack to go away with her, pointing out that his wife had given evidence against him in the case of the assault upon the police officer, for which he got seven years in prison.

Slack's evidence was given very incoherently but eventually his testimony was heard. On the Sunday before the crime, March 17th, they had met in an empty house, 66 St Helen's Street, where he had once done some painting, and they agreed to meet up the following day, at the theatre, to sort things out once and for all. They met there at 12.30pm and she suggested going away together to Coventry. He said he had work to do, including mending some steps, and would see her that night, again at the theatre.

That afternoon, Lucy called him out of work. He had mentioned that she might come to Madin, and would have asked his workmate to say that he wasn't there only Lucy saw him first and called him down to see her. They spoke together for ten minutes or more, she saying that she was angry that he had told her he wouldn't be in Avondale Road and so was obviously trying to avoid her. She would not let him go, so to get rid of her, he promised to meet her again later that afternoon. When they met again, in Highfield Road, Lucy threatened to drown herself in a local stream known, as the Donkey Racecourse, unless he came away with her. Slack walked back into the road but she grabbed at his jacket and almost knocked the pram over. Lucy then called him a rogue and insulted his wife. By now, Slack had the hatchet out of his pocket and suddenly he lost his temper. Everything seemed to go dark just as if there was going to be a great storm and the deed was done.

The defence now called Elizabeth Slack, the prisoner's wife, who said that Slack had told her that he was going to use the hatchet to repair some steps at his sister's house. A boy named Philpott had brought some wood for this purpose. This was confirmed by Clara Ford, Slack's sister, who said her brother called at her house in Knifesmith Gate, at 12.55pm on March 18th and said he would be back later to repair her steps. She also reported that Slack had suffered from sunstroke in India and was a much-changed man when he came back to England.

Clara's husband, Patrick Ford, told of an incident which had taken place in the Sportsman's Inn at Grassmoor some time before. He and Slack had been enjoying a drink together when a man came in. Slack fancied that the man was staring at him and said, "I shall certainly go for him." But for Ford holding him back, there would have undoubtedly been a serious altercation.

Sergeant Hudson said that he had been attacked by Slack in 1899. There had been no provocation or cause. Slack had spoken to Hudson in the street as his wife had left him and he wanted help in finding her. When Slack convinced himself that nothing was being done, he attacked Hudson with two knives and inflicted 16 wounds.

One of the final witnesses was Dr C.A. Greaves, the medical officer of Derby prison. He said that he had examined Slack a number of times since his reception in the jail. He described Slack as an excitable man with a touchy, irritable temper, although he was perfectly sane and certainly knew right from wrong. During the judge's summing up, Slack interrupted a number of times, saying that points he was making were irrelevant. When Lord Coleridge mentioned a pocket inside Slack's painter's jacket, in which he had held the hatchet, Slack shouted, "It was there for carrying whitewash brushes." Told to be quiet by the judge, Slack finally calmed down and apologised but added for good measure, "You are suggesting things that are not right." Later on, though, there were other outbursts, Slack demanding that witnesses be called who could prove what he was saying. He also claimed that any man on the jury, and even the judge himself, would act the same way if someone insulted their wives as Lucy had insulted his.

Although the constant interruptions meant that the summing up lasted for well over an hour, the jury deliberated for less than a minute and did not even bother to leave the box before announcing that Slack was guilty. Asked if he had anything to say, Slack shouted an obscenity, telling the judge exactly where he might put the black cap. As the first words of the death sentence were uttered, Slack shouted, "I've told you what to do with the cap. It's no use talking."

With some difficulty, Lord Coleridge continued but halfway through his speech, Slack turned and with a cry of, "Oh, I'm not going to listen to this," tried to leave the dock. Warders had to restrain him while Lord Coleridge continued but as the words ' . . . to a lawful place of execution,' were intoned, Slack tore a small tuft of hair from the side of his head and threw it into the air, shouting, "That's what I care. That's the man I am." Finally, as the judge said, " . . . and may the Lord have mercy on your soul," Slack shouted, "There is no God, or I should not be here for this. He would not have allowed this woman to have come up to me. But I don't care." He was then taken down to the cells, kicking and screaming all the way.

There was to be no reprieve and exactly three weeks later, on Tuesday, July 16th, 1907, William Edward Slack stood on the scaffold at Derby at 8.00am. He was hanged by Henry Pierrepoint and John Ellis and to the end maintained the bravado he had shown at his trial, muttering loudly as the priest intoned the prayers.

Only now did the *Derbyshire Times* publish the long text of a letter it had received from Slack a few days before the execution. In this Slack, determined to tell his own story, explained that he had first met Lucy Wilson when he was painting the theatre where she worked, in July 1905. They fell into conversation and soon she invited him to her house while her husband was working. From then on, Slack claimed that he would go to Spa Lane as many as four times a week. Eventually a child was born, on June 26th, 1906, and Lucy persisted in telling Slack that it was his and began suggesting that they run away together, even hinting that she might give her husband something to see him off as he was in the way. The letter went on to give all the details of the relationship and explain how Slack had tried to extricate himself before the entire thing boiled over into that terrible attack on Lucy.

The whole truth will never be known. Was Slack a romancer who invented a relationship in order to justify his subsequent actions in killing Lucy Wilson, or were they really lovers? What is true is that two people lost their lives, one under the sharpened blade of a hatchet and one at the end of an unforgiving rope.

Chapter Nine

Police Involvement

IN the early hours of Sunday, May 19th, 1912, a curious incident took place in Park Street, Birdholme, Chesterfield. Alfred Johnson was found shot dead, a gaping wound in his chest and his heart blown to pieces. This was not, however, a simple case of murder, for the killer claimed that the wrong man had died.

It was 2.45am when Maud Beeston was disturbed by someone hammering on her front door at 2 Hadfield's Yard. Going to investigate, Maud was surprised to see John Mowbray, a man she had been having a relationship with for the past three years and who was the father of her baby. He seemed to be deeply concerned about something so Maud asked him in and told him to have a seat in the kitchen. Mowbray then announced, "I've come to have half an hour with you and the child before they fetch me." Maud asked, "Who is going to fetch you?" and Mowbray replied, "You'll see in a minute or two." He then paused before adding, "I've killed a man." Maud asked if he knew who he had killed but Mowbray said, "No, I didn't know who it was. I've shot the wrong man."

Asked to explain himself further, Maud's agitated guest said, "When I was going home on Saturday night, I got down and had a sleep and when I got up, I was going home when someone rushed at me and hit me in the earhole." He went on to say, "There were two of them and one was a policeman but I don't know who the other man was. I went to shoot bobby Burns." By this last statement, Maud Beeston knew that the man Mowbray had wanted to kill was a policeman, Constable John William Burns, a man well known to the people who lived in the area.

Having told his story and unburdened himself, Mowbray then fell asleep for half an hour. It was then that Mowbray's landlord, William Lloyd, came to ask if Maud had seen him. Maud showed Lloyd where Mowbray still lay asleep. Lloyd woke his lodger and after some discussion over what had taken place, Mowbray, Lloyd and Maud Beeston went out into Wheeldon Lane. It was there, at 4.10am that they were seen by Sergeant James Birchall who arrested Mowbray and escorted him to the police station. On the way, Mowbray remarked, "I wish it had been that other bastard Burns I had shot instead of the man I have shot. Burns is the bastard I intended it for." Later, at the station, Mowbray repeated this sentiment saying, "I wish it had been that bloody Burns. I planned it for him to put his bloody light out but the bugger ran away like a bloody greyhound dog and that's the man that's so brave, the bloody cur."

It was on Monday, May 20th, that the police court proceedings opened but after evidence of arrest had been given by the Chief Constable, Mowbray was remanded until May 28th. The inquest on the dead man opened that same afternoon at the Municipal Hall, Chesterfield, before Mr M.S. Brodhurst. The first witness was Herbert Edmund Johnson, one of Alfred's brothers, who gave evidence of having identified the body at the mortuary. He stated that Alfred had been 31 on November 24th last. He was a married man with six young children and had lived with his family at 78 Park Street, Birdholme, for the last few years. Herbert also said that he knew Mowbray well, and had done for the past 12 years or so, pointing out that he was not only a close friend but they had often worked together and had never had an argument. Upon hearing this, Mowbray burst into tears.

The next witness was Dr William Johnstone Symes, who had been called to the mortuary at 4.30am where he had viewed the body, which in his opinion had been dead for three to four hours. On the clothing, in the region of the left breast, was a scorched ragged hole, the material around it being soaked through with blood. There were corresponding holes in each item of clothing which Dr Symes removed from the upper body and once the victim was undressed, a large circular wound, some three inches in diameter, was observed near the left nipple. The greater part of the heart had been completely blown to pieces and one-third of it was protruding through the wound. The right lung was also blown to pieces and a number of ribs were shattered. There was a smaller wound in the right armpit and Dr Symes stated that the shot which killed Johnson had entered at the left nipple and emerged in the armpit. The gun used to fire the shot would have been actually touching the victim's clothing when it was fired, and death would have been instantaneous. Only one shot had been fired and Dr Symes produced the pellets he had removed from the body to show that they had been flattened from contact with the victim's ribs.

The inquest continued with some extraordinary testimony which was given by the intended victim, Constable John William Burns. He said that in the early hours of May 19th he was on duty on the footpath which ran down from the top of Park Street. He was talking to Alfred Johnson, who had been with him since 11.00pm, when he noticed a man walking along the footpath from the direction of Boythorpe. Checking the time, Burns saw that it was 1.10am and wondered what someone might be doing out at this time. He shone his torch on the approaching figure to reveal that it was the prisoner, Mowbray.

According to Burns, Mowbray immediately launched into a verbal attack upon him crying "Keep your bloody f***ing light off! It's Mr bloody f***ing Burns. You're the man that I want. I have something in the house that I'll fetch and put your bloody f***ing lights out!" Faced with this abuse, Constable Burns claimed that he merely told Mowbray to be on his way and he saw him go into his lodgings at 37 Park Street, although he was still swearing violently at the time.

Burns and Johnson continued to talk until 1.25am when Burns left and walked down the path towards Langer Lane. From there he proceeded down into Derby Road which ran at the back of Park Street and it was then that he heard what sounded like a shot. Going back up Park Street, Burns returned to where he had been talking with Johnson, but saw no sign of anyone. From there he went to Johnson's house but there was no answer so he continued on to the police station in Storforth Lane to see if Johnson had gone there. Returning to Park Street, Burns then removed his helmet and tunic so that anyone who saw him would not recognise him as a policeman, and again went in search of Johnson. He finally found the man lying in a large pool of blood in Park Street, face down with his hands stretched out in front of him. Johnson was obviously dead, so with the assistance of Mr Millward, a neighbour, Burns took Johnson to his house from where later he escorted the body to the mortuary.

At 2.25am, Constable Burns met Constable Albert Buggins in Derby Road and asked him to accompany him to Mowbray's lodgings at 37 Park Road where they recovered a gun, some percussion caps, powder and shot, from a corner in the kitchen. The weapon was not loaded at the time but had recently been fired. Finally, Burns denied emphatically that he had ever laid a finger on Mowbray, saying that if he had hit him, then Mowbray would have had some marks to show for it. Burns also claimed that the reason for Mowbray becoming so incensed at seeing him and Johnson together was that he believed Johnson was giving the police information about his poaching activities.

The main problem with this story was that Mowbray denied it completely, claiming that Constable Burns had first beaten him and then provoked him into coming out of his lodgings for more of the same. When other witnesses were called their testimony appeared, if anything, to confirm that it was Mowbray who might well be telling the truth.

Annie Elizabeth Gallimore lived at 39 Park Street, next door to where Mowbray lodged. She was lying on the sofa in her front room at about 1.30am when she heard Mowbray at his front door. She did not see him, of course, but did recognise his voice as he shouted at someone, "I'll put you to sleep you bastard!" Mowbray then went into number 37 and Annie heard him shout for Mr Lloyd, twice. Annie drifted off back to sleep then but was woken again by someone banging about next door. Deciding that she might be better off in bed, Annie was on her way upstairs when she heard the sound of a shot. Looking out of her bedroom window she could plainly see a man's body lying in front of the houses. When the figure had not moved half an hour later she went out to take a closer look and saw that it was Alfred Johnson.

Elizabeth Lloyd was William's wife and lived with him at 37 Park Street. Mowbray, a collier, had been lodging with them for three weeks and on May 18th he left for work as usual after he had eaten his breakfast. She next heard of him in the early hours of May 19th when he was at the foot of the stairs, calling for her husband. Mowbray shouted, "Bill, come on down, there's two of them." At the time, William Lloyd was asleep. He had come home rather drunk earlier that night and she didn't want to disturb him and so told Mowbray to be quiet. She then heard him rattling about downstairs in the kitchen and she thought he might be making himself some supper.

In due course, another voice, this time from outside, shouted, "Are you coming? If you're coming out, bloody well come." Mowbray called back, "If I do come, you'll know about it." Once again the voice from outside shouted for Mowbray to come out and again Mowbray replied that if he did, the man would know about it. After this had gone on for some time, Elizabeth heard Mowbray go to the front door and immediately whoever had been outside ran away. Mowbray must have followed, though, because minutes later she heard him come back into the house and say, "Come on down Bill, I want to tell you something. I've done it."

Elizabeth went downstairs herself and followed Mowbray into the kitchen. He looked terrified and she asked him what had happened. Mowbray replied, "Missus, I was coming through the fields and I never said a word to anyone. They both started on me. One come out of the closet [meaning an outside toilet]." There was a gun on the kitchen table, which belonged to Elizabeth's son, Oswald, who had now come downstairs himself. Both he and his mother heard Mowbray repeat that he wanted to tell Bill something before Elizabeth went to call a neighbour, Mary Millward. When she returned home, she found Mowbray trying to reload the gun and Oswald attempting to take it from him.

Elizabeth feared that Mowbray was trying to do away with himself but moments later, Mowbray jumped to his feet and ran out of the back door, leaving the gun behind.

The latter part of this testimony was confirmed by 14-year-old Oswald Lloyd. Once his mother had left the house, Mowbray picked up the gun and said, "I'll do them." He then repeated that two 'bobbies' had been hitting him and he had recognised one of them as Constable

Burns. Later, Oswald went outside, saw Johnson's body and then returned to the house and woke his father.

William Lloyd had been out drinking with Mowbray on the evening of May 18th but when he returned home, Mowbray stayed on at the pub. The first he knew of this incident was when he was woken and saw the body of a man some ten or 12 yards away from their house. Lloyd went out to look for Mowbray and found him with Maud Beeston. It was Lloyd who first told Mowbray the name of the man he had shot dead, to which he replied, "I didn't know it was him. I didn't mean to shoot him," adding that he had taken the gun to look for Burns and that as he walked down the street someone had sprung at him and the gun went off. He then told the same story about coming home and being attacked by two men, one of whom was Burns, who had struck him twice with his fists. Then the police arrived and took Mowbray into custody. One problem for Mowbray came with the testimony of William Thomas Britt. Earlier, the entire Lloyd family had said that although there was a gun in the house, there were no caps or powder for it. Mr Britt was assisting in his ironmonger's shop in Chesterfield on May 18th and he testified that at 8.00pm, Mowbray had come into the shop and purchased a half pound tin of powder and some shot. This, of course, was long before the alleged attack upon him from the two policemen. Mowbray had explained this by stating that he wanted to shoot some rabbits.

The jury considered all the evidence for less than ten minutes before returning a verdict that Johnson had been murdered and Mowbray was responsible. On May 28th, Mowbray was back before the magistrates where he was represented by Mr A.J. Hopkins and prosecuted by Mr Rooke Ley. All the testimony having been repeated, Mowbray was sent to face his trial at the next assizes.

Those assizes opened at Derby the following month and Mowbray appeared before Lord Coleridge on Tuesday, June 25th 1912. The prisoner was defended by Mr E.L. Hadfield while the case for the Crown was led by Sir W. Ryland Adkins who was assisted by Mr Drysdale Woodcock.

When Constable Burns repeated his testimony, Mr Hadfield made a most telling point, stating that it was impossible for Johnson to have been the man heard shouting for Mowbray to come out, and later running away from him, since such a scenario would have meant that he would then have been shot in the back, not the chest. Mr Hadfield then suggested that the person running away was Burns himself, but he denied this. He also denied that he had taken his tunic and helmet off so that he might more easily fight Mowbray if indeed he did come outside.

It was all a question of whom the jury chose to believe. If they believed that Mowbray had been assaulted, either by two policemen or more likely by Burns and Alfred Johnson, then they might decide that he had been provoked and was guilty only of manslaughter. If instead they came to accept that Burns was telling the truth and there had been no assault upon Mowbray, then this was deliberate murder. The defence had also intimated that Mowbray was so drunk at the time that whatever his intentions, he was not responsible for his actions.

After 35 minutes of deliberation, the jury returned to the courtroom to announce that they had found Mowbray guilty as charged. Mowbray made no comment as the death sentence was passed. As he was escorted down to the cells, Maud Beeston burst into tears.

The original execution date was fixed for July 16th, at Derby prison, but this was postponed when notice of appeal was given. This was heard on July 15th before Justices Darling, Channell and Pickford. Once again the suggestion was that Mowbray was so drunk at the time that he could not form the intention to kill, but Mr Justice Darling, in dismissing the appeal, said that there was no reason to interfere with the conviction because of anything which had taken place at the time and the matter was now in the hands of the Home Secretary. A new execution date of Tuesday, July 30th was now set.

A petition was organised, asking for a reprieve on the grounds that Mowbray was drunk at the time of the offence and that while in this condition he was under the impression that he had received considerable violence at the hands of another. It was well supported, especially in the Chesterfield area, and by the time it was forwarded to the Home Secretary, held over 14,000 signatures. Whether it was that petition, or official doubts as to what really happened on that May night, the Home Office were moved to interfere with the sentence and on July 24th, announced that Mowbray's' sentence had been commuted to one of life imprisonment.

Chapter Ten

One Wife Too Many

ON New Year's Day, 1922, Thomas Gore, a shunter for the Midland Railway Company, was walking alongside some allotments at Chaddesden near Derby when he noticed his dog scratching furiously at one particular patch of earth. There was a slight mound and Gore immediately thought that something must have been hidden there. He determined to return the following day and investigate further.

It was 11.00am on January 2nd when Gore, now equipped with a small fork, returned to the allotments and began digging at the spot which had interested his dog the previous day. Perhaps he felt he might find some stolen goods, the proceeds of a robbery on which there might be a reward, or maybe some other valuables had been secreted away. However, as the soil was scraped away, it was not treasure or contraband which Gore found but items of clothing which appeared to be covering a body.

Thomas Gore ran off to fetch a policeman but it was not until 12.15pm that he found Constable Frank Holmes. The officer returned to the allotments with Gore and together the two men continued digging. In due course, their efforts revealed a fully-clothed young woman.

By her head was a hat and a shawl and lying near to the body was a broken spade. Constable Holmes returned to the police station to inform his superiors what he and Gore had found.

Before the body was removed, Dr John Acton Southern, a consulting surgeon at the Derbyshire Royal Infirmary, was also summoned to the scene to carry out an examination. Dr Southern noted that the hole was approximately two feet deep. The woman was lying on her left side, with her hands drawn up to her head. The left hand lay under the woman's head while the right lay on her face. Once the poor woman's body had been taken to the mortuary, Dr Southern also noticed a small amount of blood, perhaps no more than a tablespoonful, where the head had lain.

Although the body was badly decomposed, identifying it did not prove to be too difficult. A clothing card which contained a man's name and address was found on the body. It was noted that this man's wife had recently been reported as a missing person. It was this fact which led police officers to call at 25 Francis Street, near Derby Racecourse, a house rented by Mr and Mrs Atkin.

Percy James Atkin, a railway worker, and his wife, Maud, had lived at 25 Francis Street for some time. Maud, who at 27 was the right age to be the body in the grave, had not been seen since Monday, November 21st and her husband, two years Maud's senior, had now also disappeared. Luckily for the police, the Atkin family had had two lodgers, a married couple named Butcher and they were asked to take a look at the body which had been recovered from the allotment.

Henry Lewis Butcher also worked on the Midland Railway and he told the police that he and his wife had moved into Francis Street on June 6th, 1921. Both he and his wife, Hilda, positively identified some of the clothing which the woman was wearing, Hilda remarking especially on the boots which she had given to Mrs Atkin. The body was undoubtedly dressed in the clothing worn by Maud Atkin and since her husband and two children had now vanished, an urgent search was organised. Part of that search involved large numbers of police constables digging over the entire allotment in case further bodies might be buried there. No other human remains were found, however.

Henry Lewis Butcher and his wife were able to tell the police some of the recent history of Percy Atkin and his wife. Maud had been staying with her family in Buckden, Huntingdonshire, helping with the harvest, when the Butchers first moved in. She had returned to Francis Street on October 24th, with the two children. On November 14th, 1921, Atkin had told Henry Butcher that he was leaving the area to go to live in Normanton and had given one week's notice to the owner of 25 Francis Street. Atkin went on to suggest that if Henry and Hilda wished to stay on in the house, they should contact the owner themselves and take over the tenancy. Meanwhile, on November 19th, Atkin had moved out much of the furniture so that there was very little left in the house. Indeed, that night, Maud Atkin had had to sleep on the floor.

Hilda Butcher had next seen Percy Atkin at 9.20am on November 20th when he left the house, only to return at 11.30am when he collected a suitcase and went out again. The next day, the 21st, Atkin came home from work at 1.35pm when he was seen by both Henry and Hilda Butcher. The last that the lodgers saw of Maud Atkin was when she left Francis Street with her husband, at 2.15pm. As they left the house, Maud called out to Hilda, "I'm not going for good Mrs Butcher. I'll call to see you again. I'll leave the irons and I'll fetch them on Thursday." At 6.30pm that evening, Percy Atkin had returned to Francis Street to collect the rent his lodgers owed him, and to pick up what little remained of his furniture.

The investigation into the disappearance of the Atkins was not very old when the youngest child, Nellie, was found alive and well, living with Percy's mother in Buckden. There was still no trace of Atkin himself though, or his son, Leslie, and so, on January 3rd, the police issued details of the man they were urgently seeking. The description of the missing man read: "Age 29; height five feet six inches, or seven; clean shaven, grey eyes, long dark hair brushed back from forehead; stiff build; upper teeth false, two believed missing in front; tattoo resembling triangle on right wrist; addicted to biting his finger nails; recently suffered from boils on one arm. Total abstainer but a smoker." The report went on to detail Leslie Atkin's description, stating that he was three and a half years old, and rather small for his age. It was also revealed that Atkin had, recently, gone through a form of marriage with another woman who only now was finding out what her new 'husband' had really been up to.

Margaret Milton lived at 35 Co-operative Street, Derby, and she had first met Percy Atkin at a whist drive in September 1920. They had fallen into conversation, found themselves attracted to each other and had started going out together soon afterwards. Atkin, of course, neglected to mention that he was a married man with two children and informed Margaret that he was single and living in lodgings at Nottingham Road, near to which was Francis Street.

The new relationship flourished and eventually Atkin proposed marriage and was accepted. A date for the wedding was set and the loving couple prepared to set up home together, Atkin at one stage telling Margaret that some friends of his were going abroad and he had bought some furniture from them for the new home with Margaret. Things progressed nicely until, on November 10th, Margaret's next door neighbour, Mrs Keys, told her that she had discovered that Atkin was already married. Margaret confronted her husband-to-be, who explained that he had indeed been wed once but his wife had died a few months before, at Buckden, and claiming, rather strangely perhaps, that she had succumbed to 'galloping consumption'. Atkin went on to tell Margaret that he hadn't told her all this before because he was afraid she would not have him if she knew the truth.

For a time, Margaret remained angry that she had been deceived in this way and told Atkin to take away the furniture he had left at her house, and the young boy who had been living with them. Eventually, though, she forgave Atkin and told him that the wedding could go on, providing she saw the death certificate of his former wife. Atkin explained that he had left the certificate with his mother for safe keeping but would write to her and ask her to send it on to him. Margaret seemed to be satisfied and said that the wedding could now take place as planned. Margaret Milton also accepted Atkin's explanation when it came to the two children he produced and left at Co-operative Street. First a young boy appeared and then, the day before the wedding, a little baby girl. Atkin said that these were his dead brother's children. They were, of course, his own son and daughter.

On November 14th, Percy James Atkin married Margaret Milton at Bakewell Parish Church, on the edge of the Derbyshire Peak District, and for a time they lived happily enough together back in Derby, at Co-operative Street, with the two children. The connubial bliss was rather shattered, though, on December 12th, 1921 when Mrs Cook, who lived at 15 Francis Street and knew Atkin and his legal wife very well, brought some visitors to Co-operative Street, looking for Maud. They told Margaret that her husband was still married, although his wife was now missing. Once again Margaret confronted her husband when he returned home from work. At first, Atkin flatly denied that there was any substance to this story, but as Margaret pressed him for the truth, he became very upset and said that if she did not stand by him he would be 'had up for bigamy'.

Atkin gently explained that he had no idea where his legal wife was. He had last seen her on Derwent Bridge, which connected Derby's town centre to Nottingham Road, at 9.30pm on November 21st when they had quarrelled and he had walked away from her. This time, though, Margaret Milton was not to be convinced so easily and Atkin left Co-operative Street that same night, saying that if he cleared off out of the way, the bigamy wouldn't get in the newspapers. Atkin took both children with him, telling Margaret that he was going to leave them with his mother, but he soon returned with Leslie, saying that his mother was unable to take both and asking Margaret for time to arrange something.

Margaret next saw Atkin in Manchester on December 17th. Soon afterwards he returned to Derby and picked up his son, Leslie. The last time Margaret, or indeed anyone else, had seen Atkin was on Christmas Eve, 1921.

In fact, Percy Atkin had not run very far. As a matter of routine, all his relatives were interviewed and when police called at his sister's house in New Malden, Surrey, on the evening of January 2nd, they found Atkin and his son and took him into custody. That same day, Sergeant Joseph Humphrey Ridd travelled down to Surrey and brought Atkin back to Derby where he was charged with murder. Atkin replied, "I would rather not say anything."

On January 4th, the inquest opened before Mr Reginald William Sale. Evidence of identification was given by Henry and Hilda Butcher and by Frederick Ekins, who was Maud's brother. He reported that he had recognised the body due to the small head, long tidy hair and rather large front teeth, although Mr Ekins also had to admit that the features were so bloated and decomposed that he would not have known that it was Maud if other circumstances hadn't indicated that this was the case. Once this testimony was given, Mr Sale adjourned the proceedings until January 12th.

It was also on January 4th that Atkin made his first appearance at the police court, where Mr Bendle W. Moore appeared for the Director of Public Prosecutions and Mr T.H. Bishop represented the prisoner. The only witness was Sergeant Ridd, who gave evidence of arrest, and Atkin was then remanded until January 6th. On that date, though, Atkin did not even appear in the dock as a further remand was ordered, this time until January 13th.

January 12th saw the resumption of the inquest and Atkin took careful notes as 18 witnesses were called. Having listened to all the evidence, the jury took only five minutes deliberation to decide that the body was indeed that of Maud Atkin and that she had been murdered by her husband. One further remand followed at the police court and it was not until January 16th that all the witnesses were heard and Atkin was duly sent for trial.

That trial opened at Derby on February 16th, 1922, before Mr Justice Horridge. The case for the prosecution was put by Sir W. Ryland Adkins and the prisoner was defended by Sir Henry Maddocks. The proceedings lasted for two days.

Ernest Harry Cook, the husband of the woman who had visited Margaret Milton on December 12th, testified that he knew Atkin and Maud very well, having lived with them for a time until about three years before. On November 21st, Maud had called at Cook's house in Francis Street at 9.30am. Later that day, at about 2.30pm, Cook had seen Maud on a footpath between Chequers Lane and the Cattle Market. She and her husband, the prisoner in the dock, had been walking towards Derby. Cook said that he never saw Maud again but on December 8th, he did see Atkin who was on Derwent Bridge. They had a brief conversation, during which Atkin said he was suffering badly with boils on one arm. Cook asked after Maud and was told that she had gone home to her family because her father had just died.

Other witnesses had also seen Maud on the day she disappeared. Thomas Greasley lived at 30 Highfield Cottages, near the Nottingham Road cemetery, and knew Atkin well. At 2.10pm on November 21st, Greasley met Atkin near the railway sidings at Chaddesden and they spoke about moving Atkin's furniture from Francis Street to Co-operative Street. As they walked, Greasley saw a woman walking slowly towards them along the canal bank and remarked, "Who's the tottie Percy?" Atkin told him that it was his 'missus', whereupon Greasley apologised for his remark. At 6.30pm that same day, Greasley went to Francis Street to find only Atkin and Henry Butcher there. As the few remaining sticks of furniture were loaded up, Greasley saw Atkin pick up a small hammer and put it into his jacket pocket. For some reason, Atkin did not accompany Greasley to Co-operative Street, but told him that the door would be open and he should just put the furniture inside somewhere.

Isaac Allsop was another railway worker, but on November 21st he had been to a football match with a friend of his, David Adams. As they were walking home after the match, they saw Atkin strolling down the canal causeway towards Highfield Lane. There was a woman walking a couple of feet behind him but Allsop could not hear any conversation between them. This testimony was confirmed by Mr Adams but neither man knew Maud and so were unable to say if this woman was her.

Two other people who knew Atkin were Henry Belderstone and Elijah Hilton, both goods guards for the Midland Railway Company. Belderstone testified that he had been on Chequers Lane at 11.00pm on November 21st when he had been passed by Hilton who was riding a bicycle. As Belderstone turned into Nottingham Road he saw Atkin wearing his railway uniform. He was with his wife, who Belderstone had known for several years. He had exchanged a cordial 'good evening' with them.

Elijah Hilton had known Atkin for eight or nine years and he told the court that he had seen him with a woman on Nottingham Road, walking in the direction of the cemetery, at 11.00pm on November 21st. At the time the couple were near the Chesterfield Arms public house and Hilton described the clothing the woman wore. This description matched the articles found in the shallow grave and which were now produced in court.

The route Atkin and the woman were taking led to the allotments where Maud had been found on January 2nd. Two witnesses were now called whose testimony seemed to show that Atkin might well have spent the next few hours concealing Maud's body. The first of these was Richard Sharman who lived at 21 Nottingham Road. He, too, had known Atkin for a number of years and said that he had seen him at 10.45am on November 22nd, coming from the direction of Highfield Cottages. Atkin looked as if he had been out all night and his clothes and boots were very wet.

The second witness was William Thomas Tomlinson, a clerk for the railway company, who stated that Atkin had come into work at 6.20am on November 22nd and said that he was ill and couldn't take his duty. He was very hoarse at the time and Tomlinson could hardly hear what he was saying. Somewhat surprisingly, though, Atkin was in work at his usual time on November 23rd, and seemed to have made a remarkable recovery.

Maud Atkin's body had been found buried on an allotment rented by the man now accused of her murder. The prosecution called Robert Raiseberry Eggleton, the secretary of the allotments association. He said that he had visited the allotments, at the request of the police, on January 3rd, 1922. Eggleton confirmed that the spot indicated by the police was the only part of Atkin's allotment where he had ever been seen digging. Atkin had held the land since April 1918 but had failed to cultivate it and complaints had been made. As a result of this, Atkin said he was going to plant an apple tree and had been observed digging a single hole.

Annie Ekins, the wife of Frederick who had given evidence of identification at the inquest, told of a letter she had received from Atkin on December 2nd. In part this read, "I am writing to let you know that poor Maud passed away last Sunday, and we buried her today. She went out last week, and caught a nasty chill. Towards Sunday she began to get worse, and she passed away about 3.00pm on Sunday of ammonia *(sic)* [Atkin probably meant to say pneumonia]. I am nearly off my head. I don't know which way to look." Relatives were immediately despatched to Atkin's home. On their arrival they were told that the couple had moved. A neighbour, Mrs Cook, who knew Atkin's new address, took them around to see him. The door was answered by Margaret Milton and upon being asked the whereabouts of Mrs Atkin, she replied that she was the woman they were looking for. The relatives were taken aback and immediately reported Maud's disappearance to the police.

Although no one at this stage suspected that Atkin might have done away with his wife, there was discussion about her disappearance and Atkin taking up with another woman so soon. Some of this filtered back to Atkin himself, who appeared to be quite perturbed by it. The prosecution now called Constable Richard Hodson, who had been on duty in High Street, Buckden, on December 19th when he had been approached by Atkin who said, "What is all this gossip about me?" Hodson had suggested that Atkin ought to know best what it was about, to which he had replied, "My wife is dead and buried." He then went on to explain that a few weeks before they had moved from one side of Derby to the other and the bedding got wet in the rain. Maud had refused to sleep on the bed that night but lay down on her coat instead. The next morning she felt queer and the next day she died." Atkin had then gone on to say that he had married his new wife after Maud had died and that if there were any further talk about him, he would see a solicitor and get it stopped.

Atkin, though, was not being consistent with his story of Maud's death. To most people he was suggesting that she had died in late November but he told a different story to Charlotte Annie Bonnett of Francis Street. At the end of November, when Charlotte asked after Maud, Atkin said she had gone to her father's funeral and on December 8th, Atkin told her that he was going to collect Maud the following Saturday. Final proof that Maud Atkin had not died a natural death and been buried was given by Mr Reuben Day, the superintendent of the cemetery where Atkin claimed his wife lay. Mr Day had carefully examined his records and stated that no one named Maud Atkin had been interred between November 14th and December 21st 1922.

Medical evidence was given by Dr Southern, who in addition to examining the body at the scene had also performed a post-mortem. The body was in an advanced state of decomposition with the head, face and neck all blackish brown in colour. Dr Southern found no external signs of violence but once the skin had been removed, he saw a small amount of blood under the tissues of the neck and small bruises on the left temple. Although it was difficult to be precise, Dr Southern, who at first thought Maud had been strangled but had found no marks to substantiate this, now believed that Maud had been stunned by a blow to the temple and then placed into the grave while still alive. At the inquest, Dr Southern had expressed the view that there should have been soil in Maud's throat if this were the case but he had now realised that the position of her hands was such that her mouth would have been covered.

When Percy Atkin stepped into the witness box to give his own version of events, his story was incredible to say the least. He began by claiming that Maud had known about the existence of Margaret Milton as he had confessed all to her on November 20th. Maud had cried and threatened to call in the police but Atkin managed to calm her down and eventually she agreed to go home to her parents while he made a home for the children. Maud was to catch a train at midnight on November 21st.

On that date, Atkin said he worked from 6.00am to 2.00pm, after which he went home to find Maud in the back yard. They left together soon afterwards and went to see Greasley about moving the furniture. Atkin left Maud in town while he went back to Co-operative Street for his dinner. At 6.15pm, he met her again at the corner of St Mark's Road, off which ran Francis Street, and after going for a walk, parted while he went to help Greasley load his dray. During the afternoon, Atkin said he had visited the allotments to collect some wood, which explained the sightings of him there.

That night, he met Maud again and they walked off towards the allotments. Maud told Atkin she had changed her mind about leaving the children and wanted to take Leslie with her. Atkin refused, telling her that her family could not provide a suitable home for him and they then began arguing about the matter. As they passed down Nottingham Road, Maud suddenly took off her wedding ring, threw it into the street and ran off down a lane. He spent some time looking for the ring before following Maud but could find no sign of her. Just as he was going to give up the search, his foot caught against something and he saw that it was the body of a woman. Looking closer, Atkin saw that it was Maud and she was bleeding from the nose, ears and mouth, having apparently fallen from a bridge on to a large pile of stones. Finding no pulse, he panicked and decided to conceal the body in case anyone should think him responsible for her death. Recalling the hole he had dug for the apple tree, Atkin now carried Maud to his allotment and lay her there before returning home. The next morning he returned to the allotment at 5.25am and found that Maud had not moved so he covered her with earth. However, when Dr Southern was recalled to the stand, he said that he had found no signs that were any way consistent with such a fall and that he stood by his earlier testimony that Maud Atkin had been buried alive after being stunned by a blow of some kind.

The jury retired at 5.10pm and took just a few minutes to dismiss Atkin's unlikely explanation and return a guilty verdict. Atkin did not speak as the death sentence was intoned and paused only to take a last look at Margaret Milton, who was moaning with grief, before he was taken down to the cells. Outside the courtroom, the crowd which had gathered to hear the final verdict shouted their approval.

An appeal was heard on March 20th before the Lord Chief Justice, Lord Hewart, and Justices Shearman and Salter, the main grounds being that the alternative defence of manslaughter had not been put before the jury by the trial judge and that the jury should have been warned to accept the doctor's evidence with the greatest caution. Giving the judgement, though, the Lord Chief Justice stated that the summing up had been most favourable to the prisoner and there had been little room for the defence of manslaughter in this case. As such, the appeal must fail.

On Friday, April 7th, 1922, Percy James Atkin was hanged at Nottingham prison by John Ellis who was assisted by Robert Baxter. It was only the third execution in an English prison that year, although another 13 men faced the same fate before 1922 came to a close.

Chapter Eleven

The Bodies
In The Pit

AT some time before 10.00am on Sunday, March 4th, 1923, James Wood, who ran a fish shop from 5 Freetown, Glossop, was pleased to see his four-year-old nephew, Thomas Johnson Wood, come into his shop. Laughing at the little boy's antics, James handed over a parcel of fish and told Thomas to run home and give it to his father, Frederick, who lived at 96 Back Kershaw Street, telling the boy to come back later and he would give him some sweets.

Thomas did as his uncle had asked and by 10.30am, he was back at the shop where he stayed for half an hour before announcing that he was going to see his grandparents. Although the child was very young, everyone in the area knew him and it was a trip he had made many times before without escort. James waved as Thomas skipped off down the street.

Thomas Wood's grandparents lived, coincidentally, at 60 Wood Street, Glossop, but the little boy did not arrive for dinner that Sunday. Although he came nearly every week, there were occasions in the past when, for one reason or another, he had stayed at home, so there was no immediate cause for concern. It was only when Thomas' mother called to pick him up that night that the family realised that the little lad had been missing since he left his uncle's fish shop around 11.00am. The police were informed and an immediate search started.

It was not very long before a number of witnesses were found, all of whom reported seeing Thomas Wood after 11.00am on March 4th. Irvine Broadbent was in Hollincross Lane between 11.00am and 11.30am and he had seen a young boy, perhaps four years old, walking along the lane with a man. The man gave the boy an apple and as they walked on, the boy finished his treat and then handed the core back to the man who threw it away in Slatelands Road. The man Broadbent had seen was well known to him and he told the police that he was 62-year-old Albert Edward Burrows.

Samuel Buckley Robinson was a 17-year-old farmhand and he, too, had seen Burrows with a small boy in Slatelands Road. Robinson put the time at almost exactly 11.30am, and the two men had exchanged a few words. Half an hour later, a man fitting Burrows' description, holding the hand of a small boy, was seen by Jane Tregarthen Sidebottom who was on her way to visit her sister at Charlesworth. The man and boy were also heading in the same direction. Yet just 30 minutes after this, at 12.30pm, Burrows was seen again by two people, and now he was alone. Frank Burgess was working at Hargate Hill Farm at 12.30pm when he saw Burrows coming down from the direction of Simmondley Moor. Burgess was able to pinpoint the sighting precisely because Burrows asked him what time it was. It was also the same time that Mary Harrison was delivering milk in the area and she also saw Burrows, alone, and confirmed that it was at 12.30pm.

There was in fact one other witness who had seen Burrows that day, and he was a serving police officer. Constable Fred Bradbury had been on duty in Simmondley Lane at 12.50pm when he saw Burrows coming from the direction of the moors. The two men fell into conversation and walked together to Junction Bridge. On that short journey, Burrows pointed out that his legs were soaking wet as far as the knees and explained that this had come from walking through the fields.

When Burrows was spoken to, at his home address of 94b Back Kershaw Street, he readily admitted that he had seen Thomas Wood. As a near neighbour, he knew the family well and had often taken the child for long walks over the fields and moors. Burrows claimed that he had been for a walk on Sunday, March 4th, and when he got to Bridge Field he saw Thomas Wood watching a group of boys playing in the brook. The boys were George Dale's sons and as Thomas watched, a car almost hit him and Burrows pulled him out of the way and suggested he should go home. Burrows then went on his way, leaving Thomas in the company of three boys who were older than him. They were all looking over the top of a hen run in Slatelands Road and later Burrows heard that one of the older boys had thrown Thomas' purse over the wall, into the run.

For the time being, the matter was allowed to rest there, but the next day, March 5th, Burrows began behaving rather strangely. To begin with, at 9.00am, he went to visit Annie Wood, the missing boy's grandmother, at 60 Wood Street. Burrows expressed deep sympathy with the family's plight, saying that this was an awful business. By now, the police had informed the Wood family of Burrows' claim that Thomas had been with a group of boys who had thrown his purse into the hen run. Burrows offered to take Mrs Wood to show her where the run was. Mrs Wood, and two of her neighbours, Mrs Parker and Mrs Hammond, accompanied Burrows to the spot, with the owner of the hen run, and after some searching, they found the small purse, a dark brown leather item no more than a couple of inches square. While the search was taking place, Annie Wood asked Burrows, "Are you worried because you didn't bring the little boy home?" Burrows, with a faltering voice replied, "Yes I am Mrs Wood."

Later that day, Burrows paid a visit to the police station where he handed a written statement to Constable Samuel Roe. This was a rather rambling two-page document which began, "Sir, I am writing this because there are so many reports of Thomas Wood that are not true." Burrows went on to mention his meeting with Constable Bradbury and claimed that it was after he parted from this officer that he saw George Dale's sons who were playing in the brook with their dog. Thomas Wood was watching the group and it was then that Burrows snatched him out of the way of a car which was driving down Slatelands Road. He also said that when he saw Thomas, the boy was carrying a toy whip with him.

It was when yet another witness came forward that Burrows' story came under much closer scrutiny. Frank Steele lived at 82 Victoria Street, Glossop, and he also said he had seen George Dale's sons at about

1.00pm. This agreed with Burrows sighting but the difficulty came when Steele said that he had also seen Burrows at 1.25pm and he had mentioned something about a young boy being lost. This was hours before the family's concerns had been raised. How could Burrows have known about the missing child before anyone else? It was decided to speak to Burrows again.

On March 6th, Sergeant George Clayton saw Burrows in Victoria Street and asked him what he knew about the missing boy. Burrows replied, "I will tell you all I know about the boy." He then went with Clayton to the police station and made a second, single-page statement. This document read, "At 1.30pm on Sunday March 4th I was at Bridge Field and on turning into Slatelands Road I saw Thomas Wood, the missing boy. He had a whip with a brass furl on the end. It would be about three feet six inches in length. I spoke to the boy and told him he would get run over. I also got hold of him and pulled him out of the way of a motor car which was going down Slatelands Road at a nice pace.

"I last saw the boy in company with three other boys older than himself. He was leaning over the wall of the hen run in Slatelands Road, looking for a purse of his which one of the other boys had thrown over inside the hen run. I heard the boy Wood say, 'That bugger has thrown my purse into the run.'

"On Monday morning about 10.00am, I went down to the hen run with a man who lives in Hollincross Lane. He had keys to the run and he found the purse and handed it to Mrs Parker or Mrs Hammond. His grandmother was there also."

The officer in charge of the investigation was Inspector John Ellis Chadwick and he read both the statements Burrows had written – one which he had handed in to the police station and one he had made before Sergeant Clayton. They were substantially the same but neither fitted in with the established facts. As a result, Inspector Chadwick formally interviewed Burrows on March 7th, and asked him to give a detailed account of his movements. Burrows then made a third statement, which ran to ten pages.

Burrows' third statement began by saying that he had left home at 12.30pm on Sunday, March 4th. He then detailed a walk across the fields, ostensibly to see a farmer named Clarkson, but when he arrived at the farm he was told that Clarkson now lived at Ludworth. Returning to Glossop he saw John Lavin, an insurance agent, and then met Constable Bradbury who he finally parted from outside the Junction Inn. From there, Burrows went to try to see another friend who worked at the electricity works before returning to the Junction Inn from where he walked down Primrose Lane, and saw Constable Bradbury in front of him. Near the nurseries he saw Tom Wilson and three other men and engaged in a brief conversation with them about empty houses. Parting from them, Burrows went up Slatelands Road where he saw Thomas Wood with the other boys, none of whom Burrows knew. The story of the missing purse was then retold, after which Thomas had walked on a little way, with Burrows, to where George Dale's sons were playing with their dog. Leaving Thomas there, Burrows then walked on up Slatelands Road where he met Thomas Shortland and spoke with him for ten minutes.

The statement continued to outline Burrows now needing to relieve himself and going into one of the fields to do so. By the time he returned, the boys had all gone, so Burrows went home via Hollincross Lane, it now being about 1.50pm. The rest of the document related Burrows' movements later that same day and his sighting of a strange boy, about 13 years of age, who appeared to be the one Thomas Wood had earlier claimed had thrown his purse away. Burrows also claimed that he had first heard that Thomas Wood was missing at 5.00pm, told the boy's father that he had seen him earlier, and then went out to help in the search, not getting home until after 8.00pm.

All the details in the statement were checked and while some were found to be accurate, there were major discrepencies with the crucial times when Thomas Wood was supposed to have been seen with the older boys. George Dale's oldest son, John, confirmed that he was out playing with his brothers but they had seen nothing of Thomas Wood, although they had indeed spoken to Burrows who called out, "If you see young Tom Wood send him home, he is lost." There was also the fact that the police had witnesses who swore that they had seen Burrows with the missing boy over a period of an hour or more.

On March 9th, Burrows was again in Victoria Street and this time he was seen by Inspector Chadwick, to whom he handed yet another statement, his fourth. Written in red ink, over both sides of a single sheet of paper, the statement was headed, "Correct Statement by A.E. Burrows of

Thomas Wood. No other statement any truth in them." It went on, "Followed the Salvation Army band to top of Derby Street. Played around the band a long time. Was in Arrowsmith's eating at 1 or 1.30. Went out. Walked down to Bridge Field, seen by me at 20 past or half past or might be 25 min to 2. Seen at 2 o'clock by two girls of Marhurst and Clough's little boy at the weir against Hamilton's house. Seen an hour later against Entwistle's nursery. Seen at half past 4 by Mrs Fagan, Primrose. Also later people say by Mr Marsden, farmer, but I don't know if that is true as I have not seen Mr Marsden at all so I am not able to prove the last statement. All the rest is the gospel truth as I have proved it.

"I remain respectfully Albert Ed Burrows and I defy any other person to contradict this statement but they won't come forward like I did. I have worked hard to find this out. They all talk but they won't speak without they are made."

Chadwick checked Burrows' statements and became convinced that the boy Burrows had claimed to other witnesses to be Thomas, was in fact another boy entirely. This persuaded the inspector that Burrows was intimately involved in the disappearance of Thomas Wood. Going back over the various witnesses statements, Chadwick realised that Burrows had been seen with a young boy, almost certainly Thomas, heading in the direction of Simmondley Moor and had been observed returning alone from that same location. The boy had to be out there somewhere but all likely spots such as streams, hedges and woods had already been checked. Frank Burgess was interviewed and took police to the spot where he had last seen Burrows. It was then that Inspector Chadwick recalled two old mine shafts close by and decided to have a look at them for himself.

On March 10th, Chadwick went up to the first of the two air shafts and noticed that part of the square, brick-built structure that protected it was damaged. One of the walls had a hole in it and inside the brick-work, at the top of the shaft, blackberry bushes were broken and crushed as if something had been thrown or dropped down there. Burrows was seen again, on March 12th, and was even taken to the moors and the top of the open air shaft. Now, although he did not make another written statement, he told a different story again. Now he had indeed taken Thomas Wood up on to the moors with him, while he was searching for rabbits. At one stage he had turned around, only to find that the child had vanished. Burrows had no idea what had happened to the boy but was certainly not guilty of harming him in any way.

Inspector Chadwick noticed that Burrows persistently repeated that it was this particular spot where Thomas had vanished. Again and again he swore that he had not taken the boy across the road towards the other air shaft, the one with the wall around it and the broken and damaged blackberry bushes. Knowing that the veracity of Burrows was seriously in doubt, Inspector Chadwick decided that the best place to look was the shaft where Burrows said he certainly had not been.

At 1.00pm on March 13th, Constable Roe and a gentleman named Albert Connor began to search the second shaft by means of grappling hooks. After some unsuccessful attempts, during which various unwanted items were recovered, Connor announced, at 1.30pm, that he had found something. When the hooks were pulled to the surface, they saw that they had grabbed on to the right-hand side of a pair of trousers, near the hip. At long last, Thomas Wood had been found.

Inspector Chadwick immediately ordered the arrest of Albert Burrows but he had known about these operations at the air shaft and was now missing from home. Parties of men were sent to scour the moors. Burrows had not gone very far, though, and it was not long before a group of five men, William Newton, Daniel Birchall, Thomas Shortland, John William Aubrey and Ralph Hinchcliffe, found him cowering in a holly bush in a gully. Burrows threw himself to the ground and began pleading for mercy shouting, "I don't know what made me do it," several times. Some twine was produced and Burrows' hands tied behind his back before he was marched back to Glossop where he was handed over to Sergeant Richard Wilson.

The first thing Wilson did was to remove the twine and replace it with a pair of handcuffs. As he did this, Burrows remarked, "I have a brother in the asylum." Later, while walking to the police station, he said to the crowd who were following him, "I shan't be like Charlie Peace. (a notorious Victorian criminal who was hanged for murder in 1879) I shan't tremble when I get on the scaffold." Once he had arrived at the station, Burrows was charged with murder and taken down to the cells.

The inquest on Thomas Wood opened on March 14th before Mr G.H. Wilson at the Town Hall in Glossop. Evidence of identification was

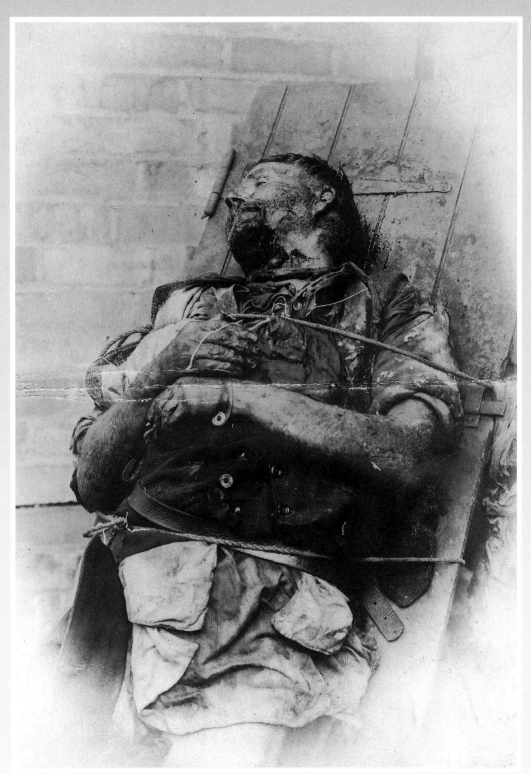

The body of Thomas Campion, strapped to a door by the police so it could be photographed. See Chapter 2. (Public Record Office)

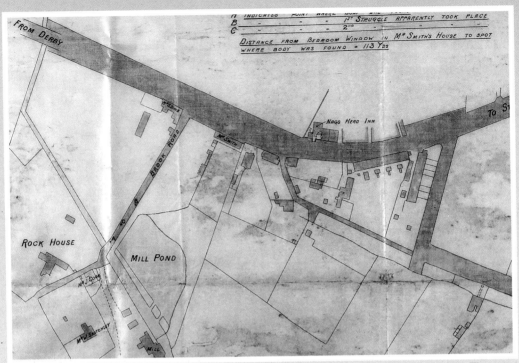

A contemporary map of the area where John Harrison murdered Thomas Campion. The spot where the body was found is labelled 'A' in Brook Road. See Chapter 2. (Public Record Office)

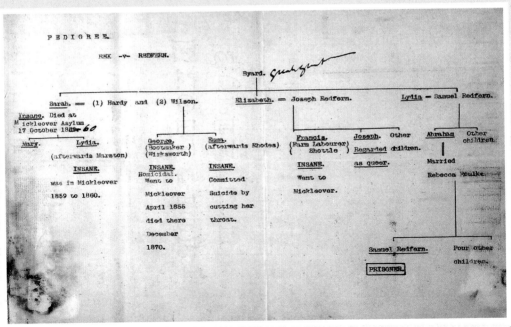

The family tree of Samuel Redfern. Used in evidence at his trial, this shows many members of the family had been certified as insane. See Chapter 4. (Public Record Office)

How the *Derbyshire Times* reported the early court appearance of William Edward Slack (pictured left) who tried to hack the head of Lucy Wilson (right) from her shoulders in Highfield Road. See Chapter 8. (British Library, Colindale)

The *Derbyshire Times* reports the murder of Alfred Johnson (pictured with pipe), who was shot to death by John Mowbray. The police officer involved, PC Burns, is also pictured. See Chapter 9. (British Library, Colindale)

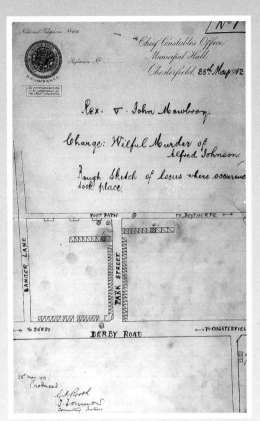

A map of the area where Alfred Johnson died. Johnson's home is marked '1', the spot where his body lay is marked '2' and the killer's house is marked '4' See Chapter 9. (Public Record Office)

The body of Maud Atkin, lying in its shallow grave on the allotments at Chaddesden. See Chapter 10. (Public Record Office)

The letter sent by Percy James Atkin to his wife's family, explaining that she had died. See Chapter 10. (Public Record Office)

The walled mineshaft where Albert Edward Burrows disposed of four bodies. See Chapter 11. (Public Record Office)

A close up of the mineshaft wall, showing the loose bricks. It was through this hole that Inspector John Ellis Chadwick noticed the damaged blackberry bushes. See Chapter 11. (Public Record Office)

The second mineshaft. Note that the one where the bodies were actually found can be seen in the distance. See Chapter 11. (Public Record Office)

The *Glossop Chronicle* reported the murder of Thomas Johnson Wood, who was Albert Burrows' last victim. If Burrows had not assaulted and killed this poor child he would almost certainly have got away with three murders. See Chapter 11. (The Glossop Chronicle)

TOMMY WOOD ! ! !

LITTLE FELLOW DISCOVERED IN HUNDRED FEET OF DARKNESS.

SENSATIONAL RECOVERY FROM SIMMONDLEY PIT SHAFT.

Chase over Hills after Wanted Man.

BURROWS DECLARES "I HAVE A CLEAR CONSCIENCE."

Public Feeling Runs High: Amazing Police Court Scenes.

HOW THE POLICE GOT BURROWS AWAY AFTER REMAND BY MAGISTRATES:

Inquest Opened.

Up to early this week there had been no solution of the mysterious disappearance of Thomas Wood, the four-year-old son of Mr. and Mrs. F. Wood, of Back Kershaw Street, Glossop, which had baffled police and public for nearly a fortnight.

SUNDAY'S SEARCH OVER THE SIMMONDLEY MOORS

OVER 100 MEN WITH DOGS TAKE PART

SEVERAL HOURS' SEARCH PROVES FRUITLESS.

On Sunday a numerous band of searchers — over 100 men accompanied by dogs taking part — turned their particular attention to Simmondley district. Acting on a prearranged plan, which co-ordinated their efforts, they made a thorough search of the fields and moorland district which skirt Simmondley on the top side and on the Nab and Charlesworth sides, ravines and other secluded spots being thoroughly investigated. Patiently they searched, covering a large area of ground, but late in the afternoon they had to give up the task without having found any trace of the missing boy. Other parts of the district were also scoured by smaller ...

TOMMY WOOD.

Dramatic and Tense Moments ! Little Body Recovered from Dark and Dank Air Shaft 111 feet Deep

...vs watching Police from ...

effect that the body had been recovered, but all these statements were, of course, void of truth up to Monday night.

...heights above, gave a few short, sharp directions to his men, and they followed an evidently pre-conceived and clever plan, to close all outlets in the direction of Charlesworth. Information came that Burrows had been seen on the tops near Simmondley, and quickly a body of civilians followed the direction Burrows was alleged to have taken, going towards the Chunal end of Glossop, just below the Plantioteods, the men in charge got a glimpse of the man they were wanting, and in a field known as Garside's Intake—commonly called "The Intack,"—Burrows was found hiding under a holly bush.

Many are the rumours one hears of what was said by pursuers and pursued, but for the present we prefer to say nothing about them. It was not long after the securing of Burrows by civilians that Detective-Sergt. Wilson arrived on the scene, and took charge of the wanted man. He was given no chance of escape, for the body of civilians stuck to arms, legs, and scarf round the neck, and in a thorough motor lorry of the Sanitary Department, Burrows, the men who had caught him, and Detective Wilson made the journey from Chunal to the Police Station.

NEWS OF DISCOVERY, CHASE AND CAPTURE SPREADS WITH LIGHTNING-LIKE RAPIDITY.

Meantime news of the finding of the boy's body, and the chase after Burrows, spread throughout the town with lightning-like rapidity, and by the time the motor lorry with its human cargo reached Glossop Police Station, an angry and restless crowd was ing vengeance ha... congregated in the roads leading to the ...lice Station. Again, however ... ut his men very roughly ..., and unresting Bur... ...ved fr... ...he b...

The recovery of Thomas Wood's body. Inset is a photograph of Burrows taken some years before. See Chapter 11. (Daily Mail)

...he ... ...removed from the lorry to ...ors closed on the excited throng.

Late on Tuesday night Dr. Milligan (the Medical Officer of Health) and Dr. Waddell

...which had come to our knowledge.

"On Monday he volunteered a statement that about 11-30 a.m. on Sunday, March 4, he took the boy for a walk through the fields to Simmondley, and

leg of the boy's trousers on the right side, I think, and level with the pocket!

Albert Connor, 60, Freetown, said he was a labourer. On Tuesday, March 13th, he was present at the air shaft whilst the

(Copyright Photo by "Daily Mail," reproduced by kind permission of Publishers).

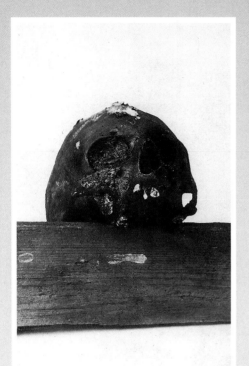

The skull of Hannah Calladine, found at the bottom of the shaft, along with the bones of her two children. See Chapter 11. (Public Record Office)

The postcard which Burrows sent to Hannah Calladine's family which he purported to be a picture of the son he had already murdered. See Chapter 11. (Public Record Office)

given by Frederick Wood, the boy's father, and the proceedings then adjourned until Tuesday, March 20th. In fact, there were so many witnesses to call that the resumed inquest continued on to March 21st, when a verdict of murder was returned and Burrows was ordered to be sent to the next assizes to face his trial. It was also on Wednesday, March 21st, that the police court proceedings reopened and Burrows was remanded again, until March 29th.

On Saturday, March 17th, Thomas Wood's body was buried in St James' Church, Glossop. Thousands of people lined the streets and there were hundreds of floral tributes. The cortege started out from the grandparent's home in Wood Street and the coffin bore a small brass plaque on which was engraved "Thomas Johnson Wood. Died March 4th, 1923. Age 3 years and 11 months."

A number of other remands followed for Burrows and it was not until Thursday, April 5th, that all the witnesses were heard. Frederick Wood told of the last time he had seen his son alive and confirmed that Burrows had previously taken Thomas out for walks many times. The family had made no objections to this and there had never been any ill-feeling between him and the prisoner.

According to Burrows' last remarks to the police, he had been over the fields with Thomas when the child had suddenly disappeared from his view. He had, of course, been seen returning from Simmondley Moor by Frank Burgess, who testified that he was alone at the time. Burgess now also stated that Burrows made no remarks about having lost a child, as he might have been expected to do if he was not involved in the child's death.

Constable Bradbury told of his own encounter with Burrows on March 4th. Although it was a cold day, Burrows was sweating and appeared to be particularly talkative. His trousers were wet and although that might well have come from tramping through the fields as Burrows suggested, his boots were also covered in mud as if he had been in a ditch. John Dale, a chemist's assistant, who lived at 90 Victoria Street said he went to Whitfield Church that Sunday morning with his two younger brothers, Irvine and George. The three brothers went home for their dog and then went back out to play around the stream near Dingle Cottage. The boys saw Mr Oliver near the hen pens and a few minutes later they met Frank Steele to whom they spoke for about ten minutes. By now it would be about 1.00pm and they met up with four other lads who played with them and the dog for about 20 minutes or so. John then told of seeing Albert Burrows, who told him that Tom Wood was lost, but he had seen no other boys, nor had he seen Thomas Wood that day. This testimony was confirmed by Frank Steele, who said that he, too, had seen no sign of Thomas Wood anywhere near the other boys.

Thomas Shortland, the next witness, said that he had met Burrows in Slatelands Road at 1.20pm on March 4th. The two men talked together and as they spoke, Shortland noticed a group of boys playing together although they were all around eight or nine and there was no child as young as four there. At one stage Burrows had pointed down to the boys and said, "There's Fred Wood's lad down the road, would you take him home; if I do his father would only curse me." Shortland replied that Burrows shouldn't interfere with other people's children but Burrows said he would go down and look for him. He and Shortland then went down to the hen pens and Burrows immediately pointed out something which he claimed was Thomas Wood's purse and said that one of the other lads had thrown it in there. That afternoon, Shortland met Burrows again and they went for a walk together, during which the prisoner behaved strangely as if he did not want to be left alone. Shortland thought at the time that for some reason, Burrows wanted to be seen with him.

The next day, Burrows called at Shortland's house and asked him to go out searching for the missing boy. They went over the fields towards Simmondley and at one stage Burrows said, "Let's go round that air shaft in James' field where they put cows and that down." Shortland insisted on going the other way, though, and it turned out that his wishes prevailed.

Various police witnesses spoke of the four written statements Burrows had made and then Constable Roe spoke of the two air shafts. The one where the body was found was in James' field was 112 feet from the bottom of the shaft to the top of the wall around it. There was eight feet five inches of water in the bottom of the shaft and the square wall around it was six feet six inches high. The other shaft was across the road and was 135 feet deep with more than 16 feet of water at the bottom.

Details of the capture of Burrows on March 13th were then given. Albert Crossland testified that he was with George Barker, Isaac Lomas and another man on Simmondley Moor when they saw Burrows, in a crouching position, running away from them across the moor. Suddenly Burrows dropped flat on the ground and, puzzled by this behaviour, the group of men went to where he lay, only to find him kneeling in a ditch which was full of water and bulrushes. Crossland asked, "What are you doing there? Have you no more sense than to lie in water?" Burrows replied that he was trying to avoid the gamekeeper as he was out looking for rabbits. Minutes later, Crossland and his friends came upon another group of men who explained that they were looking for Burrows, and Crossland informed them where they had seen him last.

On the second day, testimony was given by Dr James Henry Dible, the senior assistant in the Department of Pathology at the University of Manchester, who had performed the post-mortem on the dead child, at 9.15am on March 15th at Glossop police station. He reported that the body was that of a well nourished child and that there was no rigor mortis present when he made his examination. The body appeared to have been submerged in water for some time and the tongue protruded beyond the teeth and had been slightly bitten. The body was very pale, but the face was red in colour and there was a colourless, foamy material issuing from the nose. There were a few bruises on the body, the principle ones being grazes on the knees and a well marked bruise about the size of a human palm over the left shoulder. Other marks were visible on the forehead.

The internal examination showed that the upper air passages were not obstructed, and showed no signs of violence. There was a tear in the spleen and this had caused a haemorrhage into the chest cavity. In the stomach, pieces of apple were found, which confirmed the evidence of earlier witnesses. There were also particles of food in the gullet, which indicated vomiting at the time of death. Dr Dible stated that in his opinion, death was due to drowning. He also added that the child's anus was widely gaping which was not usual in cases of death by drowning although he was unable to confirm that a serious sexual assault had taken place.

Dr Dible also stated that he had heard that the two air passages on Simmondley Moor were connected, being part of the same mine workings which had been last used in 1864. It had been pointed out that although the body was found in the shaft which had the wall surrounding it, this was the lower of the two and it was believed that a stream of water connected them. It was possible that the body had initially been dropped down the other, open shaft and been carried to the point where it was subsequently found, some 156 yards away. He also stated that there was a small pond just over 100 yards away from the shafts and it was possible that the child had been drowned here before his body had been put down the shaft. Further medical testimony was given by Dr Ernest Henry Marcus Milligan who had assisted at the post-mortem. Referring to the condition of the child's anus, he said that he saw no other way to account for it other than by an act of sodomy.

Having heard all the evidence, the magistrates ordered that Burrows be sent to court to face his trial for the murder of Thomas Wood but other matters were also being investigated and it would be some time yet before Albert Burrows faced a judge and jury at the assizes.

More than three years before the death of Thomas Wood, Burrows had had other problems to occupy his mind. In 1919, he was living at 94b Back Kershaw Street with his wife, Clementine Burrows, but was also involved with another woman, 28-year-old Hannah Calladine.

Burrows and Hannah had first met in 1917. She lived in Royal Wood, Newhall, near Nantwich, Cheshire, and already had a daughter, Elsie. Hannah soon became Burrows' lover and as a result, on October 26th, 1918, a child was born. Hannah named the child, a boy, Albert Edward after his father and, to be on the safe side, took out a bastardy order against Burrows on September 8th, 1919 when the boy was almost one year old. Burrows now had to pay 5s expenses, 18s court costs and a sum of 7s each week to Hannah. In due course, Burrows even went through a form of marriage with Hannah, for which he was sent to jail for bigamy.

One thing led to another and on December 17th, Hannah and the two children went to Glossop to stay with Burrows. His legal wife took exception to this and two days later, on December 19th, she left him and moved in to 2 Hollincross Lane. On December 30th, Clementine issued a summons against her husband for cruelty and the case was heard at the Town Hall on January 12th, 1920. As a result, Burrows was ordered to pay his wife £1 every Monday, starting January 19th.

During the investigation into the disappearance and death of Thomas Wood, the police had not failed to recall that Hannah Calladine and her two children had also vanished. Hannah and the little boy had last been seen on Sunday, January 11th, the day before Burrows was due to appear in court, and Elsie had not been seen since January 12th. Further inquiries were now made. On May 7th, 1923, fresh recovery operations began in the two air shafts on Simmondley Moor. The bottom of the shaft contained a large quantity of debris and metal sheeting and this had to be removed before the contents of the water could be properly examined. This took some considerable time and it was not until May 23rd that some human remains and clothing were recovered. From then on, bones and other items were recovered on an almost daily basis.

On May 31st, the lining of a woman's coat was found and some blue woollen cloth along with various human remains. On June 1st, more remains were found including a pair of child's clogs in one of which was a skeletonised foot with some leg bones still attached. The operations continued until June 6th, by which time enough material had been recovered for the police to realise they were looking at the body of an adult female and two small children. The mystery of the disappearance of Hannah Calladine, her daughter Elsie Calladine, also known as Elsie Large, and one-year-old Albert Edward Calladine, also known as Burrows, had been solved.

The inquest on Hannah and her children was held on June 12th and following this, Burrows was brought before the magistrates and remanded. The funeral of the three victims took place at Glossop cemetery on June 15th.

Burrows was charged with these three further murders and appeared at Derby on July 3rd, 1923, before Mr Justice Shearman and a jury of nine men and three women. The case for the prosecution was led by Sir Henry Maddocks, who was assisted by Mr Norman Birkett and Mr Loseby. Burrows was defended by Mr T. Norman Winning who was assisted by Miss Geikie Cobb, the first time a woman barrister had acted in a murder trial in this country. The proceedings lasted for two days.

In the event, evidence was not called on the murder of Thomas Wood and the prosecution concentrated on the second set of remains found in the same air shaft on the moor. The prosecution began by explaining that Burrows was a general labourer who had lived in Glossop for the past 24 years. During the Great War, he had worked in munitions near Northwich and this is where he had first met Hannah Calladine who worked in the same factory. Sir Henry then went on to outline the bastardy order which Hannah had obtained in September 1919. Almost from the outset, Burrows fell into arrears and was in trouble with the courts.

Inspector Chadwick, who had worked so hard to solve the mystery of the disappearance of Thomas Wood, told the court that on November 7th, 1919, he had arrested Burrows for arrears of the order and had taken him to prison by train. There was another man also going to jail, Thomas Taylor Mellor, who was seen off by his brother, Robert Shenton Mellor. This latter gentleman testified that while waiting on the platform he heard Burrows say, "When I've done my time, I'll get this woman. I'll either do her in or throw her down a pit shaft" Chadwick was also able to say that he had personally served the cruelty summons on Burrows, on December 30th, 1919. At the time there had been a woman and two young children in the house.

The inspector gave even more damning evidence against Burrows. On March 7th, while making inquiries about Thomas Wood, he had mentioned Hannah Calladine and asked after her. Burrows had said, "She is in Manchester and has got a good situation." He had also taken the pair of child's clogs, found in the pit shaft, to Nantwich where, on June 5th, he had shown them to Philip George Robinson, a master clogger. Robinson had confirmed that he made the clogs and was able to pinpoint the year of manufacture from the end of 1918 to the beginning of 1919 because the effects of the war meant that he could only obtain this particular kind of leather. Mr Robinson was unable to say who had actually purchased the clogs but was able to say that Hannah Calladine was a regular customer of his at the time.

Eliza Hammond lived at 94 Back Kershaw Street, a house directly opposite to Burrows' across a common yard. Their doors were only two or three yards apart and Eliza knew the Burrows family very well. She knew, too, of the court summons for cruelty and the fact that Hannah Calladine and her children had moved into Burrows' house.

At around 6.00pm or perhaps a little later, on Sunday, January 11th, 1920, Eliza saw Hannah Calladine at the door. Eliza remembered this day particularly because she knew that Burrows was due in court the next day. Hannah was wearing dark clothes and this was the last time that Eliza ever saw her. The next morning, at 8.00am, Eliza saw Burrows walking down the street with a large stick in his hand. Shortly afterwards she saw him again and remarked, "You have been having your walks early this morning." Burrows replied that he had just been taking Elsie to her mother and when Eliza asked where they had all gone, he said, "That's a secret between me and her. I promised her I would never tell." Since that time, Eliza had spoken to Burrows many times and had often asked after Hannah and the children. Burrows had told her that they were all doing well and Hannah was working in a bacon shop down Stretford way in Manchester, although he refused to divulge her address. Since then, Eliza had received a postcard signed 'Nance' which was the name by which Hannah was known. Postmarked 'Manchester' the card had, coincidentally, arrived when Burrows was working in that city and when he returned that weekend, he had asked Eliza if she received the card. On another occasion, Burrows had also told her that Nance had met another man and given birth to twins which had unfortunately both died.

Margaret Ann Street also recalled the day that Burrows was due in court in January 1920. That morning, Margaret's husband was going to work at around 6.30am and as he left their house at 2 Hollincross Lane, he called her attention to Burrows passing the house with a little girl. They watched together as Burrows passed the church gates and went in the direction of Pike's Lane towards Simmondley Moor. The little girl, who was about four years old, held on to Burrows' hand. Later, at 9.30am, Margaret saw him returning, with a large stick in his hand, but Burrows was now alone.

About four or five days after this, Burrows spoke to Margaret in the street and said that Nance had a good job working in Seymour Mead's bacon shop which was owned by one of his relations. He also added, somewhat cryptically, "She'll never trouble me any more. We've made it up, they will never come here to bother me again." Burrows' wife, Clementine, had gone to stay with Margaret after the trouble with Hannah arriving, and this was why Burrows told her all this. Eventually, Clementine returned to her husband, but only after the court hearing was concluded.

It had been shown that Hannah and her son were last seen on January 11th, and her daughter on January 12th. Three witnesses were now called to show that soon afterwards, Burrows was disposing of articles which had belonged to them. Harriett Mellor said she had been given a navy blue lady's costume jacket which was torn. This was about two weeks after Hannah had last been seen.

Marie Hibbert of 101 Kershaw Street said that about the same time, Burrows had sold her a child's go-cart and William Cartwright, who also lived in Kershaw Street, said that he had bought a parcel of clothing from Burrows who said he had got it from his sister. That clothing, along with a pair of boots which he bought the next day, had since been identified as belonging to Hannah Calladine.

Mary Elizabeth Calladine was Hannah's sister and testified that Hannah would have been 33 on April 18th this year, meaning that she was 29 when she vanished. A skull had been found down the air shaft and Mary had identified this as Hannah's due to a rather prominent front tooth which was very distinctive. She confirmed that she had last seen Hannah alive on December 17th, 1919, at 3.00pm when she left Royal Wood with the children, saying that she was going to Glossop. Since that time, various letters and postcards had been sent to the family from Burrows, stating that they were all still together and enjoying life. One deliberate piece of subterfuge was exposed to show just how clever Burrows had been in covering his tracks.

A postcard had been sent, showing a young boy aged two or three, and the message on the back, from Burrows, indicated that this was the child Hannah had borne to him. The postcard was professionally produced and therefore bore the photographer's name – Wray Photographic Studios of 40 St Petersgate, Stockport. On June 7th, that postcard had been shown to Beatrice Cheetham who was the manageress there and upon checking her records, she found that the negative was taken at their studio on September 9th, 1921 and was of a child named Williamson. Two dozen postcards had been ordered but subsequently only one dozen was sold to the family. The rest would have been put on general sale. Burrows, it was suggested, had spotted the card on one of his trips to Manchester, thought that the boy in the picture was about the right age, and sent it to Hannah's family stating that it was their child.

Many of the remains found in the pit shaft had been bones and these had been examined by various experts. Professor John Sebastian Bach Stopford was head of anatomy at Manchester University and he examined the bones of the adult skeleton which he was able to determine was a female whose height he estimated at four feet ten and half inches when alive. Hannah Calladine was known to be just under five feet tall.

Dr James Dible, in addition to performing the post-mortem on Thomas Wood, had also examined the other remains and determined that they were of an adult female and two children, one of which was female and between three and four years old. He also stated that there were no skull injuries and it was impossible to determine the cause of death in any of the remains.

Further evidence of Burrows' financial problems towards the beginning of 1920 were given by Lemuel Bowden, the owner of 94b Back Kershaw Street where Burrows lived. Mr Bowden stated that Burrows was at the time paying 2s 8d per week rent but at the beginning of January he was £6 13s 2d in arrears.

John Thomas Rodgers had been in prison with Burrows after his arrest for the murder of Thomas Wood. Rodgers reported a conversation that had taken place in which Burrows asked him to write a letter saying, "I and the children are all right and hope to see you soon." It was to be signed, "H. Calladine". Rodgers was told to put some kisses at the bottom and Burrows also remarked, "For God's sake, don't tell anyone else what I have asked you to do." Burrows told Rodgers that he had seen Hannah on the moors the day Thomas was killed. The boy went off to play with Hannah's son and soon he ran back to say that Thomas had fallen through a hole in the wall around the shaft. It was this request which first led the police to suspect that there might be further bodies down the shaft since if Hannah was alive and well, as Burrows had claimed, and he was in touch with her, why did he not simply contact her directly and ask her to confirm that this story was true?

In his summing up for the defence, Mr Winning said that it was the theory of the Crown that Hannah Calladine was murdered on the night of January 11th, 1920, and yet there was evidence that she was still alive on January 15th. Part of a blue costume, had been found down the air shaft and it had been shown that this was posted to Hannah by her sister, four or five days after she died. Were the prosecution really claiming that after murdering Hannah, Burrows had received this costume and then made a special trip up to the pit shaft to throw it down? Mr Winning believed that Hannah had been depressed over the situation with Burrows and it was just as likely that she had committed suicide. There was no evidence that she had been murdered and Mr Winning urged the jury to acquit the prisoner.

The jury retired at 12.26pm on the second day of the trial and took only 13 minutes to reach their verdict. Burrows was guilty of the two charges which had been proceeded with: the murders of Hannah and their son, Albert Edward. Asked if he had anything to say before sentence was passed, Burrows stood firm and replied, "I am not afraid of death, but I am not guilty. I loved those children and the woman too. As true as I hope to meet my God, I am innocent."

Once Burrows had been taken down, Sir Henry Maddocks said that he wished to commend the wonderful work done by Constable Roe in the dangerous confines of the shafts. Mr Justice Shearman added his own commendation and then stated that the other two charges, those of murdering Thomas Wood and Elsie Large, would be held over to the next assizes. By that time, of course. Burrows would either have had his current sentence respited, or would have perished on the gallows.

An appeal was entered and heard on July 23rd before Justices Darling, Salter and Swift. Here it was again suggested that there was no evidence which did not show that Hannah Calladine might have committed suicide. The woman was easily depressed and had argued with her family over the kind of life she was leading. Sir Henry Maddocks pointed out that the trial judge had precluded all mention of a further indictment, that of the murder of Thomas Wood, and that the evidence in all the cases was perfectly clear.

Giving the court's judgement, Mr Justice Darling agreed with Sir Henry and said that there was no doubt whatsoever that Burrows was guilty. He had been rightly advised by his own counsel not to go into the witness box at the trial. This was an atrocious murder and there was nothing in the appeal.

The last act in this astounding drama was played out at Nottingham jail at 8.00am on Wednesday, August 8th, 1923, when Albert Edward Burrows, a native of Cheadle Hulme in Cheshire, was hanged by John

Ellis and William Willis. Women outside the jail scaled the railings to try to catch a glimpse of Burrows on his way to pay for his crimes, but the high walls obscured their view. It was the 11th English execution of 1923 and at the same time, the 12th, that of Hassen Mohamed, took place at Durham.

Chapter Twelve

Death in the Attic

THE house at 1 Bethel Street, Ilkeston, was divided into three floors. On the ground floor, the front door opened into the living room at the back of which was a scullery. Stairs in the scullery led up to the first floor where there were two bedrooms, and in the back bedroom, the stairs continued on up to another room built into the attic. This, too, was used as a bedroom, the only natural light coming from a skylight in the roof.

In 1927, there were five people living at 1 Bethel Street. The owner of the house was George Knighton, an invalid who slept on a bed in the living room. His wife, 55-year-old Ada, slept upstairs in the attic with their 16-year-old daughter, Doris Ivy. The back bedroom on the first floor was vacant, but the front bedroom was shared by a grandchild of George and Ada, Reginald Knighton, and their 22-year-old son, William, who worked as a miner.

On Monday, February 7th, 1927, Doris Ivy Knighton went to work as usual and did not return home until 6.20pm. Doris' mother wasn't at home at the time but arrived 25 minutes later. Ada stayed in the house for only ten minutes, though, and left at 6.55pm, saying she had some shopping to do. She returned at 7.30pm and after the family had enjoyed a meal together, she went out for a few drinks at 9.15pm. Her son, William, was also out and both mother and son were apparently rather fond of a drink and were not expected home until the pubs had closed.

Doris went to bed at 10.00pm that night, by which time neither her mother nor brother had returned home. The young girl was soon asleep and did not hear Ada come in. Ada certainly did retire later, though, because when Doris woke, in the early hours of February 8th, Ada was lying in bed beside her. In fact, it had been Ada who woke Doris. She was moaning and moving about quite a bit and Doris asked what was the matter. Ada did not speak but grabbed Doris' arm and tried to sit up in bed two or three times. Doris assumed that her mother was simply having another of her fairly regular coughing fits, and when Ada settled down again, Doris was even more certain that she had been correct in her assumption.

Although the room was quite dark, Doris could plainly see the silhouette of a figure at the foot of the bed as someone entered the room a few minutes later. There was no cause for concern, though, for Doris recognised the shape of her brother who said, "What's the matter with her?" Doris replied, "I don't know, she's been like it some time." She asked William Knighton to strike a match so that she could see what time it was. Knighton moved around to her side of the bed, struck a light and held it before the clock which was near Doris. It was 1.45am and Knighton then crept out of the room. Doris heard his footsteps as he went down to his own bedroom on the floor below and even heard his bed creak as he climbed into it. Once again, the house settled down for the night.

At 6.00am, George called upstairs to wake his family, as he did every working morning. Doris rose and walked around to her mother's side of the bed to rouse her. Since it was still quite dark, Doris struck a match and lit a small candle and the first thing she saw was a large pool of blood on the floor at the head of the bed. There also seemed to be blood on her mother's face and Ada, who was lying on her right side, was not responding to Doris' gentle shakes.

Doris dressed quickly and ran downstairs to tell her father that something was wrong. As she did so, she saw her brother coming out of his own room and going down before her. By the time Doris had

109

reached the ground floor, both her father and brother were in the kitchen, William on his way out into the yard at the back to use the outside lavatory. Breathlessly, Doris told George that she thought her mother was ill. Since there was a good deal of blood, Doris' first thought was that a particularly strong coughing fit might have caused Ada to burst a blood vessel. As she finished her story, William came in from the yard and washed his hands. George told him what Doris had said and asked his son to go upstairs and take a look for himself.

Coming back down a few minutes later, William confirmed that there did seem to be something the matter with his mother. George poured some brandy into a cup and told William to take this up, hoping that it might revive Ada but when William came back downstairs again he said she hadn't been able to take any and added, "It seems hopeless."

George now suggested that his eldest daughter, a married woman named Lois Wake, might know what to do and asked William to fetch her. Like a dutiful son, he left the house without delay to make the short journey to his sister's house.

Lois Pretoria Wake lived with her husband, John William Wake, at 19 Eyre's Gardens, also in Ilkeston. It was 6.55am when they were woken by someone hammering on their front door. John Wake walked over to his bedroom window, threw it open and, looking down, saw his brother-in-law standing outside. William Knighton shouted up, "Tell Lois to come at once, mother's ill." The message was passed on and soon Lois was opening the door to let her brother in.

He began by asking for a cup of tea which he drank with relish as he explained that none of the family had been able to rouse Ada, and that she seemed to have lost a good deal of blood. Lois asked if this was a sudden attack, or if Ada had been ill all night, to which Knighton replied, "I don't know. Dad wants you to bring a blanket and a sheet." Soon, brother and sister were leaving the house together to return to Bethel Street.

At the end of Station Road, William Knighton suddenly announced that he was going to see one of his closest friends, a man nicknamed Brookie, and without further ado, left Lois to continue the journey alone. When Lois arrived at Bethel Street, she immediately went upstairs to see her mother and it was only too plain that something was seriously wrong with Ada. She was lying still, on the right side of the bed, a pool of blood on the floor. Lois ran downstairs and told her father that she thought her mother might be dead and she was going to call the doctor.

William Knighton, meanwhile, had not gone to see his friend, but had instead walked to the nearest police station which he entered at 7.25am. Constable Thomas Cowlishaw was on the desk and it was to him that Knighton said that he wished to speak to the inspector. The constable knew that his inspector was a busy man and asked Knighton if he might assist him instead. Knighton replied that it was important that he see the inspector, adding "It's a case of death."

Five minutes later, Knighton was speaking to Inspector Frederick James Wheeldon and told him, "I want to see you inspector. I have done the old woman in. I have cut her throat with a razor. The razor is lying by the side of the bed." Knighton was immediately cautioned and taken down to the cells while Inspector Wheeldon went to investigate William Knighton's astonishing claim.

By the time Lois Wake returned to Bethel Street with Dr Stokes, the police were already there. Dr Stokes examined Ada Knighton and confirmed that she was dead and Inspector Wheeldon then called for the police surgeon, Dr Francis Bennett Sudbury, to make his own assessment. Dr Sudbury arrived at 8.15am, and made his own examination as the inspector searched the room. Later he returned to the police station and it was there, at 9.45am, that he charged William Knighton with the murder of his mother.

Matters proceeded rapidly over the next few weeks. The inquest opened on February 9th before Mr Arthur Norton Whiston and, after evidence of identification had been given, was adjourned to February 17th when a verdict of wilful murder was returned. William Knighton, meanwhile, appeared in the police court on February 8th, and again on February 17th when he was sent for trial on the capital charge.

The assizes opened soon afterwards and Knighton faced his trial at Derby on February 26th, before Mr Justice Branson. Mr Maurice F. Healy presented the case for the prosecution while Knighton was defended by Sir Henry Maddocks and Mr T.R. Fitzwalter Butler.

Since Knighton had confessed to the crime, the defence were not attempting to deny that he was responsible for his mother's death, but sought to show that he was insane at the time. The first witness was the prisoner's sister, Doris. She confirmed that both her mother and her brother had been drinking rather heavily of late and after relating the events of February 7th and 8th, she told of an earlier incident, which took place on Saturday, February 5th.

On that date, Doris had gone to bed at her usual time of 10.00pm. At the time, William was downstairs having only recently come into the house, and he was much the worse for drink. Doris slept soundly that night until some time between 2.00am and 3.00am when she was woken by Knighton calling up to his mother for some matches. Doris could not see her brother and from the sound of his voice, believed that he was standing on the stairs outside their bedroom at the time. Ada had shouted back that he should look for some matches in his own room and not disturb the rest of the house. For a time, no further noise was heard.

It was perhaps half an hour later that Doris heard someone come into the bedroom. She knew that this was her brother and saw his darkened figure walk around to her side of the bed. He gently placed his hand on her face and arms and stroked her before climbing into bed and getting on top of her. Young Doris had no idea what he was playing at, but could feel that he was dressed only in his shirt. It was only when she felt him enter her that she screamed and woke her mother.

William Knighton immediately rolled out of the bed and was nowhere to be seen when Ada turned over and asked Doris what was the matter. Doris said that there was a man in the room but avoided mentioning that it was her brother, or what he had done to her, for fear of causing trouble. Ada, of course, could see no one and told Doris not to be silly. Five or ten minutes later, though, Ada did see someone about to leave the room and called out, "Is that you Bill?" Knighton admitted that it was and when asked what he was doing there, replied simply, "Nothing," and went back to his own bedroom. Continuing her testimony, Doris said that she had known her brother have fits and had seen him suffer two such seizures lately.

Lois Wake told of Knighton's visit to her house and of him leaving her at Station Road. When she went upstairs to her mother, Lois had noticed a bucket at the side of the bed. This was usually kept there for Ada and Doris to use as a toilet if the need arose during the night but looking into this, Lois saw that in addition to the usual contents, there was also a good deal of blood in the bucket. Lois also testified that Knighton had always been on the most affectionate of terms with his mother. She, too, knew that he had suffered fits which left him dazed and shaky.

Dr Sudbury stated that when he entered the attic bedroom he found the deceased lying on her right side. There was blood on both of her hands and on her forearms. There was a wound in the throat some four inches long at about the mid-line of the neck. His examination took place at 8.15am and by then, Ada had been dead at least four hours. Looking around the room, Dr Sudbury saw that there was a large pool of blood on the floor and at the edge of this pool was the bucket which contained blood and other fluids. Dr Sudbury also performed the post-mortem and found no other injuries apart from the wound in the throat which had taken considerable force to inflict. Finally, he thought it highly improbable that the wound was self-inflicted, although it was not impossible.

Constable Cowlishaw spoke of the prisoner coming into the police station and asking for the inspector. At the time, Knighton was calm and rational and was perfectly sober. Inspector Wheeldon, the final police witness, said that he had found the razor lying underneath the bed, almost opposite the victim's feet. The blade was opened out and bore heavy bloodstaining.

In his summing up for the defence, Sir Henry stated that the only evidence against his client was his own confession. Knighton had said that on waking up he had found the bloodstained razor in his pocket and after seeing what had happened to Ada, had simply assumed that he must have done it. This was what made him go to the police station and confess. Although medical evidence had not been called to prove it, there was a good chance that Knighton was an epileptic and, as such, was unaware of what he was doing when he carried out this terrible attack. The jury, though, were not convinced and returned a verdict that Knighton was guilty of murder.

An appeal against the death sentence was entered and this was heard on March 21st before Justices Avory, Shearman and Sankey. The defence agreed that there could be no complaint in regard to the trial judge's summing up but the verdict of the jury was unsatisfactory and the court should substitute a verdict of guilty but insane. The evidence had shown that there was no motive and that William Knighton had been on the best of terms with his mother. In addition, he had made no attempt to escape and had surrendered himself to the police, even providing them with the only real evidence against him, his confession. There was also an application to call further medical evidence as to the prisoner's sanity.

Giving the court's judgement, Mr Justice Avory stated that it was for the Home Secretary to consider the matter of the prisoner's sanity and that could not be gone into by them. The evidence had been put properly before the jury and they had come to the only conclusion they could. The verdict could not be described as unsatisfactory and the appeal must be dismissed. A new execution date was now set.

The matter was now in the hands of the Home Secretary and when, in addition to all the trial evidence, he received fresh evidence from the defence, he took the unusual steps of cancelling the execution again and sending the matter back to the Court of Appeal.

William Knighton's second appeal was heard on April 12th before the Lord Chief Justice, Lord Hewart and Justices Avory and Sankey, two of the judges who had presided over the first appeal. The defence now sought permission to call Knighton's sister, Doris, to give further evidence which suggested that her father and not her brother, was responsible for the crime. Having read Doris' new statement, though, Lord Hewart stated that the court was satisfied that her story was untrue and therefore it was not necessary to call George Knighton to refute this charge on oath. There had also been the suggestion that since Doris' second story had been shown to be untrue, then the prisoner's conviction should not rest on the evidence of her first story. The court ruled that this was not the case. The conviction did not rely on any of Doris' evidence and there was ample other evidence to show that Knighton was responsible for his mother's death. The second appeal was also lost.

On April 25th, what faint hopes might have remained were dashed when the Home Office communicated with Knighton's solicitors and informed them that no grounds had been discovered for interfering with the sentence. Just two days later, on Wednesday, April 27th, William Knighton was hanged at Nottingham by Thomas Pierrepoint. It was only the third execution in an English prison in 1927.

Chapter Thirteen

The Ten Minute Murder

ALTHOUGH Arthur Collinson was the landlord of the New Inn public house at Little Hayfield, he also worked as a sandpaperer at a factory in Glossop. This meant that each working day, he travelled in to his job while the pub was left in the hands of his wife, Amy Collinson. Things were no different on the morning of Friday, November 11th, 1927.

It was shortly before 6.00pm, when Arthur returned home and to his surprise, found the inn door bolted. Since Amy was supposed to open for business at 5.30pm, and had never been known to be late before, Arthur was concerned and walked around the building, trying to find an open window through which he might gain access. Even as Arthur called out for his wife, and tried the windows and other doors, a close neighbour, Amos Dawson, walked up to him and asked what seemed to be the trouble.

Amos Dawson rented some outbuildings at the inn, and he told Arthur that he had called for a drink at 3.10pm and the pub door had been locked then. At the time Amos had looked through the windows of the tap room and parlour but saw no sign of Amy Collinson. All Amos could see was the wooden forms still placed upside down on the tables, and thinking that this was most out of character for Amy, he had called again at 4.30pm, but the situation had been exactly the same. Luckily, Amos Dawson had a key to the stable and access to the pub could be gained through this. He had, of course, not wanted to use this approach until Arthur came home. It was, after all, his house. Using Amos' key, the two men finally got into the pub through the stable which led through several rooms into the living room. It was in that room that they found Amy, lying on the floor, underneath the window. She had been battered about the head and her throat had been cut from ear to ear. The carving knife used to inflict this terrible wound still lay embedded in her neck. There was no doubt that Amy Collinson was beyond all human help but Amos Dawson ran to fetch Dr Lynch and, of course, the police.

It was 6.20pm by the time Constable Thomas Glynn arrived at the New Inn, in the company of Dr Horner Hamilton Carswell Lynch. As the doctor examined the body, Constable Glynn noted that a rug by the fire had been kicked up and that there was an opened tin of polish and a duster lying in a pool of blood. This implied that Amy had been cleaning and so had not been on her guard when she was attacked. Either a stranger had forced an entry or the attacker had been someone Amy knew. Constable Glynn checked all the doors and windows for any sign of a break in, but everything was secure. It was likely that the person responsible for this crime had been known to Amy and was, in all probability, a local man.

It was important to narrow down, as far as possible, the time that Amy Collinson had been attacked. A local man, Charles Hobson, had delivered milk to the pub at some time between 9.30am and 9.45am on November 11th. The front door was locked at the time but when Hobson rattled the letter-box, Amy came to the door and she closed it after him when Hobson left.

Arthur Lomas, a roadsweeper, told officers that he had passed the inn at some time between 9.45am and 10.00am and he had seen Amy sweeping out the lobby. They had exchanged a few words but when Arthur walked back, at 11.40am, the pub door was closed. Another witness was George Frederick Walter Hayward who lived at the White House, some 600 yards from the New Inn. He was visited, at 10.45pm on November 11th by Constable Glynn and Inspector W.E. Cordin, who was now in charge of the investigation. Hayward told the two officers that he had called at the inn sometime between 10.10am and 10.15am when Mrs Collinson had been cleaning the grate. Hayward said he had purchased a packet of cigarettes and stayed in the house for perhaps ten minutes. Hayward went on to explain that he had then walked to the bus stop where he caught the 10.45am to New Mills to sign on at the Labour Exchange. This timing seemed to be confirmed by Arthur Lomas, who said that he had seen Hayward at about 10.40am, walking on the footpath towards Hayfield, and they had chatted for about three minutes. Since this same witness had noted that the pub door was closed at 11.40am it now seemed reasonable to assume that Amy Collinson had been killed some time between 10.30am, when Hayward left her, and 11.40am, when Lomas passed the New Inn for the second time that day.

The police, meanwhile, had discovered the motive for the brutal attack upon Amy. After checking the premises, Arthur Collinson confirmed that there was a large quantity of treasury notes missing from the house. Although he could not be sure of the precise figure, there had been some cash in a trunk in the bedroom and this, together with the contents of the till, meant that somewhere between £30 and £40 had been stolen.

The trunk which had held the cash had not been forced, though, and the key used to unlock it was normally kept in a large purse in a separate cash box, next to the trunk. This cash box had been opened, the key removed and left on the floor after the trunk had been unlocked. This again reinforced the belief that the killer was a local man who knew both the inn and the habits of the Collinsons.

The police were certainly most thorough in their efforts to find all possible clues. In the early hours of November 12th, a number of officers, including the Assistant Chief Constable, Mr J.M. Garrow, searched the inn from top to bottom. It was during that search that it was noticed that the key to the lavatory was missing. It normally hung on a hook in the bar. When the door to the lavatory was finally opened, a disused cistern in the toilet appeared to have been disturbed. It was covered in cobwebs, some of which appeared to be broken, and upon lifting the hinged lid, a piece of lead piping was found which had sticks of some kind jammed inside it. The fact that this was wrapped in bloodstained paper indicated that it must have been used to batter Amy Collinson, before the wound on her throat was inflicted.

George Hayward might prove to be a most valuable witness in this case. He had already told Constable Glynn and Inspector Cordin that he had left the inn at about 10.20am. It was likely that he had been the last person to see Amy alive apart from her killer and so, at 10.45am on November 12th, Inspector Edgar Banham paid a call at the White House where the door was opened by Hayward's wife. She explained that her husband was out but Inspector Banham said he would wait. Hayward finally came back at 11.15am and was informed that Superintendent Macdonald wished to see him to confirm the times of his visit to the New Inn.

Upon hearing this, Mrs Hayward interrupted and asked her husband why he had told her that he hadn't been anywhere near the inn on the day that Amy Collinson met her death. Hayward appeared to be rather evasive and would only say, "Don't get upset, I shall soon be back." Mrs Hayward persisted and demanded to know why she had been lied to, whereupon Hayward replied, "I went to get a packet of cigarettes." It had not escaped Inspector Banham, though, that Hayward had told one story to the police and another to his wife. When he arrived at the New Inn, to be interviewed by Superintendent Macdonald, Hayward persisted in his story that Amy had been alive when he left her, saying, "I have not murdered the woman. You can examine my coat if you like. I was wearing this coat yesterday." At this stage, there was certainly not enough evidence to hold Hayward, and after answering further questions he was allowed to return home. Meanwhile, Inspector Banham had spoken to Mrs Hayward who told him that her husband had given her a new pair of gloves and £2 in cash, on November 11th.

At 2.00pm that same day, another police officer, Detective Constable Leonard Butterly, also visited Hayward's house and was given permission to look around. At the back of the house, Butterly noticed that the waste outlet pipe was loose and that a portion seemed to have been sawn off the end fairly recently. Recalling the bludgeon found in the cistern at the New Inn, Constable Butterly took this information back to his superiors.

By 5.30pm, Inspector Banham, Constable Butterly and Detective Sergeant Trevor Holland, were back at the White House where Banham cautioned Hayward and then asked him about the £2 he had given to his wife and the pair of gloves he had told her came from his sister in Manchester. Hayward replied, "I don't care to say." Continuing his questioning, Banham asked Hayward to say where he was at about 1.30pm on November 11th. Hayward thought for a moment and then said, "I was not in Hayfield or even Derbyshire at 1.15pm. I can prove I was in Manchester. At present I won't say where I got the money and gloves from as it may incriminate someone else, but not in this case." Then, as proof that he was indeed in Manchester on the day of the murder, Hayward told the police that he had collected his watch from a repair shop on Corporation Street at 1.50pm.

The police were far from satisfied and at 9.00pm they were back at the White House, this time with a builder, Alfred Thompson, who removed the waste pipe from Hayward's sink so that it could be examined more closely. When it was seen that there were three pieces of cane embedded in the body of the pipe, exactly the same as had been found in the bludgeon found in the cistern at the New Inn, Hayward was taken into custody while further enquiries were made, and removed to the Chapel-en-le-Frith police station. The next day, November 13th, the police were back at Hayward's house, again with Alfred Thompson, and a full-scale search of the premises was now organised. After some time, it was Constable Butterly who saw a bag hidden up the chimney breast, and asked Thompson to retrieve it for him. It turned out to be a Lloyd's Bank bag and stamped with the Oswestry branch address. When the bag was opened it was seen to contain 14 one-pound notes, 34 ten-shilling notes and just under £1 6s in silver and copper, a total which was a halfpenny short of £32 6s 0d. Hayward was taken into custody and at 9.55am on November 14th, he was charged with murder by Superintendent John Archibald Macdonald.

Hayward made his first brief appearance before the magistrates later that day. Evidence of arrest was given and some brief details of the prisoner outlined. Hayward, it was said, was 31 years old and had been married for two years, he and his wife having one child who was three months old. Superintendent Macdonald asked for a remand until November 21st, which was granted.

Two days after this, on November 16th, the body of Amy Collinson was laid to rest at Glossop cemetery. There was a large crowd gathered around the graveside and Amy's relatives were utterly devastated by the occasion.

On November 21st, Superintendent Macdonald explained that the Director of Public Prosecutions was not yet ready to proceed and a further remand was granted. Hayward was back in court on November 24th when he was remanded yet again, this time to New Mills, on November 30th. On that date, some of the evidence was finally outlined, during which Hayward spent most of his time staring out of the courtroom windows. A further remand was requested and Hayward said that he had no objections but asked that he be granted legal aid. He was told that this would be given, if he ended up being sent for trial. He was then taken from the court by means of a side door and returned to Strangeways prison, Manchester. The final police court hearings extended over three days, from December 6th to December 8th. Hayward, who was now quoted as being 32 years old, was not legally represented but listened to the prosecution case outlined by Mr G.R. Paling. Many witnesses were called and on the third day, Hayward was sent to face his trial at the next assizes. The prisoner seemed to be somewhat unconcerned, though, for on this final day he whiled away his time sketching people in the courtroom and showing his efforts to the police officers set to guard him in the dock.

The case of the Crown against George Hayward opened at Derby on February 20th, 1928, before Mr Justice Hawke in what was to be his first murder trial after being appointed to the bench on February 8th. The prosecution case was led by Sir Henry Maddocks who was assisted by Mr T. Norman Winning, while Hayward was defended by Mr A.H. Davis. The proceedings lasted until February 24th.

Sir Henry began by outlining the basic facts of the case, stating that Hayward, a man who had been unemployed and short of money, had not only given his wife £2 on the day that Mrs Collinson was killed, but that he had also purchased a £4 postal order in Salford. In addition, by his own admission, Hayward had been in the New Inn close to the time of the attack and had lied about this visit to his wife. After the long opening speech was completed, the first witness, Arthur Collinson, was called.

Mr Collinson stated that on November 11th, he had risen at his usual time of 6.00am. He began the day by helping Amy with the clearing up and as he left for work, at 7.45am, his wife was preparing to begin her daily chores. Upon returning to the inn, at about 5.55pm, he found the doors bolted and a concerned Amos Dawson, who himself had been unable to gain entrance during the day and had even had to take delivery of a shipment of porter that had been made to the pub.

Discussing Amy's daily routine, Collinson said that she was a creature of habit. After he had gone to work, she would make the beds and do other jobs upstairs before coming down to collect the delivery of milk. She would then clear up the breakfast things and sweep out the lobby and do the fireplaces starting with the living room.

Turning to the money held on the premises, Collinson said that this was normally kept until the sum was large enough to pay into the bank. The last time Amy had done this was some three weeks before and this was what led him to estimate that there would have been something in excess of £30 there, although it was his wife who dealt with such matters and only she would know exactly how much there was at any given time.

Arthur Collinson did, of course, know Hayward very well indeed. He was a regular customer at the pub and it seemed that he did have financial problems, especially since he had lost his job. In the middle of October, for instance, Hayward had sent a letter to Amy, asking for 12s or 13s which he had paid into a Christmas club known as 'The Pudding Club'. The letter had read something like, "I will pay the money when I restart work so that you will not lose business."

The second day of the trial began with Arthur Lomas confirming that he had seen Hayward some time around 10.45am on November 11th. At the time, Hayward was 300 or perhaps 350 yards from the New Inn. Next, the prosecution called Emma Warrington who said that she had also seen Hayward on the 10.50am bus which ran from Hayfield to New Mills. She recalled the time precisely because this was Remembrance Day and the bus stopped soon afterwards to observe the two minutes' silence. Mrs Warrington was also travelling all the way to New Mills and as she alighted, she saw Hayward again, walking off in the direction of the Labour Exchange. Corroboration as to the time was also given by John William Johnson, the bus conductor, who said that his vehicle left Hayfield at 10.48am.

Confirmation that Hayward had attended the Labour Exchange was given by Mr John Thomas Sleight, one of the clerks there, who added that Hayward had been given 25s benefit. Further evidence as to his movements was given by Elsie Sophia Luke, a Post Office clerk at Piccadilly, who sold a £4 money order to Hayward. Mrs Luke was unable to pinpoint the exact time this transaction had taken place but said that it must have been between 3.00pm and 5.00pm.

The next witness was Constable Glynn, who after detailing what he had found when he attended the inn on the day of the murder, referred to his interview with the prisoner. Hayward had admitted that he had visited the pub saying, "Yes, I left home about 10.05 in the morning. I arrived at the New Inn about ten past ten to a quarter past and remained there ten minutes. I bought a packet of Black Cat cigarettes. Mrs Collinson was down on her knees cleaning the grate when I was in."

It was also on the second day of the trial that Dr Horner Lynch was called to describe the wounds inflicted upon the dead woman. He testified that he had first arrived at the inn at 6.20pm and noted that the body was lying on its right side with the right arm outstretched. The right hand was clenched and the left arm lay over the body. The right hand lay in a large pool of blood but there were no defence cuts or abrasions on either hand. Amy's throat was cut from under the lobe of her right ear to below the lobe of the left. Many blood vessels and organs of the neck had been severed and the knife still lay embedded in this wound with the point of the blade resting on the floor and the handle pointing to the left.

Once the body had been removed to the mortuary, Dr Lynch shaved the head so that he could examine the scalp wounds. There were three distinct wounds, all of which had bled profusely. Having performed a post-mortem, Dr Lynch was able to say that the direct cause of death had been haemorrhage and shock from the throat wounds and suggested that Mrs Collinson had first been battered, in all probability from behind, and her throat cut while she lay on the floor. He confirmed that the pipe found in the cistern, could have inflicted the head wounds.

It was while these graphic details were being related that one of the juryman was overcome. The case had to be adjourned while he received medical treatment but after 20 minutes, it was decided that he was not fit enough to continue. A new jury, consisting of the 11 existing members and a new one, was then sworn in and the case started all over again.

On the third day of the trial, witnesses were called to narrow down the time of the attack upon Mrs Collinson. Hayward had said in his first interview with the police that he had left his home at 10.05am. John Ferguson Barr, an engineer at Clough Mill, was in the boiler house at some time between 10.10am and 10.20am on November 11th when Hayward called on him. The two men talked about a gramophone for a few minutes before Hayward, who was wearing a mackintosh at the time, left and headed off towards the New Inn.

Mrs Mary McBain, who lived close to the New Inn, was cleaning her front steps on the morning of November 11th when Hayward walked past, going towards the inn. As Hayward walked on, a train passed and since this was checked and shown to be on time, it was 10.23am when Hayward was seen by Mrs McBain. This encounter was also seen by Emma Bradley who ran a shop in Clough Lane. She had known Hayward as a customer for the past couple of years and she was at her upstairs window as he walked past. She too confirmed the time as just before 10.25am.

In some ways, this presented a problem for the prosecution. Hayward had been seen close to the inn at 10.23am, but was boarding a bus which left Hayfield at 10.48am, just 25 minutes later. Since that bus stop was some 1,500 yards from the inn, and the police had measured that as approximately a 12-minute walk, Hayward had only 13 minutes in which to commit the crime but, when it was remembered that Arthur Lomas said he had spoken to Hayward for perhaps three minutes, that time span was now reduced to just ten minutes, if indeed Hayward was the killer.

The weapon used to batter Amy Collinson was the short length of lead pipe found in the cistern at the New Inn. Witnesses were now called to show that this piece of pipe had definitely come from Hayward's home.

Maud Lilian McBain was only 12 years old, but she proved to be a valuable witness. She had been helping Mrs Hayward with her baby for the past three months and knew the family well. Indeed, it was Maud who delivered the letter from Hayward, asking for his Christmas club money but added that this missive had been given to her by Mrs

Hayward, not the prisoner. Maud, though, was also able to say that on November 5th, six days before the murder, she had been at the White House all day. During the evening, Mrs Hayward complained to her husband that the waste pipe in the kitchen was blocked and Maud saw him remove it. In an attempt to remove the blockage, Hayward had hammered a piece of stick up the pipe, but this became wedged and only served to make the problem worse.

The pipe found at the New Inn had three pieces of wood wedged inside it and these had been examined by John Edmund Shirt, a master joiner. He compared the wood with that found in the pipe in the cistern and confirmed that they had once been joined to form one larger piece by comparing the texture of the grain. The same was done with four small pieces of wood also removed from the same pipe.

William Henry Grey, a plumber, had examined the pipe itself. He could say that the pipe had been cut by means of a fine toothed saw. He was also able to show that the piece found in the cistern had exactly the same cross-sectional dimensions as the waste pipe at Hayward's house. As if further links were needed, the prosecution then called Dr Gerald Roche Lynch of St Mary's Hospital. He had found several traces of blood on Hayward's clothing but had also made a microscopic examination of the teeth of a saw found in an outbuilding at the White House. Dr Lynch confirmed that there were minute particles of silvery metal adhering to the teeth and that he had found similar particles in Hayward's jacket pocket.

George William Welch was the managing director of Hazlehurst & Sons, a company employed in the manufacture of soap. He told the court that Hayward had been employed by the company since April 1927, receiving a basic salary and commission on sales he made. On October 11th, Hayward had been dismissed since he had been tardy in sending cash received on to his employer. Mr Welch asked Hayward to send any outstanding monies to him but there were constant delays and requests for more time. This situation was allowed to continue until November 1st when Mr Welch discovered that Hayward had been telling his customers that he still worked for Hazlehurst & Sons, and had carried on collecting money. By now he owed the company £63 0s 3d and Mr Welch wrote to Hayward to say, "Let us have your undertaking that you will not attempt to make any further collections from our customers. We shall at once take such proceedings as we may be advised to protect our interests."

Other witnesses tied up a few of the loose ends in the case. Noel Henry James Bailey was a bank clerk based at Lloyd's in Oswestry and he stated that the bag found in Hayward's chimney had been one issued during the 1914-1918 period to soldiers based at Park Hall. Hayward, who had served in the Army from 1914 until his demob in September 1918, had at one stage been stationed at Oswestry.

Herbert Mountain worked for John Harrop, a house furnishers in Piccadilly, Manchester, and he testified that Hayward had ordered £57 11s 4d worth of goods in May 1926. The monthly instalments were just £2 but payment had been erratic and attempts were made to recover the debt. Hayward had written to Mountain at the end of October, promising that the payments would be brought up to date and true enough, on November 12th, he received a note from Hayward with a £4 postal order enclosed. Other debts were detailed by Edwin William Kershaw, the owner of White House, who said that Hayward's rent was in arrears to the tune of £6, and the shopkeeper, Emma Bradley, who said that Hayward owed her £2 16s 10d.

On the third day of the trial, Hayward stepped into the witness box to give evidence on his own behalf. He confirmed that he had known Amy Collinson well and had visited her on November 7th to see her about some soap he had ordered in her name. In fact he had been quite a regular visitor but had tried to cut down on his visits since he had become unemployed. This was why he had lied to his wife about being in the New Inn on the day that Amy was killed, in case she thought he was spending money he could ill afford. Although Mrs Hayward was also friendly with the Collinsons, she had objected in the past about the amount of time and money he spent there.

Turning to the waste pipe, Hayward said that his wife had first tried to clear it by pushing some cane down it but this had got stuck so she asked him to sort it out. He had hammered some wood down but this also got stuck so he cut a piece off the pipe, hoping that he would then be able to get the wood out. He still couldn't shift it and threw the entire pipe into his shed. Mrs Hayward complained about there being no pipe at all now so he put the longer piece back and threw the small piece away. As for the small portions of metal in his pocket, Hayward explained that he quite often carried small tools in his jacket as he was interested in repairing wireless sets.

Referring to his financial concerns, Hayward admitted that he had been using his former employer's money for some time and it was money from them that he used to pay off the furniture debts, buy some gloves for his wife and give her the £2. Hayward pointed out that Mr Welch had testified that there was more than £63 owed and the money found in the chimney breast was from this cash, not from the New Inn.

The final day was largely taken up with speeches for the prosecution and defence. For Hayward, Mr Davis said that Hayward had simply not been in the public house long enough to commit the crime of which he was accused. Even the prosecution had agreed that he would have had only ten minutes, at the very most, in which to put Amy Collinson off guard, batter her over the head, take a knife from the kitchen drawer and cut her throat, take the cash from the box upstairs and then hide the cosh he had used in the toilet cistern. For the prosecution, though, Sir Henry Maddocks pointed out that the crime must have been committed by someone who knew the layout of the inn and no stranger had been seen in the area by any of the witnesses.

In his own summing up, Mr Justice Hawke praised the efforts of Mr Davis and told Hayward that whatever the outcome, he should have nothing but gratitude for the man who had represented him. The jury retired to consider their verdict and after half an hour, returned to court to announce that they had found Hayward guilty as charged.

Asked if he had anything to say, Hayward replied, "Only that I am not guilty. I am quite innocent my Lord." Mr Justice Hawke then passed his first death sentence.

An appeal was entered and this was heard on March 26th before the Lord Chief Justice, Lord Hewart and Justices Avory and Talbot. The main defence argument was that at the trial, medical evidence had stated that the doctor had put the time of death somewhere between 10.00am and noon, with the later time more likely. If this was the case then Hayward must be innocent as he was in Manchester. Even if the earlier time was accepted, then Hayward did not have time to commit the murder. Two separate pools of blood had been found at the scene and evidence was given that Mrs Collinson had been bodily carried from one location to the other, by her killer. The first pool of blood was of such a size that the doctors believed she must have lain there for a full five minutes before being moved. This reduced even further the time available in which Hayward might have committed the crime.

Giving the judgement, Lord Hewart said that the coincidences in this case were very strong. The prisoner had been in the pub on the day of the murder; there was blood on his clothing; he had financial problems and yet a good deal of cash was found in his home; and the piece of pipe used to batter the dead woman had certainly come from Hayward's house. The circumstantial evidence was overwhelming and the appeal must be dismissed.

In due course it was announced that there would be no reprieve. By now, Hayward had been moved to Bagthorpe jail in Nottingham and it was there, on the morning of Tuesday, April 10th, 1928, that he was hanged by Thomas Pierrepoint who was assisted by Henry Pollard. It was already the eighth execution in an English prison this year.

Chapter Fourteen

Something More Serious

WALTER Graham Rowland was a worried man. It had all started with a rather minor offence when Rowland, who lived at 2 Cheetham Hill, Mellor, had taken a taxi ride to Blackpool and then neglected to pay the £3 fare. As a result, he had received a summons telling him to appear in court at Stockport. The first hearing had been adjourned and now, on Friday, March 2nd, 1934, he was due to make his second appearance.

The matter had certainly preyed on Rowland's mind ever since the case had been adjourned. He had even gone to see his employer, Mr Renshaw, and arranged to borrow money from him to pay off the debt to the taxi company but this attempt to have the case dropped had not succeeded. The proprietor had explained that much as he would like to help, the matter was now out of his hands and would have to be dealt with by the police and the courts. As the days passed, Rowland even suggested to his wife, Annie May, that they should leave the area and start afresh somewhere else. When she in turn pointed out that they didn't have the money to do such a thing, Rowland had suggested breaking open the electricity meter and using the money it held to escape from Mellor. Annie May told him not to be so silly, but nothing, it seemed, could stop her husband worrying.

On the date of the adjourned hearing, Annie May woke at 9.15am. Rowland was already up and about and brought her a cup of tea in bed. Once again Rowland spoke of his worries and confided in Annie May that he did not think he was going to court, even though it would mean a warrant being issued for his arrest. Nevertheless, at 11.00am, Rowland went out leaving Annie May to take care of their two-year-old daughter, Mavis Agnes. Annie May Rowland busied herself with the household chores and by 3.00pm, she was upstairs, cleaning out the bedrooms. Some 30 minutes later, Annie noticed her husband's working trousers hanging over a chair near the window and as she straightened them, she saw that there was something hanging out of one of the pockets. To Annie's surprise, this turned out to be a woman's stocking but even as she gazed at it, she heard Rowland arriving home. Knowing that he hated her looking through his pockets, she hurriedly pushed the stocking back where she had found it.

For the next couple of hours, Rowland seemed to be on tenterhooks. More than once he went to the front door, opened it, looked out and then rushed back inside and locked the door behind him. Annie May asked Rowland what the trouble was and he explained that he hadn't gone to court after all, and was afraid that the police would come for him at any time He was still in this state at 5.20pm when Annie left the house to visit some friends at New Mills. At the time, Mavis was playing on the living room carpet and Annie told Rowland not to put her to bed before eight or even half past as otherwise she might not sleep through the night.

It was 7.45pm by the time Annie May returned home, to find the house in darkness. The front door was closed but not locked and as Annie entered the cold house, she snapped on the light to see a towel and the evening paper lying on the table. She called out for her husband, but there was no reply to her shouting so she went upstairs to see where he was, and to check on Mavis.

Checking first in the front bedroom, Annie found no trace of Rowland. In the back bedroom, nothing had apparently been disturbed but upon looking into the child's cot, Annie saw her daughter – and that Mavis was very pale and her tongue was protruding from between her lips. Pulling the bedclothes down a little, Annie saw to her horror that there was a woman's stocking tied tightly around the little girl's throat. Annie frantically untied the four knots and as the pressure around Mavis' throat was released, a sickening hissing sound escaped from the child. Annie Rowland picked up the child and ran next door for help.

Olive May Brough lived with her husband, John, at 1 Cheetham Hill. It was almost 8.00pm by the time Annie Rowland, carrying the little girl in her arms, dashed in through the back door and explained what she had found. Annie left Mavis with Mrs Brough and ran to fetch the doctor. While Annie was gone, Olive Brough walked about the room, nursing the still bundle, although she saw that Mavis' face was very white and her lips were blue. Olive also saw that the stocking was still loosely around the child's throat. There was yet another knot to unfasten before it could finally be removed.

At 8.15pm, Annie May Rowland returned to Olive Brough's house with Dr David Dougall Hepburn Craig and Police Sergeant Wilfred Coates. By now, Mavis had been placed into a pram and it was there that Dr Craig examined her and confirmed that she was dead. He noted a purplish groove around the child's neck, some quarter to a half-inch in width, and estimated that death had taken place within the last two hours, and in his opinion, the latest time of death would have been one hour earlier. This put Mavis' death at some time between 6.15pm and 7.15pm. Sergeant Coates, meanwhile, had checked the Rowlands' house and found that the electricity meter had been broken into. He then contacted his station and had details of Walter Rowland circulated to forces in the immediate area.

It was not long before a number of witnesses were found who had seen something of Rowland on the evening of March 2nd. Percy Jackson was 13 years old and a member of the local Boy Scouts group. Percy lived at 6 Green Doors on Cheetham Hill and knew the Rowland family quite well. The Scouts met every Friday night and at some time between 6.00pm and 6.30pm, Percy had been on the way to the Scout hut when Walter Rowland stopped him and asked if he had seen the newspaper deliveryman. Percy said he hadn't, whereupon Rowland picked up Mavis, who had been playing on the pavement in front of the cottages, and took her inside.

The newspaperman to whom Rowland had been referring was James

Horsfield and he told the police that he had delivered papers to the cottages at Cheetham Hill at 6.30pm on Friday evening. For a few minutes, Horsfield spoke to Mr Burdekin who lived at number three. Horsfield explained that he had to talk rather loudly as old Mr Burdekin was rather deaf. His voice probably carried quite a distance as a result and as they talked, Rowland came to Mr Burdekin's front door and asked Horsfield if he might buy a newspaper. Horsfield handed over a copy of the *Evening Chronicle* and saw Rowland return to his own house. A few minutes later, as Horsfield passed down the hill, he heard the door being bolted at number two and saw that the blinds were now pulled down. He was sure that they had been up when he had first started speaking to Mr Burdekin, because he had seen Rowland in his front room, through the window.

There was one other man who had seen something of Walter Rowland that night. James Hambleton lived at a house named Heatherick on Moor End, Mellor, and at 6.50pm, he was near the Devonshire Arms Inn. As Hambleton watched, the bus from New Mills came down Cheetham Hill and stopped at the inn. Hambledon was well acquainted with Rowland and he was certain that he was the man who got off the bus and ran across the road to catch another bus a few yards down the road. This bus went to Stockport and pulled out a minute or so after Rowland had climbed on. The search for Rowland now moved to Stockport.

Samuel Henderson lived at 28 Hayfield Street, Portwood, Stockport, and at 8.30pm on March 2nd, he walked into the Touchstone Inn where he noticed a man drinking alone. Henderson fell in conversation with the stranger and they both bought rounds of drinks. Henderson's new friend seemed to be somewhat nervous and at one stage asked which was nearer, New Brighton or Blackpool. Told that it was New Brighton, the stranger said that he was thinking of going there on business, if he could get a woman to go with him. When a few minutes later, an attractive woman came in alone, the man persuaded Henderson to go over and ask her if she wanted a drink.

Eliza Ann Burke lived at 12 Reddish Road, Stockport, and although she was a married woman, she quite often went out drinking alone. It was nearly 8.50pm when she entered the Touchstone and almost immediately Samuel Henderson went over and said that his friend wanted to buy her a drink. The three sat together for a time, the stranger introducing himself as Walter Rowland. Soon, Henderson realised that he was playing gooseberry and went off to drink by himself at the opposite end of the bar. He was still in the Touchstone when Rowland and Eliza Burke left together.

When Rowland had first explained to Eliza that he was going to New Brighton and would like her to go with him, she refused. Eventually she gave in to his charms and agreed to go with him. Rowland asked where they might get a taxi and so, at 9.20pm, he and Eliza walked down to Shephard's Garage in Wellington Road where they asked the proprietor to telephone for a cab for them. The first taxi arrived within five minutes but the driver did not relish the thought of a trip to New Brighton and said he would return to base and send out one of his colleagues. As a result, it was almost 10.00pm when a second driver, William Grimshaw, pulled up in Wellington Road.

It was not until just after midnight that the taxi arrived in New Brighton, since the male passenger had asked Grimshaw to stop once on the journey. Once they were in the town, Grimshaw was told to find a Mrs Hudson's house in Lime Grove. He had no idea where that address was and the few people he asked for directions also had no idea. Even an attendant at a garage had never heard of Lime Grove and so Grimshaw parked in Birch Grove and made no objection when his male passenger said he would go off and make enquiries while Grimshaw and Mrs Burke waited in the cab.

When his passenger had still not returned after 20 minutes, Grimshaw went in search of his man and found him close by the police station. A brief argument ensued, during which Grimshaw demanded payment for his fare. The passenger produced an envelope on which he said was his name and home address. He explained that he did not have any money on him and had thought that the woman was going to pay the fare. It was all a simple misunderstanding and if Grimshaw would call at the address he would receive his money without further delay.

William Grimshaw gazed at the envelope and noted the name Rowland and an address at Mellor. Even as he read the words, Grimshaw recalled a case he had seen in his newspapers only that afternoon in which a man named Rowland had been accused of 'bilking' or avoiding a taxi fare. Concerned that he was about to become the second victim of the same man, Grimshaw determined to bring this matter to the attention of the police.

In fact, Rowland had only just walked out of the police station situated just a few yards away. It had been 12.45am on March 3rd when Rowland went to the station desk and spoke to Constable William Allan Wesley. He explained that he had just come from Stockport in a car with three of his workmates but they had separated during the night and as a result, he had now been left behind with nowhere to stay for the night. Constable Wesley said that a colleague of his, on duty outside, might be able to assist Rowland in finding somewhere to stay, and he had gone out to see this second policeman when Grimshaw found him. Now Rowland walked up to Constable Joseph Ryan, who was on duty at the corner of Rowson Street and Victoria Road, and said that his sergeant (mistaking Constable Wesley's rank) had sent him to ask after lodgings for the night. Even as this conversation was taking place, an irate Grimshaw interrupted and shouted, "Wait a minute officer. I want this man's name and address. I've driven himself and a woman to here from Stockport and now he says he's got no money."

In order to sort this matter out, Constable Ryan suggested that they all go back inside the police station. Once again Rowland produced his envelope and was then taken into a back office by Constable Wesley who asked about the fare that had apparently been avoided. Rowland replied with, "Ring up the police at Mellor. They will tell you something more serious than that." He was immediately cautioned to which Rowland said, "Oh, I see you have been through to the police," and became somewhat agitated. He then asked to use the lavatory, a request which was granted.

Telephone calls were made to Derbyshire and at 8.00am on March 3rd, Sergeant Coates and Constable Percy Radford Merrey arrived at Wallasey, the station to which Rowland had now been transferred. There Rowland was told that he would be detained for the murder of his daughter. Upon hearing this Rowland quickly turned pale, fainted and had to be supported. He was formally charged with murder at 11.45am and, one hour later, made a full written statement.

Rowland's statement began, "At 6.20pm the evening of 2nd March I took the child upstairs and put her in a cot while I went to meet the paperman. After I got the paper I came in home *(sic)* and saw that a warrant had been issued for my arrest in regard to an offence com-mitted in Stockport for which I should have appeared in court at the hour of 11.00am, 2nd March, but did not do so. I then put on my coat and hat, fastened the back door and came out leaving the front door on the latch only.

"I walked down the road and boarded a bus near the Scout room, as far as the Devonshire. I then boarded a bus for Stockport, this being ten to seven, arriving Stockport at approximately half past seven. My move-ments from this time onward, up to being apprehended by the Wallasey police are known to the police."

Walter Rowland made his first appearance before the magistrates later that day and was remanded to Chapel-en-le-Frith until March 9th. On that date, a further remand followed, this time until March 16th. This second hearing was again very short, Rowland being content only to ask for legal aid and stating, "I am totally innocent of this crime and I would like to be represented. I have not the means to pay for it myself."

Further remands followed until March 23rd and finally until March 28th when the evidence was finally heard, over two days, Rowland being represented by Mr R. Ashworth. All the witnesses being heard, Rowland was then sent to face his trial at the next Manchester assizes.

The trial of Walter Rowland opened on Monday, May 7th, 1934. Rowland was represented by Mr H. Rhodes, while the Crown's case was led by Mr R.K. Chappell who was assisted by Mr F. Atkinson. The proceedings lasted for two days.

For the prosecution, Mr Chappell began by explaining some of the geography of the case. He stated that Mellor was only just inside Derbyshire and was situated about five miles west of New Mills. Also to the west, about 730 yards from Rowland's cottage, was the crossroads where the Devonshire Arms was situated and all these locations would play a part in the evidence he would call. Mr Chappell went on to say that Rowland had been a casual labourer but was not at work on March 2nd because he was due in court at Stockport to answer a charge. Had he attended court, Rowland might well have successfully defended the charge but if he failed to turn up at all, as indeed he did, then it was certain that a warrant for his arrest would be issued.

The first witness called by the prosecution was Annie May Rowland, the prisoner's wife, who was heavily pregnant with her second child due at the end of the month. She began by saying that she had married the prisoner on September 5th, 1931 and that Mavis had been born on February 21st, 1932. She went on to tell the court of the worries her husband had had over his court appearance and of his suggestions that they run away together, at once stage suggesting that they go to Ireland. She went on to tell of the discovery of the stocking in Rowland's pocket, her visit to relatives at New Mills later that day, and what she had discovered when she finally returned to the cottage that evening. Annie May confirmed that Rowland had always expressed love for his daughter and had seemed to be devoted to her. After he had been arrested, she had visited him and they had spoken of the crime. When Rowland had said that he was innocent, she had asked him who could have done it and Rowland had replied, "My dear, I think you must have had a brainstorm and done it yourself."

Mrs Rowland also confirmed that some weeks before this incident, she had suffered a nervous breakdown and had gone away for ten days to recover. She had no qualms about leaving Mavis in the care of her husband at that time.

This suggestion that Annie May was responsible for her daughter's death was largely dismissed by the evidence of Dr Craig. In addition to attending the scene of the crime, he had also performed a post-mortem on Mavis and this had showed a bloody froth in the child's windpipe and lungs, confirming that the cause of death was strangulation. He repeated under oath that the child must have been dead at least an hour before he made his initial examination showing that the very latest time that Mavis could have died was 7.15pm, and even this was highly unlikely, death almost certainly taking place well before this time. Annie May was then in New Mills and there was therefore no way that she could be responsible for Mavis' death.

Annie May had referred to finding a stocking in Rowland's trouser pocket. Sergeant Coates now testified that after carefully searching Rowland's home, he had found the trousers referred to but there had been no stocking there. However, when Rowland was searched at Wallasey, a woman's stocking was found on him and tests had shown that this was the twin to the one found around Mavis' throat. Referring then to the electricity meter, Sergeant Coates said that this had been forced at the hinge and when he inspected it, only one shilling remained in the cash drawer. That drawer had since been removed and sent to the fingerprint office at Scotland Yard, for examination.

Constable Wesley testified that he had asked Rowland to come into the back room at the New Brighton police station because the light was better there and he could get a better look at the man. Rowland unfastened his coat and Constable Wesley saw a newspaper there. Rowland handed it over and said that there was an article in it showing that he was wanted at Stockport but that there was something more serious at Mellor. Later, Constable Ryan had escorted Rowland to Wallasey and some time later, Ryan had telephoned New Brighton and told him that Rowland had admitted leaving something behind when he used the police station toilet. Constable Wesley checked the cubicle and on top of the cistern found a chisel. Tests had since shown that this could have been used to force the electricity meter at his house.

Rowland had always claimed that the 'something more serious' he was referring to was his forcing of the electricity meter at his home and the theft of its contents. The prosecution now called Eliza Burke, the woman who had accompanied Rowland on his trip to New Brighton. She told the court of her and Mr Grimshaw waiting in his cab and then Grimshaw leaving to find his missing passenger. Mrs Burke had seen the two men involved in an animated discussion with a policeman and had followed them all in to the police station. She heard Rowland say, "You might as well ring up Mellor police station," and point to something in the newspaper he held, saying that he was wanted for something. The policeman asked him what for and Eliza Burke heard Rowland reply, "Murder."

The final link in the prosecution's chain of evidence was to prove that Rowland had broken into the meter at his home. Jack Rothera was an engineer for the High Peak Electricity Company and he had examined the body of the meter. He confirmed that it had been forced at the hinge and that the cash register showed that there should have been 7s inside.

Alfred George Short was a prison officer at Manchester and he told the court that on March 9th he had taken Rowland's fingerprints and sent them down to Scotland Yard. The final witness was Frederick Cherrill of the fingerprint department in London who said that he had found prints matching Rowland's on top of and inside the cash drawer of the meter.

Rowland gave evidence on his own behalf. He denied Mrs Burke's suggestion that he had ever mentioned that he was wanted for murder. When he had been in the police station at New Brighton he had no idea that his daughter was dead and it came as a total shock to him when he was charged. He was guilty only of breaking into his electricity meter and had no involvement in the death of Mavis.

The jury retired at 5.15pm and the verdict, when it came, was that Rowland was guilty of murder, although a recommendation to mercy was added. Almost immediately an appeal was entered and this was heard on June 6th, before the Lord Chief Justice, Lord Hewart, and Justices Humphreys and MacNaghten. The grounds of the appeal were that all the evidence produced had been circumstantial and that Rowland maintained that he was innocent of the charge. The only thing to connect Rowland to the crime was the silk stocking found in his pocket and he could have picked this up in the house at any time. Giving the court's judgement, Lord Hewart stated that it was clear that Rowland was in charge of the child during the material time. He went on to say that the jury had, for some reason which was not clear to him, recommended Rowland to mercy, but this was not a matter for the court. The appeal was dismissed. Rowland's execution date was set for Thursday, June 21st, at Manchester but just two days before, on June 19th, the Home Secretary announced that he had recommended that the King should commute the sentence to one of life imprisonment. Rowland was taken out of the condemned cell and sent to Parkhurst prison on the Isle of Wight, to serve his life sentence.

Under normal circumstances, that might well have been the last that history heard of Walter Graham Rowland, but for World War Two. At that time, Britain needed all the fighting men she could find and a system was introduced whereby long-term prisoners could be released if they went into the armed forces. Rowland took advantage of that scheme in 1945 but hostilities ended soon afterwards and he was demobbed, a free man once again.

The story of the murder of Olive Balchin on a Manchester bomb site in October 1946 is well documented and, indeed, appears in *Murderous Manchester*, another title in this series. Walter Rowland was arrested for that crime, tried in December and, having been found guilty, was sentenced to death by Mr Justice Sellers. Despite a confession to the crime by a Liverpool prisoner, David John Ware, Rowland lost his appeal against this second death sentence and was hanged at Manchester on Thursday, February 27th, 1947. If there are people who feel that he should have paid the ultimate penalty for killing his own daughter in 1934, there are still many who believe that he was innocent of the crime which finally claimed his life 13 years later.

Chapter Fifteen

Day Trippers

CONSTABLE Isaac Vincent Heggs, who was based at the Whitworth Lane police station in Sheffield, was on duty in Richmond Road at 1.10am on Sunday, August 9th, 1936, when a man came up and said that he wished to give himself into custody for murder. Constable Heggs immediately cautioned the man before escorting him to the police call-box in Handsworth. Despite being cautioned, the man continued to talk on that journey and explained that he had killed a woman, adding that they had argued the previous afternoon and again at night. He went on to say, "I have been playing the game with her for seven years. I held her by the neck and after a time she lay still."

Constable Heggs waited with the man until a police car arrived to take him and his prisoner to Attercliffe police station. There the man identified himself as Albert Edward Batty, a 39-year-old married man who lived at 9 Halesworth Road, Handsworth in Sheffield. Further, he also explained that the woman he claimed to have killed was also married, lived in Rotherham and was named Rosa Elizabeth Blackburn. The crime, though, was not an entirely Yorkshire affair, for the body of the woman lay across the border, in Derbyshire.

Once he arrived at Attercliffe, Batty had been given over to the custody of Superintendent Willie Parnham, who asked the prisoner exactly where the alleged crime had taken place. Batty replied, "Near a footpath from Dronfield Woodhouse to Totley, about 600 yards from the road." Batty then offered to show the officers the precise spot and in due course he, Superintendent Parnham and Constable Heggs climbed into a police car to make the journey to Derbyshire. Another car, containing Detective Sergeant William Ewart Beresford, followed close behind. In due course, Batty asked for the car to be stopped and announced, "This is the place." The officers then followed as Batty strolled off down a footpath, although after walking some distance he turned and shouted, "I made a mistake, it's more than 600 yards." Soon the path divided and Batty led the police down one fork, through a gap in some hedges and then across some fields until Superintendent Parnham's torch picked out an object on the ground. Moving closer, the officers saw that this was a woman's body. She was dressed in a red frock, a fawn coat and wore brown shoes and stockings. Although a doctor would have to be called out, it was plain that the woman was dead and Batty was driven back to Sheffield for further questioning.

Since the crime had taken place in what in those days was part of Derbyshire, the police from that county would have to be involved. Superintendent Clarke was contacted and he went to the field to view the body before travelling to Sheffield where he saw Batty, at 7.30am that same day, and told him that he would be taken back to Renishaw, where he would be charged. Batty's only comment was that he had nothing to say.

Batty, though, had already made a full statement to Sergeant Beresford. In this he explained once again that he had been seeing Rosa for seven years and that he loved her very much. Batty claimed that lately, Rosa seemed to have cooled their relationship somewhat, so he wrote to her at her home, taking care to sign the letter as if it had come from a woman friend, in case Rosa's husband should see it. During the past week, they had met up every night, except one, and on August Bank Holiday Monday, they had gone to Southport together for the day. The following Saturday, August 8th, they had met, as arranged, at 3.00pm at Sheffield's Midland railway station where he had purchased two return tickets for Dore and Totley. The train wasn't due to leave until just after 4.00pm so they bought some fruit from a stall and enjoyed some plums and apricots together.

Eventually the train reached Totley, and Batty and Rosa went for a walk through some woods until they reached the main road where there were some shops. Here they purchased bread, cakes, butter, tomatoes and sweets before they went into a field near a farm where they argued about which of them should go to the farm to ask for some tea to go with their picnic. After some discussion, Batty agreed to go and when he returned to tell her that the tea wouldn't be long, they sat down and began to eat. He now thought again about how their relationship seemed to have deteriorated of late and pointed out to Rosa that at one time they wouldn't have argued about such a trivial thing as who should go for the tea, and also added that she seemed to have grown colder towards him. At this, Rosa stood up to leave but he grabbed hold of her and she fell to the ground, bruising her right shoulder. Although this did little to bring them closer together, Rosa did say that she would stay.

Batty and Rosa had their tea at about 5.30pm and stayed in the field until about 7.30pm. The atmosphere between them was somewhat cold and both seemed to be rather depressed. Rosa announced that she wanted to go for a walk and Batty followed her down a footpath into another field where Rosa said she felt ill and complained that her shoulder was hurting her. They sat down again, and then walked a little further before stopping to rest once again. By this time another 45 minutes had passed.

At 8.30pm, Rosa said she wanted something else to eat but Batty wanted to speak about where their relationship was going and asked her to reassure him that it wasn't going to end. Instead, although she did not use the exact words, Rosa implied that it was over and it was then that Batty attacked her. His statement went on, "I got hold of her neck and she just gasped a bit. She did not struggle much." Batty said that soon Rosa fell still. He waited by her body for 15 minutes to make sure that she was dead. When she had not moved during that time, he walked away. Batty's statement ended by saying that he was not trying to provide an excuse for his actions and was quite prepared to die for the crime, at one stage saying that indeed he wanted to die. After leaving the scene, Batty said that he had thought of suicide but wanted to see his family first, so he caught the bus back to Sheffield and went home before going to find a policeman.

Albert Batty appeared in court at Renishaw on August 10th.

Superintendent Clarke gave details of the arrest and Batty was then remanded until August 17th. Told that he would be granted legal aid, Batty said that he didn't want it, but was eventually persuaded to apply.

It was also on August 10th that the inquest opened at the Eckington council offices, before Mr F.D. Worthington. Evidence of identification was given by Sidney Blackburn, the dead woman's husband, who said that he lived with her at 11 Bramwith Road, Nethergreen, Sheffield, and had last seen his wife at 2.00pm on August 8th. Rosa was approaching 40 and although a strong woman in good health, she was only slightly built. Medical evidence was also called before matters were adjourned, also until August 17th.

By the time he made his second police court appearance, Batty was represented by Mr W. Irwin Mitchell. Another remand was requested and this was granted, Batty's only request being that he be allowed to see his wife and some friends. Permission was granted and matters then adjourned until August 24th. The same day, the reconvened inquest ruled that Rosa Blackburn had been murdered and that Batty was responsible.

The final police court hearing took place on August 24th, when Mr Crump outlined the evidence for the Director of Public Prosecutions. Batty was sent for trial and appeared at Derby on November 19th, before Mr Justice Atkinson. The Crown's case was led by Mr Maurice F. Healy, who was assisted by Mr F.W. Wallace, while Batty was defended by Mr T. Norman Winning. Even as the charge was read out, Batty burst into tears and sobbed with his head resting on the rail of the dock.

George Johnson was a furnaceman who lived at 18 Richmond Road, Sheffield, and he had known Batty for the past 11 years. He also knew Rosa and was with Batty when the couple first met. Johnson knew of the relationship and had advised Batty to end it as his family were growing up. Batty had a daughter, who was now 16, and sons who were 12 and six respectively. Johnson pointed out that Batty's daughter might marry soon and have children of her own. How would he feel if his grandchildren found out that he was going out with a 'fancy woman'?

Sidney Blackburn then gave evidence as to his identification of his wife's body, and he was followed into the box by Detective Sergeant Beresford. He said that after Batty had made his statement, he noticed that the prisoner had a scratch on his right hand. Pointing this out to

Batty, Sergeant Beresford heard him admit that Rosa had done it, just after he had hurt her shoulder. Batty was then searched and Beresford found the return halves of two railway tickets for a trip between Dore and Totley and Sheffield, which had consecutive numbers.

Two witnesses were now called to show that Batty and Rosa had been in Totley together. Nellie Bargh ran her confectionery shop from 53 Baslow Road, Totley Rise, and she said she had sold some sweets and other items to Rosa on August 8th. At the time there had been a man waiting for Rosa outside the shop and he had resembled Batty, although Mrs Bargh said she could not be absolutely sure. She had been shown eight photographs by the police and picked out the one most like the man. This picture was of Albert Batty.

Ena Bramhall Salt was a domestic servant at Woodthorpe Farm and she told the court that at 6.15pm on August 8th she was in the scullery, carrying out her duties, when a man came and asked if they did teas. She had since positively identified Batty as that man. Miss Salt, continuing her testimony, said that a few minutes later, she took the tea across to the orchard where she could see a woman waiting. The woman was wearing a red dress and a red hat. Later, at about 9.30pm, Ena was with her sister and a cousin when she saw a couple sitting in another field, near Fanshawegate Lane. This woman, too, was wearing a red dress and a red hat and she was sure that it was Batty and the woman she had seen him with earlier.

Inspector William Henry Bramhill was another officer who had been to the scene of the crime and he was there when the body was moved. Beneath Rosa there had been a man's mackintosh and Inspector Bramhill later showed this to George Johnson who confirmed that it belonged to Batty.

Dr James Matthewson Webster had viewed the body in situ and noted a small spot of dried blood in the left corner of Rosa's lower lip. The tip of her tongue protruded from between her teeth and there were subconjunctival haemorrhages in her right eye. There was a bruise over Rosa's adam's apple and another on her right shoulder. The cause of death was asphyxia due to pressure on the neck and since there were no ligature marks, this was done manually using considerable force. Under cross-examination, Dr Webster confirmed that there were signs that only one hand had been used, which was unusual, and that death might have occurred in as little as 40 seconds although two to five minutes was more usual.

An attempt was made to show that Batty might not have been responsible for his actions at the time he killed Rosa. Dr James H. Murdock, the medical officer of Hull prison, had examined Batty and said that there was a family history of insanity and that Batty had been diagnosed as suffering from psychasthenia, which is a state of mental inertia. Batty had suffered several attacks of bitter weeping while held in prison and Dr Murdock felt that he might not have as much self control as a normal man under the stress of an emotional crisis.

Another prison medical officer who had examined Batty was Dr Francis H. Brisby from Leeds. He testified that there was a strong strain of insanity on Batty's mother's side and she had been in a mental hospital three times, suffering from melancholia. An aunt of Batty's had also suffered from this condition, spending four months in a mental institution, and in 1906 an uncle had committed suicide by leaping into a deep quarry.

In his closing speech for the defence, Mr Winning asked for a verdict of manslaughter, pointing out that if Batty had really wanted to deliberately end Rosa's life, he would have used both hands to strangle her. Mr Winning claimed that his client had committed a foolish and rough act, but not one of murder. The jury, though, did not agree and after deliberating for one hour, returned to court to announce that Batty was guilty as charged, although they added a strong recommendation to mercy. Batty swayed and had to be supported by a warder as the verdict was announced and he was once more in tears as the death sentence was passed.

An appeal was heard on December 14th, before the Lord Chief Justice, Lord Hewart and Justices Salter and Talbot. The main grounds were that the trial judge had omitted to fully direct the jury on the defence of insanity or that the crime was only one of manslaughter. Medical evidence had shown that Rosa had died very quickly, and that Batty had only used one hand and although these did come out in the trial itself, neither point was mentioned in the summing up. Lord Hewart stated that there was nothing in these arguments and the appeal was dismissed. Batty, who was present in court, burst into tears again as the decision was announced.

A new execution date was set but in due course the Home Office announced that a reprieve had been granted and a notice to that effect appeared in *The Times* on December 28th. The recommendation of the jury that Batty be granted mercy had prevailed.

Chapter Sixteen

A Gentleman Caller

THERE were three people living in the rather isolated farmhouse known as Quarry Cottage, on Slack Hill, Ashover. The owner of the property was James Ball and he shared the house with his second wife, Marion, and his 23-year-old daughter from his first marriage, Jessie.

Since May, 1936, Jessie Ball, by all accounts an attractive young lady, had been walking out with a 25-year-old brickyard worker named Ronald Smedley who lived at 115 Bole Hill, Wirksworth. The couple appeared to be very much in love and Smedley was in the habit of visiting Jessie every Wednesday, Friday and Sunday, when he would normally arrive, by bus at some time around 7.40pm. Jessie's parents thought that there would be no change to this routine on Friday, August 20th, 1937 and as they left the house together at around 7.30pm, they knew that Smedley would soon be over to see Jessie who had been left in the cottage alone. Indeed, as James Ball and his wife strolled off over the fields they saw the bus from Matlock at the top of Slack Hill and believed that Smedley was almost certainly on it.

Ronald Smedley had indeed been on that bus because he was with

Jessie just 15 minutes later, at 7.45pm, when she received a visit from 12-year-old Florence Bowen, her cousin who lived at Amber Lane Cottage, Kelstedge, Ashover. When Florence arrived, the front door of Quarry Cottage was slightly open but she knocked anyway and was soon greeted by Jessie who asked her in. Once inside, Florence saw Smedley, a man she had seen many times before, sitting on the edge of the sofa near the fire.

Jessie Ball sat down next to Smedley, and Florence sat at the other end of the sofa next to Jessie. Smedley had brought Jessie a large box of chocolates, knowing that she was very fond of such treats and these were now offered to Florence who took one with a polite thank you. At the time, there seemed to be a very happy atmosphere in the house and Smedley and Jessie were laughing and joking with each other. Florence Bowen stayed at the cottage until around 8.15pm when she waved goodbye to Jessie who saw her off down the lane.

It was 11.20pm when James and Marion Ball arrived back at Quarry Cottage and from the first moment, they knew that something was wrong. The garden gate, normally kept shut, was swinging open and when James tried to close it, he found that it had been bent out of shape at the hinge and couldn't be latched. Further, although the front door of the cottage was open, the house was in darkness and there was no answer when Marion Ball called out for her step-daughter.

It was Mrs Ball who first went inside the cottage and after lighting the oil lamp, she saw that there was a table overturned in the front room. The items which had been on that table – a paper, a magazine, a handkerchief and a large box of chocolates – were now scattered about the floor and there seemed to be no sign of Jessie anywhere inside the house. James Ball told his wife to stay where she was and went outside to search for any signs of what might have happened. He did not have to look very far. There, close to a pile of stones at the back of the house, he found Jessie, lying on her back, her head a mass of bruises and wounds. There could be little doubt that she was beyond all help.

Dr Walter Henry Mosberry arrived at the cottage at around midnight and confirmed that Jessie Ball was dead. Dr Mosberry noted a gaping wound across her forehead and a great deal of blood on her face and spattered around the grass on which she lay. Around Jessie's neck was a man's tie and since there was a quantity of frothy blood-stained mucus on her mouth, Dr Mosberry felt that asphyxia was the direct cause of death. Finally, he was able to state that in his opinion, the girl had been dead no more than one or two hours, putting the earliest time of the attack upon her at 10.00pm.

Since it was known that Ronald Smedley had visited Jessie on the night she died, police officers went to his home to talk to him. They soon discovered that Smedley had not returned home on August 20th, his bed had not been slept in and no one had any idea of what had happened to him. A full-scale manhunt was launched, which included bloodhounds belonging to Mr C.A. Furness of Brampton Hall. Despite the best efforts of the Derbyshire force, no signs of Smedley were found.

The inquest on the dead girl opened on August 23rd, before Dr R.A. McCrea, the Chesterfield District Coroner. The only witness was James Ball who stated that his daughter had been born on March 5th, 1914 and had worked as a mill-hand since leaving school. Mr Ball went on to describe what he and his wife had found when they returned home on the night of August 20th, and testified that he had since formally identified his daughter's body at the mortuary. After hearing this evidence, the coroner adjourned the inquest sine die, in the hope that the man wanted in connection with this crime would soon be in custody.

Ronald Smedley was still at large, though. On the same day that the inquest was adjourned, a detailed description was released to the press. According to this, Smedley was "about five feet nine inches, with high dark brown hair, blue eyes, clean shaven, and very fresh complexioned. Well-built, he was dressed in a grey worsted suit with a faint red stripe but wore no hat. He had on a white poplin shirt, with a semi-stiff collar of the same material and it was believed that he wore dark coloured socks and black shoes."

Although the police believed that Smedley was almost certainly still alive, there was always the possibility that he might have done away with himself and so large areas of water were dragged in an attempt to find his body. One such area was the pond at Old Engine Farm, situated about a mile from where Jessie Ball had met her death. Once again, no trace of the missing man was discovered.

The manhunt continued on August 24th when further details of Smedley were released. Now the reports stated that he worked for Swann, Ratcliffe & Company, firebrick manufacturers of Brassington, and that he had left his home at around 6.30pm on the night that Jessie died. At that time he was his usual cheerful self and there had been no intimation of what was to happen later that night.

On August 25th, the search moved to the hills above Matlock. A man fitting Smedley's description had been seen running from a barn on Riber Hill by George Bignall, a labourer at Riber Hillside Farm. Bignall had told his employer, Mr T. Smith, what he had seen and although Mr Smith's son, Edward, gave chase, the man escaped. That same day, Jessie Ball was laid to rest at Ashover, the service being conducted by the Reverend J.B. Nodder, the rector of the parish church. More than 300 people gathered to watch as the coffin was lowered into the ground.

Another reported sighting of Smedley took place on August 26th. A woman walking near in the woods near Willersley Castle had seen a man leap down from a tree as she approached him. The man fitted Smedley's description and once again, the search moved to accommodate this new information.

The citizens of Derbyshire were certainly doing their best to aid the police in their efforts to find Smedley. It was also on August 26th that Mr J. Page was approached in Derby town centre by an unkempt man who asked him where he might get a shave. Mr Page directed the stranger to a barber's shop and then promptly contacted the police, believing that this might be Smedley. Even as the man sat in the barber's chair, police rushed into the shop, only to find that he was not the man they were looking for.

Over the next few days, the search was scaled down, amid rumours that Scotland Yard was to be called in. By August 30th, the police were stating that they believed that Smedley had either left the district or was being harboured somewhere by a friend. Other sightings were still being reported, though, and there was even a report that Smedley had been arrested in Wales. This proved to be false and on August 31st, in an attempt to redouble efforts to trace the wanted man, 5,000 posters were circulated to various police stations, giving details of the crime and of Ronald Smedley.

On September 1st, yet another report came in to the police headquarters. Frederick Hopkinson, a labourer at Moor Edge Farm, Tansley, stated that he had been followed down a lonely lane, on Sunday, August 29th, by a man who looked like Smedley. The following morning,

August 30th, Hopkinson had found 20 empty grain sacks in the barn at the bottom of that same lane. These had been made into a sort of bed and it was suggested that Smedley might have spent the night there.

In fact, the night of September 1st was to be the last that Smedley remained free. Early the next morning, Mr Swift, who owned a farm at Cromford, reported that there was a man asleep in one of his haystacks. Sergeant Frederick Mellors and other officers were despatched to investigate, arriving there at 6.30am. Mellors knew that they had found the man who had eluded an entire police force for 12 days, as he had known Smedley before and recognised him immediately.

Sergeant Mellors woke him with a shout of, "Hello Ronald! Do you know who we are?" Smedley shook his head and after Mellors had identified himself, offered no resistance and was pulled to his feet and handcuffed. Taken to Matlock police station where he was charged with murder, Smedley would only reply, "I just lost my head, that's all. I've nothing else to say."

Later that same day, Smedley made his first appearance at the Alfreton police court where he was remanded for one week by Mr George Preston, the magistrate. On September 9th, Smedley was back in court, by now having obtained legal representation in the form of Mr Bertram Mather of Chesterfield. Once again he was remanded and further appearances followed on September 16th and September 21st. Only on this last date was all the evidence heard and Smedley sent for trial for murder.

That trial opened at Derby before Mr Justice MacNaghten, and a jury of ten men and two women, on Friday, November 12th, 1937. The case for the prosecution lay in the hands of Mr Richard O'Sullivan and Mr A.C. Caporn, while Smedley was defended by Mr T. Norman Winning who was assisted by Mr Geoffrey Smallwood.

In addition to telling the court what he and his wife had found when they returned home on August 20th, James Ball went on to say that since Christmas 1936, Jessie had worn an engagement ring given to her by Smedley. At one stage Mr Ball said, "He was a good mannered man so far as I know, and I approved of the engagement."

Marion Ball testified that before she and James had left the cottage on that fateful night, she had used a small rake, normally kept near the fire, to scrape over the coals in the grate. At that time, the rake had been perfectly straight but when it was found by the police, not far from Jessie's body, the shaft was bent.

One of the first police officers on the scene had been Constable Walter George Willis and he stated that upon searching the living room of the cottage, he had found a button which had a few threads still adhering to it. This button lay close to the front door and appeared to have been forcibly torn from a jacket. When Smedley was finally arrested, it was noted that his jacket had a button missing and the one found by Willis matched the remaining buttons.

Dr Mosberry testified that the tie fastened around Jessie Ball's throat was quite loose when he examined her. Although he had not attended the post-mortem, Dr Mosberry believed that Jessie had been struck in the face at least once, possibly more, with some sharp heavy object wielded with considerable force. The shock of this attack, together with the consequent loss of blood, would have greatly weakened Jessie but her attacker then placed the tie around her neck and throttled her to death.

The post-mortem had been carried out by Dr Griffith John Griffiths, a pathologist who practised at Buxton. He described a deep wound in the dead girl's forehead, some one and a half inches long and three quarters of an inch wide, with a depressed linear fracture beneath it. There was a small puncture wound over the left upper eyelid and a horizontal wound behind the left ear. Another wound, two inches long, lay on the crown of the head and this, too, had a fracture of the skull beneath it. There had been at least two blows inflicted and very probably three. In Dr Griffiths' opinion, the cause of death was not asphyxia but shock and loss of blood due to the multiple injuries to the base of the skull, the necktie having been placed around Jessie's throat at the very point of death, or very soon afterwards. He went on to explain that the froth Dr Mosberry had seen was cerebral spinal fluid and as such might well have been mistaken as a sign of strangulation. Under cross examination, though, Dr Griffiths agreed that the wounds he had seen were typical of those inflicted by a maniac, or someone under the influence of extreme temper. Finally, the doctor was able to state that Jessie had been ten to 12 weeks pregnant.

Scientific evidence was given by Dr Gerald Roche Lynch, a senior analyst to the Home Office. He had examined the button found by

Constable Willis, the bent rake found near the body, Smedley's clothing, the necktie and Jessie Ball's dress. Dr Lynch was able to say that the jacket Smedley wore had blood, of the same type as Jessie's, on the inside and outside of the left sleeve and on the left lapel. At the top, there was a button missing and the threads still adhering to the loose button matched the material of the jacket. The rake had a metal shaft and weighed a total of 16 ounces. There was a thin film of human blood over the raking portion itself, but none on the shaft. Blood was also found on one corner of the rake, showing that it had, in all probability, been the portion which had been brought into violent contact with Jessie's skull.

Medical testimony had shown that Jessie was pregnant when she was killed and the prosecution now called Ivor Wilkinson of 75 Dale Street, Wirksworth. Wilkinson had known Smedley since they had been at school and the two men often cycled to and from work together. Wilkinson testified that about a month before the attack upon Jessie, Smedley had mentioned that he thought she was 'in trouble' and that now he would have to get married after all. The suggestion was that either Smedley did not want the encumbrance of a wife, or he had convinced himself that the child was not his, but under cross examination, Wilkinson swore that Smedley had never expressed any such doubts to him and had not said anything about Jessie being unfaithful to him.

The final police witness was Sergeant William Anthony Wardle. He had attended the scene of the crime at 12.50am, on August 21st and had noted blood marks on the living room floor, the stone pathway outside and on the grass close to the body. Wardle had also noticed two large stones near Jessie's head. One appeared to be deeply embedded in the grass and had obviously not been moved for a long time but the other seemed to have been recently placed where it was found and bore traces of what looked like blood. It appeared that this second stone might, at some stage, have been thrown at Jessie. More important than this testimony, though, was Sergeant Wardle's report of what had taken place after Smedley had been arrested.

It was 10.35am on September 2nd when Wardle had seen Smedley at Matlock police station. Smedley said he wished to make a statement and Sergeant Wardle had given his notebook to the prisoner for this purpose. Smedley had written his statement in the notebook and signed it. That statement was now read out in court. It began, "I left home on August 20th, 1937 about 6.30pm, and got on the 6.55 buss *(sic)* to Matlock Bath and bought one box of chockalate *(sic)* from Mrs Lulsby and then got on the 7.15 East Midland and got off at the Quarry Corner and went strait *(sic)* in to my girl's home and sat talking on the couch without any intention at all of doing what I did do and in the meanwhile Florrie came up and stayed about half an hour and we all sat on the couch.

"After Florrie had gone we sat loving each other just as usual and about 10.30 she said she had seen Harry Ludlam in Matlock and that was what first started the jealousy as she once arranged to go to Chesterfield pictures with him a while back and that was what made me do the action as I could not bare *(sic)* any other boy to either look at her or even speak to her as I loved her so much.

"I had been engaged since last Christmas and I was thinking of getting married shortly as I had no intention of doining *(sic)* such a thing and then I seized her by the throat and put my tie around her neck and she ran out of the house and fell down on the ground and in my temper I through *(sic)* the stone at her and then ran off up the fields and I am very sorry for what I had done."

After this statement had been heard, Smedley stepped into the witness box to give evidence on his own behalf. He began by saying that he earned only £2 6s each week and after giving money for his keep to his mother, spent most of the rest of his pay on travelling to see Jessie and buying her presents, such as the chocolates. He knew that Jessie was pregnant and accepted that the child was his. They had discussed getting married at Christmas 1937.

Turning to the night of August 20th, Smedley described his journey to Quarry Cottage and of Florence Bowen's brief visit. At 10.30pm, he got up to leave and reminded Jessie that they had arranged to meet up the next night at Cromford. It was then that Jessie had explained that she couldn't meet him on the Saturday as she was seeing Harry Ludlam. Smedley now began to question Jessie about her involvement with Ludlam and at one stage she had referred to him as her 'second husband'. She then pointed to her stomach and said, "It might be you, it might be Harry."

A full-scale argument then began and it was Jessie who picked up the rake from the fireside and lashed out at him. He remembered losing a button from his coat and put his tie around her throat to quieten her. Jessie struggled free and ran from the house. Following her, Smedley then picked up a large stone and threw it at Jessie. It must have hit her because she fell to the ground near the gate. Smedley then picked her up and carried her to the spot where she was subsequently found by her father. Scared at what he had done, he then ran off over the fields and spent the next 12 days trying to avoid capture, and during this time the only food he had eaten was a turnip. Smedley denied ever having used the rake to strike Jessie Ball.

The jury retired at 3.55pm, and took 58 minutes to decide that Smedley was guilty as charged, although they did add a strong recommendation to mercy. There was, of course, only one possible sentence and Mr Justice MacNaghten announced that Smedley would be hanged by the neck until he was dead.

The very next day, November 13th, Smedley's defence team stated that after due discussion, it had been decided not to enter an appeal but to organise a petition for a reprieve. Smedley, meanwhile, was transferred to Leicester prison where he occupied the condemned cell and awaited his fate.

By November 22nd, over 5,000 people had signed the petition but three days later, when Mr Mather, Smedley's solicitor, travelled to London to hand it in at the Home Office, the number had risen to around 30,000 names. For a few more days, Smedley languished in his cell, waiting to see if he would keep his appointment with the hangman.

Finally, on the evening of November 29th, 1937, Ronald Smedley was informed by the prison governor that the Home Secretary had advised His Majesty to commute the sentence. Smedley's life had been saved.

Chapter Seventeen

The Chicken Farm

FOR some years, Hugo Collier had run a chicken farm from his isolated cottage on Hulland Road, Wood End, Bradley, about a mile from Ashbourne. Hugo was greatly helped in his business by his 54-year-old wife, Kate Elizabeth Collier, and his daughter, Elsie Kate. There were few real problems for the family to cope with and just about the only cloud was the fact that Mrs Collier did not really approve of the young man with whom her daughter was walking out.

Elsie Collier had, by 1937, known 32-year-old Horace William Brunt for some five years, although they had only been going out together since June, 1935. Brunt was, of course, a regular visitor at the lonely farmhouse and although Kate did not usually make her disapproval obvious, there was always an abruptness in her words whenever she spoke to him. Still, Elsie seemed to be enamoured of him and Kate tried her best not to interfere. After all, there were signs that Brunt was trying to improve himself. He had recently been unemployed for some five months but had now managed to get himself a job at the Royal Oak Hotel, Hanging Bridge, Mayfield, having taken up his duties there on

April 15th, 1937. Perhaps he might make something of himself after all.

At 8.30am on Saturday, April 24th, Elsie Collier left the farm with her father in order to sell their produce in the market at Derby. This was something they did every Saturday and anyone who knew the family at all would have been aware of this routine. While Hugo and Elsie were out of the way, Kate would get on with her household chores, not forgetting, of course, to feed the chickens their meal. It was 2.45pm when Hugo and Elsie finally returned.

Even as they approached the house, Elsie could see that there was something different about the place. The dogs should have been out and roaming about the place, but there was no sign of them. Elsie was the first into the cottage, entering through the back door, and to her horror found her mother lying on the floor with her head towards the fender and her feet up against the sink. The amount of blood around Kate left Elsie in no doubt that something terrible had taken place and she dashed out to fetch her father.

Hugo Collier had gone to check his chickens and he, too, had realised that something was wrong even before his breathless daughter came running out to fetch him. The meal which the chickens ate needed water to moisten it and this invariably took two buckets' full. Hugo had noted that the feed in the corn shed had indeed been moistened but only one bucket of water had been used. For some reason, Kate had not completed the job.

Having dashed into the kitchen after Elsie had told him what she had found, Hugo Collier also viewed the sight of his wife's body lying on the floor. As Elsie ran off towards Ashbourne to fetch the doctor, Hugo stayed with his wife and as he waited, noticed that the bucket used to carry the water to the chicken feed was in the sink. It appeared that poor Kate had been in the act of preparing the feed for the livestock when her assailant had entered the kitchen and attacked her.

By the time Elsie had found Dr Hubert Harry Hollick and taken him back to the farmhouse, it was 3.10pm. Dr Hollick made a careful examination of Kate Collier, confirmed that she was dead and noted that there was a large wound at the back of her head. Although a post-mortem would be necessary, the wound was obviously caused by shot and the gun used had been fired from very close range. Blood had issued from Kate's nose and mouth and flowed backwards over her forehead. This was a case of murder and the police would have to be contacted.

Detective Sergeant John Wilfred Downes arrived at the farmhouse after being contacted by Dr Hollick and made his own examination of the scene. There were no signs of a disturbance, indicating that the killer had either crept up behind Mrs Collier before shooting her, or was someone she had admitted to the kitchen herself. Since there were no bloodstains anywhere else in the house, it was clear that Kate had been attacked in the kitchen. As for the murder weapon, that was easy to trace. A shotgun was kept over one of the doors and Mr Collier had confirmed that this had recently been moved because someone had put it back the wrong way round. When this gun was inspected, a spent cartridge was found still in the weapon although it was a different type to others which had been found inside drawers at the house. It seemed that the killer, whoever he was, had brought his own cartridge with him. This confirmed that they had known of the existence of the gun and where it was located, suggesting that they were almost certainly someone known to the family. Further, the motive for the crime appeared to be one of robbery, for Mr Collier also stated that some money, which had been in the house at the time, had been taken, including a crisp new one-pound note.

In addition to the Colliers, the doctor and the police, there were other people at the farm as the investigation progressed. On her way to fetch the doctor, Elsie Collier had called at 35 Compton Street, Ashbourne, a house occupied by an old friend of the family, Charles Roy Lumbard. Elsie told Lumbard what had happened at the farm and as she went on to the doctor's surgery, Lumbard climbed into his car and drove out to the farm to see what help he could offer. Later, after the police had finished their initial inspection of the premises, it was Lumbard who called on Sarah Ann Parker, who lived at 14 Sturston Road, Ashbourne, and asked if she would come back to the farm with him, to lay out the body. Sarah went back to Wood End, performed her unpleasant task and was still at the farm when Horace Brunt came cycling down the lane.

Seeing Sarah, Brunt asked her what she was doing there and it was she who broke the news to him that Mrs Collier had been found shot dead. Brunt seemed to be quite upset at hearing the news, even though he and the dead woman had never really got on. Brunt went inside the farmhouse and spoke to Hugo Collier who told him, "It's a terrible job we've got." Brunt asked, "What, the missus?" and Collier nodded before adding, "You've no cause to bother about her. There was no love lost between you. She told you off last night." Brunt shrugged off this comment but the words had been overheard by Sergeant Downes.

Once Horace Brunt had climbed back on to his bicycle and ridden off towards his work, Sergeant Downes spoke again to Hugo Collier and heard details of the atmosphere that had existed between Brunt and the dead woman. Further, Hugo was able to expand upon his comment about Kate having 'told off' Brunt the previous night. On April 23rd, Hugo and Kate had been erecting a new fowl pen when Brunt arrived on the scene and offered his help. Although he had previously worked as a farmhand, Kate had abruptly told him that he wasn't needed and suggested he go into the house to see Elsie.

Sergeant Downes soon turned up two other witnesses whose statements proved to be most valuable to his investigation. John Henry Baldwin lived at Ladyhole Cottages, Feldersley, but on April 24th, he had been at Lady Hole Farm repairing a fence. From that fence, Baldwin could see the chicken farm and he confirmed that he had seen Kate Collier walking across to the pens with a bucket in her hand. This was very close to noon and since it had already been established that the bucket was used to carry water to the feed, and that task had never been completed, it was highly probable that the shooting had taken place soon after Baldwin had seen Kate. The other witness was Frederick Leslie Hallam, a coal dealer from Ashbourne. It was around 12.30pm when he returned to his yard at Belper Road and as he was backing in his lorry, he saw Horace Brunt, a young man he knew quite well, cycling past and heading towards Ashbourne. More significantly, the route which took Brunt towards Ashbourne was also the direction he would be travelling in if he was coming from Wood End.

It was 8.10pm when Detective Sergeant Downes called at the Royal Oak and asked Brunt to come to the police station at Ashbourne to explain his movements of earlier that day. Brunt readily agreed and after a brief interview, made a full statement. It began, "I am 32 years of age and am a yard hand at the Royal Oak Hotel, Mayfield. I reside at Rose Cottage, Upper Mayfield, with my mother, Lucy Brunt, who is a widow."

The statement went on to explain that Brunt had risen at 5.50am that morning and arrived at the Royal Oak at 6.05am. He began by milking a cow which Mrs Agnes Alice Bassett, the licensee, owned and feeding her chickens. The first work period ended at around 7.40am when Brunt returned to Rose Cottage for his breakfast. Arriving back at the pub at 8.25am, Brunt claimed that he then swept the yard, and the front of the pub, fed the pigs and cleaned out the cowshed. Once all this was complete, it was about 11.00am. Other jobs, such as watering the plants in the greenhouse, then took Brunt up to 12.10pm.

It was now that the statement began to disagree with facts already known to Sergeant Downes. Brunt claimed that he did not leave the Royal Oak until 12.50pm, when he again returned to Rose Cottage for his dinner. He arrived home at about 1.00pm and while there, saw a friend, Jack Grundy, who was putting up a shed in their backyard. Brunt also claimed that in addition to his mother and his sister Dolly, his two brothers, Roland and Sidney, were also there. He finally left home at 1.35pm and got back to the pub at around 1.45pm. Other work meant that Brunt did not leave the pub again until 4.30pm when he cycled into Ashbourne to get some groceries from a shop in St John's Street, getting back to the Royal Oak at 5.05pm. Finally, Brunt arrived home at 5.25pm when he washed, changed and had a bite to eat before cycling to Wood End to see Elsie.

Since it was plain that Brunt's statement was in conflict with what other people had said, he was detained in the police station pending further inquiries. Sergeant Downes and his superior, Inspector Herbert Edgar Mayfield, then spoke to some of the other employees at the Royal Oak in order to check the timings quoted in Brunt's statement.

Katie Bramwell was the daughter of Mrs Bassett, the pub licensee, and lived on the premises. She confirmed that she had seen Brunt sweeping the yard at 10.30am or perhaps a little later. However, according to Katie, it was 11.30am, not 12.50pm, when he left on his bicycle and although he did return for work at the correct time, she did not actually see him again until 3.30pm. That same evening, at some time between 7.30pm and 8.00pm, just before the police had arrived to speak to Brunt, Kate had seen him drinking ginger beer in the bar. He seemed deep in thought and when she asked him what the matter was, he replied that someone was dead and when she inquired who, said that it was Mrs Collier from Bradley.

Mary Alice Waltho lived at Sturston Fields Farm on the Belper Road near Ashbourne and on April 24th, at 11.50am, she had been walking towards Ashbourne with her daughter, Lilian. They saw a man on a bicycle, peddling leisurely towards Belper and since that same man had once applied for a job as a hand at the farm, Mrs Waltho was able to identify him. The cyclist was Horace William Brunt.

Told that there were problems with his testimony, Brunt made a second brief statement in which he tried to produce other witnesses who could confirm what he had said. He now claimed that when he had left for his dinner at 12.50pm, he had seen Esther Lomas, who lived next door to the Royal Oak, and had spoken to her. Unfortunately for Brunt, when Mrs Lomas was interviewed she said that her conversation with Brunt took place at 11.10am, and just 20 minutes later she had seen him preparing to mount his bicycle and Brunt had told her that he was going to his dinner early as his mother wanted him to run an errand to Ashbourne.

Once again Sergeant Downes went back to Brunt and informed him that his alibi did not check out. After thinking things over, Brunt then made a third statement, during the early hours of April 25th. This document read, "I went up to Mrs Collier's and she run at me with poker and after that she got the gun down to me. I took it off her and the trigger went off and no intensions *(sic)* of a cartridge been in, it was quite a *(sic)* accident that it did happen. It was before dinner, 12.30pm." Brunt was then charged with murder and searched, whereupon a fairly new £1 note was found in his possession. Brunt explained that this had been in his pay, which had been given to him by Mrs Bassett. This lady was spoken to again, and she said that Brunt had indeed been paid 24s on April 18th, but this had been in the form of eight half-crowns and two florins. Faced with this, Brunt now made a fourth statement in which he admitted taking cash from the premises, claiming that he had since hidden the rest in a wood, in a small tin, close to three old buckets. Detective Sergeant King searched the area but was unable to find the tin, so Brunt was taken to show him exactly where it was. Although the three buckets were visible from the road, even Brunt was unable to find the tin he claimed contained the money. The police then offered a reward to anyone who could find the missing tin but the reward was never claimed.

The bucket in the bedroom where William Knighton cut his mother's throat. See Chapter 12. (Public Record Office)

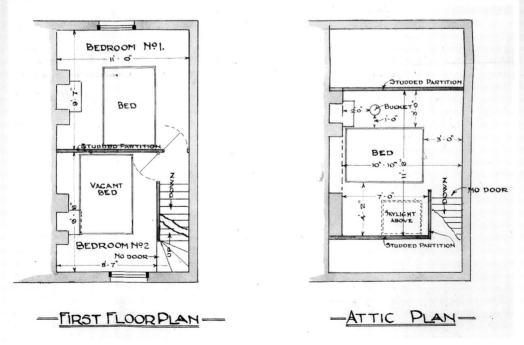

Plan of the house at Bethel Street, Ilkeston, where Knighton killed his mother. His bedroom was the one labelled 'Bedroom No.1' See Chapter 12. (Public Record Office)

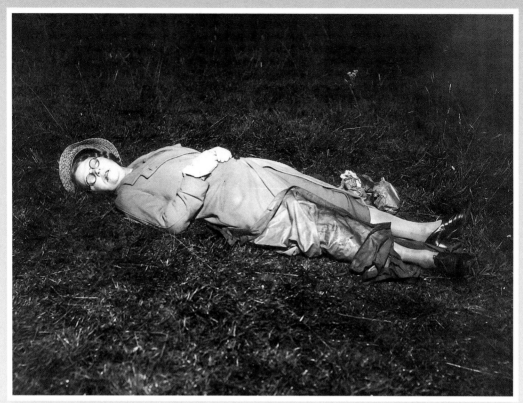

The body of Rosa Elizabeth Blackburn, lying in a Derbyshire field. See Chapter 15. (Public Record Office)

The broken wooden gate at the farmhouse where Jessie Ball died. See Chapter 16. (Public Record Office)

A rear view of the farmhouse. See Chapter 16. (Public Record Office)

The body of Jessie Ball, lying in situ. See Chapter 16. (Public Record Office)

Derby
Evening Telegraph

LATE FINAL E.DN.

INCORPORATING THE DERBY DAILY EXPRESS

VOL. CL—No. 17,498   TELEPHONE 2400 (5 LINES)   THURSDAY, SEPTEMBER 2, 1937.   *REGISTERED FOR TRANSMISSION AS A NEWSPAPER*   PRICE ONE PI

SMEDLEY FOUND AND ACCUSED OF MURDER

ARRESTED IN BARN NEAR CROMFORD, A MILE FROM HIS HOME

CROWDS WATCH DEPARTURE FROM MATLOCK

REMAND AFTER BRIEF APPEARANCE AT ALFRETON COURT

DRAMATIC SEARCH OVER

RONALD SMEDLEY, 25-years old Wirksworth brickyard labourer, was arrested in a lonely, unoccupied farm near Cromford, about a mile from his home to-day by two police officers, and later he appeared at a special Alfreton police court, charged "that he did feloniously kill and slay one Jessie Ball at Ashover on August 20." He was remanded in custody for a week.

Smedley was arrested by Police-sergeant Mellors and Police-constable Shorthose, stationed at Matlock Bath and Cromford respectively, who were members of a party making a routine search of pastureland and woodland round the farm.

They found Smedley asleep in the hay in a Dutch barn, and he was taken to Matlock Police Station where he was given a shave and wash and a change of clothes until a car came to take him to Alfreton.

When Smedley walked between two police officers to the car there were hundreds of people outside the police station to watch his departure, and he turned towards them and smiled.

There was also a crowd outside Alfreton Police Station when the car arrived. Smedley, however, was admitted by a side entrance. He was later taken to Leicester Prison, and he will reappear at Alfreton next Thursday.

RONALD SMEDLEY (marked with a cross), in the c... two police officers, leaves Matlock Police Station to-Alfreton, where he was brought before a special court exclusive "Derby Evening Telegraph" photograph

**SIR MALCOLM GO...
ONE BETTER**

The *Derby Evening Telegraph* reports how Ronald Smedley was escorted from Matlock police station to Alfreton for his first court appearance on the charge of murdering his girlfriend. The prisoner is marked with an 'x' over his head. See Chapter 16. (Derby Evening Telegraph)

The farmhouse at Bradley where Horace William Brunt shot Kate Elizabeth Collier. See Chapter 17. (Public Record Office)

Another view of the farmhouse. It was this view that John Henry Baldwin had as he repaired the fence in the foreground. See Chapter 17. (Public Record Office)

Inside the kitchen at the Bradley farmhouse. It was in this room that Mrs Collier was shot. See Chapter 17. (Public Record Office)

The murder weapon over the door. Notice that Brunt had replaced it upside down. See Chapter 17. (Public Record Office)

County Hall, Derby, where so many of the trials in this book took place.

The haystack at Breadsall Village where the body of Frances Stevens was found. Her feet can be seen sticking out from the stack, in the centre of the picture. See Chapter 18. (Public Record Office)

The body of Frances Stevens, once the hay had been removed. See Chapter 18. (Public Record Office)

Chesterfield's famous twisted spire, taken from St Mary's Gate. The Phoenix Inn, referred to in the story of Ernest Prince, is on the right. See Chapter 19. (Public Record Office)

Eyre's store where Thomas Bown worked and where he died. See Chapter 19. (Public Record Office)

The bedroom inside Eyre's store, used by firewatchers. Bown was found in the bed numbered '1' See Chapter 19. (Public Record Office)

Horace Brunt made his first appearance before the magistrates on April 26th. A special hearing was convened in the superintendent's office at Ashbourne police station and after hearing brief evidence of arrest, Mr H. Thackery Schwabe ordered that Brunt be remanded for three days.

The inquest on Kate Collier took place on April 27th before Mr Reginald William Sale. The jury were informed that they need not apportion blame as a man had been arrested in connection with this case and would be dealt with in the courts. The verdict finally given was that death was due to severe haemorrhage caused by a gunshot wound. The following day, April 28th, Kate Collier was laid to rest at Bradley, the service being conducted by the Reverend W.C. Riddings.

The second magistrate's hearing, on April 29th, was again quite brief and Mr F.W. Barnett who represented Brunt made no objection to a further remand until May 6th. Other appearances followed, on May 6th and May 13th, but it was not until May 19th that all the evidence was heard and Brunt was sent for trial.

The case of the Crown against William Brunt opened at Derby on July 2nd, 1937, before Mister Justice Singleton. The case for the prosecution was led by Mr Richard O'Sullivan, assisted by Mr Graham R. Swanwick while Brunt was defended by Mr Maurice F. Healy and Mr A.J. Flint. The evidence was heard over two days.

Mr O'Sullivan began by relating that Brunt had been a lorry driver until he had lost his job. After being unemployed for some time, he had started work at the Royal Oak which was some three miles from the scene of the shooting at Bradley. Brunt had been seen cycling towards the farmhouse at the crucial time and for what possible reason could he go there when he knew that Elsie and her father would be out selling eggs in Derby? In addition, the crime would appear to be premeditated since evidence would be called that Brunt had taken his own shotgun cartridge with him. The prosecution suggested that there was only one possible thing in Brunt's mind as he peddled towards the isolated farmhouse on April 24th.

In addition to the witnesses already referred to, the prosecution called George William Fearn, a lorry driver who knew Brunt well. Fearn had left his depot at 12.35pm on April 24th and had been driving along the Belper road when he saw Brunt coming from the direction of

Bradley, on his bicycle. It was then 12.40pm, a time when Brunt had originally claimed he was still working at the Royal Oak.

There could be little doubt that after visiting Bradley, Brunt had gone home to Rose Cottage. His family confirmed that he had arrived there just after 1.00pm. In addition, John Grundy stated that he had been putting up a shed at the house and he had passed the time of day with Brunt when he arrived on his bicycle. Grundy put the time at about 1.10pm.

Of slight concern for the prosecution was the evidence of Esther Ann Lomas, a general servant at the Royal Oak. She had seen Brunt coming into the yard from the fields at the back of the pub and he had asked her the time. Esther now testified that it was 12.50pm and Brunt had then remarked that he had to go to his dinner as he was late. That night, at some time before 8.00pm, Esther had spoken to Brunt in the kitchen of the pub and he had said, "It's a rum affair. Elsie found her mother lying in a pool of blood. She went out to call her father and said, 'Something has happened to my mother!' She's either been shot or knocked on the head." Esther added that as he related this, Brunt appeared to be very emotional and upset.

Detective Sergeant Downes referred to the various statements which Brunt had made while at the police station. Brunt had first been told at 11.40pm on April 24th that he would be detained on suspicion of causing the death of Kate Collier. The following morning Brunt had asked to see Downes and had said, "If you will let me see Elsie, I will tell you all about it." Miss Collier was allowed in to the prisoner at 8.30am and Downes heard Brunt tell her that he wasn't responsible for her mother's death.

Inspector Mayfield described what he had found when he attended the scene of the crime and reported that upon examining the double-barrelled gun over the door he had found that neither trigger was cocked but there was a discharged cartridge in the left barrel. None of the other cartridges found at the farm were of the same type but when Constable Robert Cope searched Rose Cottage, Brunt's home, after he had been arrested, he found some live cartridges in a recess in a landing on the stairs. These were of the same type as that found in the gun at Bradley and Brunt said that he had purchased them the previous April.

Sergeant Frank Ernest King was in charge of Brunt at 10.50am on

April 25th. Brunt had suddenly announced, "I'll tell you and Downes all about it. I went there and she got a poker to me, and then got the gun down. Well, you know what I did then."

The shotgun had been examined by Edgar Lester Urton, a gunsmith of 129 Ashgate Road, Chesterfield. He stated that the weapon was a Bonehill 12-bore double-barrelled, bar lock hammer gun. Both barrels were rather dirty but there were signs that the left one had recently been used. The pull of the weapon was up to eight pounds and Mr Urton had found no way in which the gun could be discharged accidentally. From his own experience, Mr Urton believed that the barrel had been six to eight feet away from Mrs Collier when it was fired.

The post-mortem had been carried out by Dr Griffith John Griffiths of Buxton. He described a wound two inches above the nape of the neck, which consisted of 14 separate puncture wounds and which was blackened and tattooed by powder. The spinal cord had been largely destroyed and three vertebrae were splintered. Shot was found deep in the tissues and the cartridge wad was embedded in the wound. In Dr Griffiths opinion the shot had been fired from shoulder height at a distance of about six feet.

Brunt gave evidence on his own behalf, stating that he had known the family for perhaps seven or eight years in all. He had not believed that Mrs Collier had anything against him and had not been offended by her remarks of April 23rd and in fact had stayed for supper that same night.

Turning to his visit to the farmhouse on April 24th, Brunt said that he had gone to collect a jacket and some overalls he had left there on a previous visit. As he cycled into the yard he saw Mrs Collier crossing back to the house with a bucket. They talked for a while and he offered to take the second bucket of water out to make up the meal while she fetched his clothing. As he placed the bucket in the sink, Mrs Collier made for him with the poker. He managed to wrestle this from her only to see her get the gun down from above the door. She was not aiming the gun at him but tried to hit him with the butt. As they struggled for possession, he pulled the gun backwards and it fell against the floor and went off accidentally, without him even touching the trigger. He had not known that it was loaded at the time. However, under cross examination, Brunt was unable to explain why he had then taken cash from the house and why, if this was a tragic accident, he had not summoned medical help. Finally, Brunt admitted that he had used the gun quite often before, with Mr Collier's permission.

The jury took just 40 minutes to decide that Brunt's story was a complete fabrication and that he was guilty as charged. An appeal against the death sentence was heard on July 28th before Lord Hewart, the Lord Chief Justice and Justices Du Parcq and Goddard. Here the defence team tried to suggest that some evidence which tended to corroborate Brunt's testimony had not been put to the jury but Lord Hewart refused to accept this, saying, "This appeal is a mere waste of time. There is nothing in it except that it arises out of a case of murder. It is dismissed."

Just over two weeks later, on Thursday August 12th, 1937, Horace William Brunt was hanged at Manchester prison. It was only the fourth execution of the year, although later that same month, two more men, Leslie George Stone and Frederick George Murphy, would both lose their lives on an English gallows.

Chapter Eighteen

The Haystack Murder

AT 2.00pm on Saturday, November 11th, 1939, Richard William Jarvis Bridgett, a farmer, drove a horse and cart up to a field on Mill Farm at Breadsall, near Derby, intending to collect some hay for his animals. In fact, there were a couple of other jobs which required attention in this field and Richard Bridgett spent some time repairing fences before he climbed back into his cart in order to load up the remaining hay. It was now 2.45pm.

As Bridgett stood on the back of the cart so that he could climb up on to the stack itself, he noticed a shoe sticking out of a pile of hay which lay on the ground. Intrigued, Mr Bridgett jumped down from the cart and gave the shoe a gentle poke with his hayfork. The way the shoe moved showed plainly that there was a body hidden in the hayrick. Richard Bridgett touched nothing else and ran to fetch the police.

Constable James Hardie Scott was on duty at Little Eaton when Bridgett dashed up to him and told him what he had found in one of his fields. Constable Scott passed a message about the discovery to his divisional headquarters before going back to Lime Lane and the field where the body lay. He noted that the hayrick was in the furthest corner of the field, some 120 yards from the road. After careful examination of the hayrick, Constable Scott discovered that the body, that of a woman, was lying close to the foot of the stack, almost in the centre of the side that was furthest from the road. The entire body, apart from the feet, was covered by hay and Scott remained on guard at the scene until some of his colleagues arrived.

Detective Constable James Richardson arrived at the scene at 3.40pm. He began by checking the area around the haystack to make sure that there was no evidence which might be disturbed when the straw was removed from the body. Finding nothing, Richardson then moved the hay from the opposite side of the stack from where the shoe lay. This revealed the face and neck of a woman who had sustained obvious facial injuries and had a scarf tied tightly around her neck. A piece of the same material which made up the scarf lay on the ground eight inches from the woman's head.

Slowly and carefully the officers removed all the hay from the body. Once this had been done, a crumpled, bloodstained petticoat was found, lying between the woman's left arm and her body. Later, although it was plain that the woman was dead, Dr Frederick William Schofield attended and he confirmed that she had perished some days before. The body was then removed to the mortuary so that a post-mortem could be carried out.

One of the first tasks that the police had to concern themselves with, was identifying the body. Extensive inquiries were made in Breadsall, Chaddesden, Morley and Smalley. This painstaking approach led, on November 13th, to the confirmation that the woman was 41-year-old Frances Stevens from Ockbrook, who was known to her friends as Fanny. She had been living in the Derby area for the past six weeks and prior to that had been staying in Uttoxeter.

This identification was made by Mrs Isabella Roache, who lived at 29 Suffolk Avenue, Chaddesden. She had known Fanny well and the dead woman had actually been living at her home for the past month or so. On Sunday, November 5th, Isabella's husband, Peter Roache, had been in hospital and she and Fanny had gone to visit him at around 1.40pm on that day.

As the two women approached the infirmary gates, Fanny saw a soldier who she said she knew, and went over to speak to him. Isabella went into the infirmary alone and had not seen Fanny again until she identified her body at the mortuary. Isabella was also able to tell the police that during the time Fanny had been living with her, she had received visits from five different soldiers. Three of these had come inside the house, the other two contenting themselves with a chat at the front door.

Since the last sighting of Fanny Stevens had been made on the afternoon of November 5th, the police now issued a newspaper appeal for any witnesses who might have seen her after this time. In the *Derby Evening Telegraph* of November 13th, 1939, an article on the front page gave details of the identification and gave a detailed description of the dead woman. According to this she was "Five feet four inches; weight eight stone seven pounds; dark brown hair, shingled, without a parting and untidy; blue eyes; fairly even front teeth; oval face."

The article went on to say that Fanny had worn a bandage on her left leg, just above the ankle, and that this had covered a festering sore about the size of a half-crown. It continued, "When the body was found the woman wore a coat of rough, fawn tweed, with a brown and orange fleck, and a half-belt at the back. She had a sandy fawn skirt of hopsack tweed and under this a frock of dark brown flowered print which appeared as a blouse above the skirt. She had a small grey felt hat, brown artificial silk stockings and dirty brown shoes, size five, with a single strap."

On November 14th, the inquest on the dead woman was opened at the Old Hall, Breadsall, before the district coroner, Mr Reginald William Sale. Only the most basic evidence of identification and cause of death was given before matters were adjourned sine die so that the police inquiries could continue unhampered.

Meanwhile, the police appeal for help had brought forward other witnesses who reported that Fanny Stevens had been seen a number of times in company with a 36-year-old farm labourer named Joseph Myatt, who lived in a lodging house at 10 St Alkmund's Churchyard, Derby, a quaint part of the town that had survived largely intact since Georgian times. At 6.00pm on November 14th, Detective Chief Inspector Gray and Sergeant Oliver Fairbrother went to the lodging house where they first saw Myatt. He readily admitted that he had known the dead woman and agreed to accompany the officers to the police station to make a written statement, describing his movements on November 5th.

This first statement, made from 6.15pm until 8.05pm, was a most curious document. Myatt began by saying that at 11.15am on November 5th, a fellow guest had approached him and said that there was a woman outside asking for him by name and requesting that he take her for a walk around nearby Darley Park. At first, Myatt had refused and asked the message carrier to tell her to go away. Eventually, though, he did go out to her and although he had never set eyes on this woman before, agreed to go for a walk with her. The statement went on to say that they stayed in Darley Park until 3.15pm, during which time Fanny stated that she was meeting a man with a car, at Brailsford. As a result, Myatt walked with her to the bus station in Derby and saw her get on the Ashbourne bus, after which he returned to his lodging house.

There were, of course, two problems with this statement. In the first place, Myatt was claiming that a perfect stranger had asked for him by name at his lodgings and he had gone for a walk with her, and secondly, the timetable he outlined did not agree with the last sighting of Fanny Stevens, by Isabella Roache. Consequently, Myatt was held in custody while further inquiries were made.

At 9.10pm, Sergeant Fairbrother went back to Myatt and asked him if he wished to change anything in his statement. Myatt who had, of course, had time to think things over replied, "Yes, I want to tell you the truth. I haven't slept for a week for thinking about Sunday and that woman." He then made a second statement which was completed at 10.20pm.

In this second document, Myatt admitted that he had known Fanny Stevens for a couple of weeks before November 5th and had been out with her twice. He still maintained that she had called for him at his lodgings on that Sunday, but now put the time at 2.15pm. Together they walked down to St Mary's Bridge and there boarded a bus for Little Eaton, getting off at the Breadsall turning. The statement continued, "We went up Breadsall Road till we came to the signpost which says to Breadsall Moor. When we got to the church, we went into the field opposite the church. As we got so far down the fields we came to a huge stack. She said to me, 'What are you going to do?' I said, 'Nothing.' I simply got my temper and by getting temper I kicked her in the face as she lay down by the stack. She shouted. I put the paid *(sic)* to her by finishing her off with the heel of my shoe. Her scarf was round her neck and I tied it, and the end of the scarf came off in my hand. I covered her over with some hay and came away.

"My scarf had some bloodstains on and so had the shoes. On the following Saturday night I was in a public house when I heard some people talking about the murder. I started to cry, I used my scarf to wipe my eyes. I noticed bloodstains on the bottom of the scarf, so when I got back to the kip I put the scarf behind the kitchen door, and as far as I am concerned it is still there. When I was going to bed I noticed bloodstains on the left boot toe, so I put them under my bed and the next day I asked a man who had two pairs of boots if he would give me a pair, and he gave me the boots I am wearing now. On the Monday morning I put the bloodstained boots at the bottom of the garden and covered them over with some rubbish."

Acting on this information, Sergeant Fairbrother and Chief Inspector Gray went back to the lodging house at 11.00am on November 15th but could find no trace of the scarf or the boots Myatt had referred to in his statement. At one stage, Myatt was taken under escort to St Alkmund's Churchyard and he pointed out the pile of rubbish where he claimed the boots were hidden. This was taken apart but again no trace of the missing boots could be found. Nevertheless, at 4.50pm that same day, Myatt was charged with murder. In reply to the charge he remarked, "I did her in, but I didn't mean to do it."

Even though he was due to appear before the magistrates the next morning, Myatt was still not finished with his confessions to the police. At 10.30pm he asked to see Sergeant Fairbrother to whom he explained that the first two statements were not correct and he wished to make a third. Sergeant Fairbrother advised the prisoner to sleep on this and make his decision in the morning when he was fresh. The next morning, at 10.00am, Myatt said he had not changed his mind and his third statement was then taken down.

The statement began by again outlining how he and Fanny had come to the field where her body would subsequently be found. Myatt said that there were two rows of barbed wire around the haystack but they had climbed under these, gone to the stack and had intercourse. As soon as Myatt had finished, Fanny said that she wanted some money from him but he claimed that he didn't have any. At this, she had grabbed him around the waist, shaken him and said that she could hear money rattling. He persisted in saying that there was no cash, to which she replied that she would get it off him one way or another.

Myatt continued, "I did no more but I caught her in the mouth with my fist and she fell to the ground. While she was on the ground I hit her again with my fist on the side of her face. She was moaning and I catched *(sic)* her with my boot in the face. She had a scarf round her neck, tied once. I tied another knot and I pulled it tight. The bottom of the fringe came off in my hand and I threw it down. She had light-coloured stockings on tied with string above the knee. She had no knickers on while I was with her that day. She had two frocks on, one was a white and one was a fawn one. I pulled her to the stack and covered her with hay and left her. I walked away across the fields and saw a man coming towards me, so I went in the opposite direction and that brought me on to the same road I had come along with the woman. I got through a gap in the hedge on to the road and I turned to the left and at the end of the road I turned to the left again and went past the Windmill Inn and on to Derby.

"When I left the woman it was just getting dusk so it was about seven o'clock when I got to the kip in St Alkmund's Churchyard and I stayed at the kip all night. I never went out again. I am very sorry I have come to this. I never intended to do anything like that."

Myatt appeared before the stipendiary magistrate, Mr Gerald H. Smith, later that morning and was remanded in custody until November 18th. Later that same day, the body of Fanny Stevens was laid to rest at Ockbrook. Further court appearances followed on November 18th and November 22nd. In the first of those two appearances, Myatt was asked if there were any reason why he should not be remanded and he replied, rather curiously, "I got some work to go to, but it is a bit too far away for me, but I could stop on the premises." By November 22nd, Myatt was represented by Mr H.R. Cleaver and that same day, was transferred to Leicester prison.

Further court dates followed on December 8th, when Mr Cleaver expressed concerns over the delay in the prosecution presenting their case, and December 18th. It was not until January 9th, 1940, that all the evidence was heard and Myatt finally sent for trial.

Joseph Myatt appeared at Derby on Monday, February 19th, 1940, before Mr Justice Oliver and a jury of nine men and three women. The Crown's case was led by Mr Richard O'Sullivan who was assisted by Mr Arthur Ward and Myatt's defence rested in the hands of Mr T. Norman Winning and Mr Geoffrey Smallwood.

The first witness was Detective Inspector James Brailsford who said that he had taken various photographs of the place where the body was found. When questioned by Mr Winning for the defence, though, Inspector Brailsford admitted that there were no signs of any struggle having taken place at the haystack. Further, in his statements, Myatt had referred to the field being opposite a church but Inspector Brailsford confirmed that there was no church within half a mile of the location.

Dr Schofield was then called to describe the injuries Fanny Stevens had suffered. He first stated that when he had made his first examination, at the murder scene, he had noted a number of footmarks near the body and underneath it after the body had been moved. These were of a larger shoe size than the woman's and could have been caused by someone carrying the body to the spot. However, Dr Schofield also said that in his opinion, since the body lay in a natural attitude, it had not been placed there and it was more likely that the attack had taken place close to the haystack. Cross-examined by Mr Winning, Dr Schofield confirmed that his initial belief had been that the woman had been knocked down by a motor car and then carried to the haystack, although he had since concluded that death was due to strangulation. He also agreed that there must have been a most violent struggle for the injuries he noted to have been inflicted.

The post-mortem had been carried out by Dr Schofield and Dr Gladstone Rule Osborn, a pathologist from the Derbyshire Royal Infirmary. Cataloguing the bruises and injuries he found, Dr Osborn said that there was a bruise on the side of the face, close to the left eye, and others at the angle of the jaw. Fanny's upper lip was bruised and torn and there were other marks on the left side of her forehead and on the left cheek. There were six separate bruises on the outside right forearm and others on the left hand and right elbow. A front tooth had been knocked out and two others were loose.

Turning to the scarf found around Fanny's neck, Dr Osborn said that it had been wound round three times and tied in the front with a single knot, the pressure fracturing the hyoid bone. Death had taken place two to three hours after Fanny's last meal which had consisted in part of potatoes. Dr Osborn was also able to say that the dead woman had had sex prior to death and that had the scarf not been tied around her throat, she would have undoubtedly have recovered from her other injuries. Cross-examined by Mr Winning, Dr Osborn also stated that all the injuries were consistent with a violent struggle and he would have expected there to have been signs of that struggle at the scene, along with some bloodstaining, and in addition, Fanny's attacker might well be scratched or have received injuries to his fist from Fanny's teeth. He was also able to confirm that Fanny had been suffering from venereal disease.

Isabella Roache was the next witness and she again told of Fanny's encounter with a soldier on the afternoon of November 5th, the last time she had seen her alive. Noel Beeston, the deputy lodging house keeper at 10 St Alkmund's Churchyard, was then called. He reported how he had told the police, after Myatt had first been questioned, that he had seen Myatt wearing different boots. He could not recall when the prisoner stopped wearing the old ones but thought it might have been as long as two weeks before his arrest. Beeston was also able to say that he had always found Myatt to be quiet and inoffensive and had never noticed any scratches or injuries to his face or hands.

James Frederick Powell was a fellow lodger at the house where Myatt lived and he stated that he had given Myatt a pair of boots in November. Powell could not remember precisely when this was but it was either the Thursday or the Friday before Myatt was first interviewed. These boots were a little too small for Myatt, and Powell had no idea what he did with his old pair. However, Powell also stated that the boots he had given to Myatt were not the pair he was wearing when the police picked him up.

Sergeant Fairbrother was called to describe his interviews with Myatt. Fairbrother freely admitted that after speaking to Myatt for an hour or so, he had come to the conclusion that he was far from normal mentally. The defence had produced documentation showing that Myatt had the mind of a child of 12 and Sergeant Fairbrother said that this did not surprise him.

Another police witness was Detective Superintendent Alan Evans, who had first interviewed Myatt on November 14th, after reading his first statement. Initially, there had been some confusion and Superintendent Evans had believed he was talking to another suspect, and asked why he had signed the statement in the name of Myatt. Myatt told him that he had done so because it was his name and produced his unemployment insurance card which gave his correct name and address, to prove that he was telling the truth.

Continuing his testimony, Superintendent Evans told the court that Myatt had said that he was a native of Congleton and had three sisters and two brothers. He had left the town three years before and had since done odd farm jobs in Derbyshire including some for a Mr Shaw at Breadsall. The story Myatt told in this interview was rambling and often contradictory. He had no idea who the man was who told him that there was a woman outside asking for him, and then detailed the walk they had taken, saying that Fanny had said she was meeting a man at the wholesale market. He went there with her and gave her 10d with which she bought a cup of tea and a couple of ham sandwiches, in a cafe opposite. This statement was in direct contradiction to the known facts, Fanny's last meal, according to the post-mortem, being a meat and potato pie which she had eaten with Isabella Roache. There was also the not insignificant fact that the cafe Myatt referred to was closed on a Sunday.

Myatt then said that he had walked Fanny to the bus station and seen her get on to a bus. He went on to say that she had paid 3d for her ticket and when asked how he knew, since he had remained behind in Derby, he had no answer. After relating all this, even Superintendent Evans admitted that he thought there was something wrong with Myatt. He told the court, "I formed the opinion that he was a man capable of talking rubbish." He also agreed that there was no evidence against Myatt apart from his own statements and that other men had been suspected of the crime. One man in particular had been a prime suspect. On November 5th, a blue car had been seen parked outside the field where Fanny's body was later found. The driver of this car was located and interviewed. The man had a criminal record but his story that he had been looking for rabbits was believed and he was allowed to go. Finally, Superintendent Evans said that the soldier seen with Fanny Stevens was certainly not Myatt and had never been traced.

The defence called no witnesses apart from Dr C.M. Dickinson, the medical officer of Leicester prison where Myatt had been held. Dr Dickinson outlined Myatt's family history, saying that a maternal aunt and uncle were at present in an asylum, as were some of Myatt's cousins. Myatt could only read and write very simple words and was unable to perform the calculation 27s minus 1s 6d. In Dr Dickinson's opinion, all of Myatt's statements were unreliable and he often contradicted himself in an obvious fashion. There was also the fact that when asked what he thought the punishment for this crime might be, Myatt had replied that it might be a fine of 5s.

In many ways, the summing up was as important as the trial itself. For the prosecution, Mr O'Sullivan said that the defence had implied that Myatt had heard about the case from the newspapers and had concocted his confession from those reports. However, there were several points in Myatt's statements which could not have been gleaned from the papers, including the fact that Fanny had had sex before she died, and that she was not wearing knickers.

For the defence, Mr Winning said that there was not a shred of evidence against Myatt apart from his own statements to the police. No one had seen Myatt close to the spot where the body was found and his description of the area was in error. There were no signs of a struggle at the spot and yet Myatt had described a violent assault upon Miss Stevens.

In his own summing up, Mr Justice Oliver told the jury that the defence had not addressed them on the subject of Myatt's sanity so they could not find the prisoner guilty but insane. The judge went on to refer to other points in Myatt's statements which had also not been made public, including the fact that a piece of scarf had been found close by the body, a piece that Myatt said had come away in his hands as he strangled Fanny Stevens. Also, the press reports carried nothing about the woman's stockings being tied with string.

The jury took 70 minutes to decide that Myatt was guilty although they did add a recommendation to mercy because of the prisoner's mental condition. The judge then sentenced Myatt to death and pointed out that the jury's recommendation would be forwarded to the proper quarter.

An appeal was entered and heard on March 18th before Justices

Hawke, Charles and MacNaghten. Here the defence referred again to the fact that only Myatt's own statements had convicted him. Had he stayed silent he would probably never have been charged and the statements themselves were contradictory. Allied to this, Myatt was undoubtedly well below normal mentally. However, the three judges again referred to the various points which Myatt had mentioned and which only the killer could have known about, including the piece of scarf which lay near the body. The conviction was safe and the appeal was dismissed.

In the event, Myatt's mental condition and the jury's recommendation did save his life. On March 25th, exactly one week after the appeal had been lost, the Home Secretary announced that he had advised His Majesty to commute the sentence to one of life imprisonment.

Chapter Nineteen

Money Is The Root Of All Evil

THOMAS James Bown had worked for Messrs Eyre & Sons Limited, house furnishers of Chesterfield, for 25 years. Employed as a caretaker and porter, Bown carried out his duties conscientiously and also took most seriously his work as a fire-watcher during the dark days of World War Two. He and other employ-ees carried out this task on a shift basis and often there would be two or more men peering out into the skies, looking for enemy aircraft. For that reason, the company had set up a small bedroom in one of the rooms and it held beds for three men.

At 11.30am on Sunday, March 30th, 1941, Harry Oswald Eyre, the advertising manager for Eyre & Sons, called at the factory and was admitted by Bown. The front door was immediately locked again and for the next few hours. Mr Eyre, who was a keen aeroplane spotter, stood on the roof looking out for aircraft of various types. He finally left the factory at 1.10pm, telling Bown that he would return after he had had some lunch.

Thomas Bown also went out shortly afterwards, for at 1.30pm he was in the Phoenix Inn on St Mary's Gate where he was served by Dorothy Green, the wife of the licensee, a woman who had known Bown for 17 years. She saw him take out a small purse which contained four or five bank notes and select a pound-note to pay for his drink.

At 2.30pm, Harry Eyre was back at the factory and again Bown let him in. Another session of plane-spotting on the roof followed and it was not until 5.15pm that Eyre went down to the office where he sorted out some *Aeroplane* and *Flight* magazines, calling out to Bown to bring him some string so that he could tie them up into a parcel. Bown did not reply, so Eyre, thinking that Bown must be at the other side of the building, went to the radio department of the store and got the string himself. His task complete, he then called to Bown to tell him he was going home. By now, it was 5.30pm.

Once again there was no reply and since Bown would have to let him out and lock the doors behind him, Harry Eyre went to look for him. Bown was lying in one of the beds in the fire watchers' room, his head to the wall and a blanket pulled up over his face. Eyre went to the bed and gently shook Bown to wake him but when he still did not move, Eyre pulled back the blanket to discover to his horror that Bown was suffering from terrible head injuries and there was also a gaping wound in his throat.

Harry Eyre rang for the police and a doctor who ordered that the injured man be taken without delay to hospital. On arrival there, Bown was examined by Dr Lewis Gordon Cruickshank, who pronounced him dead. The initial police investigation, though, was little short of farcical. Constable Robert Leslie Maynard had, together with Constable Newbold, answered the telephone call from Mr Eyre and gone to the factory at 5.50pm on March 30th, believing that they were looking at a case of attempted suicide. Bown was lying on his back on the bed, fully clothed except for his collar and tie, still partly covered by a blanket and with the pillow and mattress soaked in blood. There were blood splashes all around the room and a large wound in Bown's throat and deep puncture wounds in both temples. A search of the premises was made but since no bloodstained weapon had been found, and there were no signs of a struggle, the suicide theory was maintained. Although no weapon had been found, it was believed that Bown had used a razor blade which was they assumed was still embedded in the wound.

Once Bown was certified to be dead, a suicide was duly reported to the coroner. Now, though, after the post-mortem had been carried out, and no razor blade had been found, the police had finally realised that they were dealing with a case of murder, and altered their approach accordingly. Inquiries soon revealed that Bown's purse was missing, which indicated that robbery was a possible motive for this crime. Also missing were the keys Bown had charge of, and one of the three firemen's axes normally kept in boxes underneath the beds. Two remained in place, but the third box was now empty and it now appeared that just such a weapon had been used to inflict the injuries upon him. Since there were no signs of any struggle, it was assumed that Bown had been having a nap when his assailant attacked him and since there were splashes of blood all over the surrounding area, the killer's clothing was also believed to be heavily stained.

On Friday, April 4th, the *Derbyshire Times* printed a detailed report of the crime, together with a picture of the type of axe used and a description of the weapon, stating that it was 15 inches long, bore the inscription 'Chillington Arfax' on the head, had an insulated handle marked 'Tested 20,000 volts' along with the patent number 19242, and would almost certainly be heavily bloodstained. Anyone with information was asked to contact the police directly on Chesterfield 2222. The article also reported that a bunch of seven or eight keys on a split ring was also missing, and it went on to describe some of the individual keys in detail. It also described a torch which was missing.

That same newspaper report also mentioned that the inquest on the dead man had opened on Wednesday, April 2nd, before Mr F.D. Worthington, when evidence of identification was given by Mr Ernest Lorenzo Lowe of 728 Woodborough Road, Mapperley, Bown's brother-in-law. Mr Worthington then said that since police inquiries were continuing, no further evidence would be taken and matters would be adjourned for at least a fortnight and possibly longer if the police wished it. The next day, Thursday, April 3rd, Thomas Bown was buried at the Newbold churchyard, the ceremony being conducted by Father Wilson. The grave in which Bown was laid to rest had only just been closed after the burial of his mother-in-law the previous week.

The inquest resumed on April 30th and had been in progress for more than six hours when Detective Inspector Percy Nixey, who had been in charge of the investigation into Bown's death, was seen having an animated whispered conversation with the Chief Constable, Mr T. Wells, who then handed the coroner, Mr Worthington, a note. This note informed Mr Worthington that an arrest had been made and he then adjourned the inquest sine die, pending the outcome of future proceedings in the police court. The following day, May 1st, the man the police had charged appeared before the magistrates. He was named as 32-year-old Ernest Prince, a miner of 22 St Augustine's Road, Chesterfield. Evidence of arrest was given by the Chief Constable who said that some 20 minutes after Bown had entered the Phoenix Inn on March 30th, Prince had also been noted inside the bar. The two men, along with other customers, left the inn at 2.00pm and Prince had been interviewed as a matter of routine. Prince had made a statement and then been allowed to go but further inquiries had revealed that when Prince had left home that day, he had little or no money on him but later, after Bown's body had been found on the bed, Prince had been in possession of £3 10s in notes.

As a result of this, Inspector Nixey together with Sergeant Elliott and Sergeant Manton, saw Prince at his place of work, and took him in for further questioning. Prince later made a voluntary statement admitting his part in the death of Bown and subsequently some of the missing articles had been recovered. A remand was then requested while other inquiries were made and Prince was told that he would be held in custody until May 15th.

On May 15th there were strong words spoken between the prosecution and Mr Bertram Mather, who by now was representing Prince. The prisoner was being held at Leicester jail and Mr Mather stated that this was most inconvenient for him and he would prefer it if Prince were held overnight at Chesterfield, where he would be able to talk to his client more easily. The Chief Constable, Mr Wells, pointed out that every facility would be granted at Leicester but Mr Mather reminded him that his client might well soon be on trial for his life, and demanded that he be allowed to see his client at Chesterfield. Finally, a compromise was reached whereby it was agreed that Prince would remain at Leicester but would be brought to Chesterfield early in the morning and held in the police cells, at Mr Mather's convenience. Prince was then remanded until May 20th. One further remand followed and it was on May 27th that the evidence was finally heard and Prince sent to the next assizes which opened on June 18th.

Prince appeared before Mr Justice Oliver and a jury of ten men and two women at Derby on Friday, June 20th. The Crown's case was led by Mr P.E. Sandlands, who was assisted by Mr C. Gallop, and Prince was defended by Mr T. Norman Winning and Mr Francis L. Lee. The evidence was heard over two days and the verdict returned on Saturday, June 21st.

Thomas Henry Neal was the night caretaker at Eyre's and he testified that he had been relieved from duty, by Bown, at 8.00am on March 30th. He handed the factory keys over to Bown and ensured that all the doors were secure when he left. Neal also stated that there was an inside communicating door which linked Eyre's premises with those of the Stephenson Arcade Limited, next door. During business hours, this door was always left open, so that the fire watchers could come and go, but at other times it was locked. This was confirmed by Albert Edward Booth, the manager of the arcade, who said that he locked all the doors, including the communicating door, when he left the premises on Saturday, and did not open it again until 8.30am on the Monday. There was no sign of the door being forced or interfered with in any way, suggesting that Thomas Bown had himself admitted the man who subsequently attacked him.

In addition to the circumstances already mentioned, Harry Eyre said that when he returned to the factory at 2.30pm, the premises were not well lit and Bown appeared to be rather nervous and seemed to keep his distance from him. Asked what would have happened if he had believed there had been someone in the factory who had no right to be there but who had been admitted by Bown, Mr Eyre replied that for such a breach of discipline, Bown would have received a severe reprimand on the spot.

Besides Mr Eyre, Bown received two more visitors at the factory that day. At some time between noon and 12.10pm, William Kenneth Bower, an electrician, went to the premises to look at some timetables. His first knock must not have been heard by Bown because Bower had to knock again before he was admitted, and at the time the factory, which was usually well-lit, was in darkness. The key must have been in the lock for Bower did not hear the sound of it being inserted or turned. While Bower was there, the third visitor, Bown's wife, arrived with his lunch.

Sarah Elizabeth Bown also said that once she had knocked, it was a while before her husband admitted her to the building. She only went into the showroom of the factory and did not enter the room where the fire watchers ' beds were. Sarah testified that she took her husband some meat sandwiches and a piece of cake and told Thomas that she would be back at 6.30pm to 6.45pm.

When Eyre had returned in the afternoon he had told Bown that his son, Clive, might be joining him later and when he did not arrive he had assumed that he had simply changed his mind. Clive Eyre, however, said he did go to the factory at 4.00pm that day and although he knocked loudly for 35 minutes, he received no reply. He could see his father on the roof but was unable to attract his attention. This was confirmed by some friends who saw Clive there. Eventually, Clive Eyre had given up and gone home.

In addition to being seen by Dorothy Green in the Phoenix Inn, Bown was also seen by Richard Dunks. At the time, Bown was sitting with a man named Harry Copeland, and Dunks joined the two men later. At 2.00pm, Bown left the pub with Dunks and after walking back towards the factory together, they parted at around 2.20pm.

Dorothy Green had already told of seeing Bown in the Phoenix but she also testified that Prince was in the bar that afternoon too. Dorothy had not actually seen Prince come into the pub but he was certainly in the tap room at 1.30pm because she saw him sitting in his usual seat. According to Dorothy, although Bown didn't like to mix with strangers, he was quite a talkative man and told everyone his business. He was proud of the fact that he had the factory keys, and had been given this position of responsibility, and even showed Dorothy the keys while he was at the bar. Bown had also told everyone in the bar that he had received an insurance payment on the death of his mother-in-law and even showed Dorothy the money in his purse.

It was known that Bown had money with him on the day that he was killed. Other witnesses were now called to show that, at least up to the time Bown had been attacked, Prince was without funds to speak of, although he seemed to have acquired some cash by the afternoon of that day. Lily Singleton occupied the house at 22 St Augustine's Road and she said that Prince had lodged with her since March. He and his family occupied two rooms, one upstairs and one down. On March 30th, she saw Prince leave the house some time between 11.30am and noon, only returning between 4.00pm and 5.00pm. When he did come in, Prince went straight to his room and was seen doing so by Lily's married daughter Beatrice Florence Woodhouse.

At tea time that same day, another daughter of Lily's, Doris Margaret Mary Singleton, had gone out with Prince's wife, Eileen. By the time they returned, Prince was back from wherever he had been and later, Doris went with him to Brailsford's shop for some fruit. While there, Prince bought sugarette which cost 1s 3d but he paid for it with a £1 note. Earlier that same day, though, Prince had been without cash because when Lily's son, Frederick Arthur Joseph Singleton, went up to Prince's room he found Mrs Prince cleaning the grate and Ernest getting ready to go out, saying he was going to the pit to draw his money. This, though, was obviously a lie because George Hadyn Coleman worked with Prince and he testified that later that day Prince tried to cadge a cigarette from him and later borrowed 2s.

Other testimony showed that Prince had been borrowing money from as many people as he could and owed debts to others too. Albert Ambrose, a newsagent, said that Prince owed him 15s 8d, while Edward Winfield, the licensee of the Horns Hotel, said that Prince had often borrowed money from him and now owed him £1. Roger Marples, a coal cutter, told the court that he had lent Prince £1 on February 2nd and was still waiting to be paid back, while Eric Gordon Ottwell had also lent Prince money, having given him 10s three weeks before the crime for which he was now standing in the dock.

Detective Inspector Nixey told of the events leading up to Prince's arrest. As a known acquaintance of the dead man, who had been seen in his company on the day that he was attacked, Prince was spoken to as a matter of routine on April 20th, and asked to make a statement detailing his movements on the day of the murder. In this first state-ment, Prince said that he had been living at his present address, with his wife, for the past four weeks and previous to this had been living with his mother at 77 Lordsmill Street. He claimed that he recalled the Tuesday that 'Tommy' met his death, although he did not actually hear about the crime until the following Wednesday, April 2nd. The statement continued, "It would be about ten to two on this Sunday when I went into the Phoenix. I had called at the Anchor previously, from 1.15pm. When I got in the Phoenix, I saw Tommy. He was talking with Mrs Green and two other people, a man and a woman I think. I had a couple of bitters on my own. I didn't talk to anyone, and I turned out about five past two. Tommy came out and stood outside with three or four, and then I saw him set off towards Vicar Lane. He went off on his own. I should say it would be about ten past by then. When I was standing outside I was not talking to anyone, just messing about with mother's dog.

"From then I had a walk round the town, window-gazing, and then went towards the hospital to see if my sister had gone there to visit mother. I waited outside the hospital for a while, then had a look in the Army Stores until about 3.00pm, then I walked through Cavendish Street and to the bus stand. I caught the bus home. I think it was the 3.10 Storforth Lane. When I got home I had my dinner and stopped indoors until about half past eight, when I came into town again and called at the Anchor. My wife told me mother had come out of hospital the day before, but she didn't tell me until Sunday night.

"I knew Bown worked at Eyre's, but I didn't know much about him. I didn't know he had any money except what he earned. I passed Eyre's that afternoon but I didn't recognise anyone about and I did not see Tommy after ten past two."

Inspector Nixey made further inquiries and found that there were elements of this statement which were not true and also that Prince had suddenly been spending money he should not have had. As a result, Prince was taken into custody on April 30th, told that his first statement was not satisfactory and asked if he wished to make a second. Prince replied, "Let me write down what happened. I can write it better than talk." He was then given pen and paper and wrote out another statement which began, "On Sunday, March 30th, I saw the deceased person as stated previously, but omitted to say that I saw him again later.

"As I made my way across Holywell Cross, Bown caught me up on the by-pass road and walked down with me. He then said something about a position in the shop, as if he was manager or something, and asked me to go in and have a look round. While inside, someone came to the door and he switched out the lights so I should not be seen. After a short while and when all was quiet he showed me round a bit, and then the corner where the fire watchers camped. The implements were lying about and he showed me different things. I sat on one of the beds, and he made a suggestion to me which I took offence at."

Prince went on to say that Bown had then made a sexual advance towards him and he suddenly saw red. There was an axe nearby and Prince grabbed it to hit Bown with, but Bown twisted the axe and caught Prince on the side of the head. He continued, "At that I think I lost all reason and I started as if I was in a New York den. When I realised what I had done I tried to cover it up. I took the money to make it look like robbery ...If he had not acted this way I don't suppose anything would have happened. It was when he caught me with the axe and started shouting I went partly mad, I think. As near as I could say, this was about 3.15 because I was on the bus stand about 3.30. The purse and stuff I burned, bar the money, some of which I gave Eileen and told her I had borrowed it. The keys, if they are still there, are in the river under the wooden footbridge near Hyde's works. The axe is buried down the pit under several hundred tons of debris ...I alone am responsible for it, and no one else until this day knew anything about it." Prince also claimed that he came upon Bown's money accidentally when he searched his pockets to find the keys to let himself out of the building. Detective Sergeant Elliott had later found these keys in the River Rother and Detective Constable Druitt found the torch case where Prince said he had put it, in a drain in Whitecoats Lane.

The injuries which Bown had sustained were then outlined in court, both by Dr Cruickshank, who had attended to him in the hospital and Dr James Mathewson Webster who had performed the post-mortem with Dr Cruickshank's assistance. Both doctors noted that most of the injuries were to the head and neck, although there was also an incised wound on the index finger of the right hand, an abrasion to the back of that hand and another mark on the inner right forearm.

In front of the right ear was a wound which led to a fracturing of the skull beneath with bone being driven into the brain. There was a similar wound on the left side and a third just below the hairline on the forehead which was probably the result of two separate blows. Other bruises were seen over the left lower jaw and the right cheek, which made it possible that Bown had been knocked unconscious before the fatal blows had been struck. The throat showed evidence of at least two blows with some sharp cutting instrument. All of these wounds could have been caused by an axe like the ones used by the fire watchers and the sharp end of the axe would have been used to inflict them. The cause of death was cerebral laceration, fractures of the skull and external haemorrhage and shock from the incised wounds to the throat.

One of the final witnesses was Dr C.M. Dickinson, the medical officer of Leicester prison. He testified that Prince had told him that he had an uncle in a mental asylum, although there was no other history of insanity within the family. Dr Dickinson described Prince as a quiet, well-conducted prisoner who had slept well and appeared to have a good memory. He was rational and there were no signs of mental disorder.

The jury took over two hours to decide that Prince was guilty of murder. Asked if he had anything to say before the sentence of death was passed, Prince simply shook his head to indicate 'No'.

On July 11th, it was announced that Prince would appeal against the death sentence and this was heard on July 28th by the Lord Chief Justice, Lord Caldecote, and Justices Tucker and Asquith. For the defence, Mr Lee, who had been the junior counsel at the trial, challenged the summing up of Mr Justice Oliver, claiming that there had been misdirection as to Prince's defence, the medical evidence and the onus of proof. In addition, the judge had 'made observations likely to leave doubt as to whether they were expressions of opinion or directions in law'.

After considering the evidence carefully, the appeal court judges ruled that Prince should only have been convicted of manslaughter and therefore the verdict of murder could not be allowed to stand. As a result, the death sentence was quashed and a prison term of 15 years substituted. Hearing this decision, Prince smiled broadly and strode quickly from the dock. Later that day he packed up his belongings and moved out of the condemned cell at Leicester jail.

Chapter Twenty

Forgive Me

LIKE most fathers, William Frederick George Meffen loved his children. The problem was that in Meffen's case, this love was rather a possessive one and this was especially true in the case of his 38-year-old stepdaughter, Winifred Ellen Stanley.

Meffen and his wife shared their home with Winifred at 453 Nottingham Road, Chaddesden, Derby, and Meffen and his step-daughter even worked together, at the Derby Cables Company. They were not the only members of the family to work there, however. Another daughter, Lily Calladine, also worked alongside them, as did a man named George Birks. Unfortunately for Meffen, Birks took rather a shine to Winifred and started paying her close attention. Meffen made it plain that he did not approve of this attention but Winifred told him that she was a grown woman and as such would make her own decisions. She started seeing George Birks on a regular basis which bothered Meffen greatly and on one occasion he told Lily that if Winifred persisted in this liaison, he would have to give her 'a damned good thrashing'.

On the night of Tuesday, February 22nd, 1944, Winifred was again out with Birks. Meffen sat up, waiting for her to come home, but Winifred stayed out all night. Meffen was distraught and spent the entire night sitting in a chair, crying uncontrollably. Two days later, on February 24th, Meffen confronted Birks and demanded to know whether or not he had spent the night with Winifred. George Birks said that this was not the case, but Meffen did not believe him. For a few more days, the atmosphere at Nottingham Road remained tense until finally, on the morning of Tuesday, February 29th, it boiled over into violence.

There were in fact five people living in the house at 453 Nottingham Road. In addition to 52-year-old Meffen, his wife, and Winifred and Lily Calladine, there was also another married daughter, Elsie Bishop. At 6.45am, the entire family were up and about, getting themselves ready for the day's work. Winifred Stanley went into the bathroom to wash and no one took any particular notice when Meffen followed her into the room. Seconds later a terrible scream rang out.

The bathroom door was locked from the inside but eventually Lily Calladine, her mother and her sister, Elsie Bishop, managed to force an entry, only to find Meffen standing with an open razor in his hand. Winifred was lying on the floor with a gaping wound in her throat. Bravely, Lily moved forward and attempted to take the razor from her father's hand, but he would have none of it. Although he made no attempt to hurt any other member of his family, Meffen shouted, "No, I've done it now and I'll hang." He then walked calmly to his own room, changed his clothes and left the house.

William Meffen did not go far. Finding the nearest policeman, Meffen announced, "I want you to lock me up. I have just cut my daughter's throat with a razor because she has been associating with a man." Taken to the police station, Meffen was searched, whereupon officers found a hand-written note, apparently penned the night before. Addressed to his family, this missive explained his intentions and made it plain that the crime he had just committed was not accidental and had been premeditated. As a result, Meffen was charged with murder. Later that day, Meffen made his first appearance at the police court. Only evidence of arrest was given, Meffen being described on the charge sheet as a braider. A remand was ordered, until March 10th.

On March 3rd, the inquest opened and medical evidence was given that death was due to the single throat wound which could not possibly have been self-inflicted. A verdict of murder by William Meffen was returned. By March 10th, the prisoner had obtained legal representation in the form of Mr N.R. Pinder, who made no objection to a further remand, this time for 14 days. On March 24th, a final remand was made, until April 12th when, finally, all the evidence was heard.

It was Mr E.G. Robey who outlined the case for the Director of Public Prosecutions at this final police court hearing. Mr Robey outlined the history of the family and revealed that on February 22nd, when Winifred had not returned home, she had spent the night with George Birks at Whatstandwell. When Meffen had confronted Birks two days later, Birks had denied this, but only because he knew of the problems Winifred was having at home.

Turning to the night before the attack, Mr Robey stated that Meffen had been seen by members of his family, scribbling a letter. At one stage he had asked them how to spell the word 'false' and this made it clear that the letter found on Meffen after the attack had been written on February 28th, showing that he had already decided on the course of action which would bring him to the court.

The letter referred to was then read out. It began, "Forgive me for what I have done, but I loved Winifred and she loved me until she got in with George Birks and then the love between us was over. If she had not told you and I so many lies about it things may have been very different, but she would not leave him so I had to do this.

"To think a great man like him having for his wife a little one like her, it fills me up to think about it. I don't know when I shall do it, but it is bound to come for I cannot stand it much longer.

"He has made her as false as himself. Regards to Whatstandwell but a week on Tuesday, it is true they were together so I think I have done the best thing.

"So, mam, don't worry about me. Give her a good grave. I did not think it would come to this after 25 years together, so if this happens before my dear son comes home tell him his dad loved him but could not stay to see him return. God bless him and God bless you all - Your broken hearted husband and dad." Having heard this damning letter and the testimony of the remaining witnesses, the magistrates had no hesitation in sending Meffen for trial.

That trial opened at Derby before Mr Justice Singleton on June 19th, 1944. The proceedings lasted only one day, during which the prosecution case rested in the hands of Mr Walker Kelly Carter, Meffen being defended by Mr T. Norman Winning and Mr G.A. Myers-Ward.

In addition to the family, Mr Carter called George Birks of 139 Ashbourne Road, Derby, who said that he had first visited Meffen's house in November 1943 but it had been made perfectly plain that he was not welcome there. Despite this, he and Winifred had continued seeing each other, despite the fact that Meffen had issued threats against him. Birks denied that there had ever been any impropriety between him and Winifred and he had not accompanied her to What-standwell to seduce her. Winifred had said that she was going there and asked him to come just in case her stepfather should find out, follow her, and cause trouble. He added that Winifred was very nervous of Meffen.

Medical evidence was given by Dr Gladstone Rule Osborn, who reported defence wounds on both of Winifred's hands. There was also a wound on her left shoulder and another on the right side of her face. Dr Osborn noted two wounds in the throat, either of which was serious enough to cause death. Finally, the doctor stated that, as far as he could tell, Winifred had not been sexually active.

Meffen stepped into the witness box and claimed that he had no memory of the attack, or even of writing the letter on the night of February 28th. He explained that he had served in the Army and had been in India in 1909, where he contracted malaria. He now had frequent attacks of this disease, usually every four or five weeks, and during these bouts he had little or no memory of what happened to him. Meffen claimed that he had suffered just such an attack at the end of February. He said he remembered getting up, lighting the fire and making tea on the morning of the 29th, but the next thing he recollected was being in the police station. The time in between was just a blank.

The final defence witness was Dr E.V.H. Pentreath, the superintendent of the Mickleover Mental Hospital. He testified that he had examined Meffen and found him to be 'reasonably normal'. There were, however, signs that Meffen did suffer from lapses of memory and it was possible that he had a split mind which was associated with a generally hysterical condition. Dr Pentreath was unable to say whether, at the time of the crime, Meffen would have known that what he was doing was wrong.

To counter this testimony, the prosecution called two medical experts of their own. Dr G. Waring Taylor was the medical officer at Leicester prison and he said that he had formed the opinion that Meffen knew what he was doing when he attacked his stepdaughter. Under cross-examination, though, Dr Taylor agreed that Meffen did have an hysterical personality and that an emotional upset might bring on a loss of memory. Finally, Dr John Humphrey, the medical officer of Winson Green prison in Birmingham, also stated that he believed that Meffen remembered his crime but again, under pressure from Mr Winning, had to admit that it was possible he did not.

In summing up for the defence, Mr Winning referred to the letter Meffen had written and asked the jury if they thought the letter implied a man contemplating 'an atrocious crime' or a man who thought that what he was about to do was 'the best thing'. Mr Justice Singleton also referred to the same letter in his address to the jury, pointing out that the first words used were 'Forgive me' and suggested that Meffen must have known that what he was doing required forgiveness.

It was for the jury to decide if Meffen knew what he was doing and was therefore responsible for his actions when he cut Winifred Stanley's throat. In the event, they took just over half and hour to decide that Meffen was guilty and he was then sentenced to death, visibly trembling as the terrible words were intoned. On June 30th, it was announced that Meffen had entered an appeal and this was heard on July 24th by the Lord Chief Justice, Lord Caldecote, and two of his colleagues. Once again, the main grounds were that Meffen had been temporarily insane at the time of the attack. Giving his judgement, the Lord Chief Justice pointed out that all the medical evidence had been before the jury at the trial, and they had been properly directed by the judge. It was pointed out that Meffen had personally drawn up the grounds of his appeal, complaining that the medical expert he had called to give testimony on his behalf had not put his case fully to the jury. In the court's opinion though, the evidence had been put properly and the jury had reached the only possible verdict.

At 8.00am on Tuesday, August 8th, 1944, William Frederick George Meffen was hanged at Leicester prison by Albert Pierrepoint. In fact, it was a double execution, Meffen sharing the gallows with William Alfred Cowle, who had stabbed to death his ex-girlfriend, Nora Emily Payne, in Springfield Road, Leicester, in May that year.

It was the first double execution at Leicester since 1903 when Thomas Porter and Thomas Preston were hanged for the murder of a policeman at Sileby. Among the crowd of 150 who gathered outside the prison gates was a grey-haired old woman who told a reporter that she had also been in the same spot then. Double executions were it seems something she did not want to miss!

Chapter Twenty-One

False Alarm

BRIDIE Gaynor had been working at the Carlton Hotel at 116 London Road, Derby, for a only few weeks and so she did not recognise one of the regular customers when he came into the foyer at 8.55pm on Saturday, December 8th, 1951.

The man who walked into the hotel was in fact 37-year-old John Cyril Eaton who lived at 117 Havelock Road, not far from Derby County's Baseball Ground home, but the management and staff of the hotel knew him as Mr Warner. At fairly regular intervals, every three months or so, Eaton would book a room for himself and his wife, Ivy. In fact, although Ivy May Warner was the lady's real name, and she was indeed a married woman, she was not Eaton's wife. The relationship between Eaton and Ivy Warner had been going on for some time, however, and marriage had been discussed, once Ivy obtained a proper divorce from her legal husband.

As Bridie Gaynor attended to 'Mr Warner' another of the hotel maids came up and suggested to Bridie that she give him guest room number two, the one he had whenever it was available. Bridie signed the gentleman in and offered to show him up to his room, but he smiled and said that there was no need as he knew the place well. Soon afterwards, Eaton left the hotel and was not seen again until he and Ivy Warner passed Bridie on the way up to their room. It was then 9.45pm.

Cyril Eaton, alias Mr Warner, was not seen again until 8.00am the following morning when Bridie Gaynor knocked on the door of room two. Eaton opened the door and politely refused the cup of tea which Bridie offered to bring up for him and his wife, saying that he would be down shortly. In fact, Eaton went downstairs at 8.15am when he approached the hotel proprietor, Mary Ellen Knowles, and asked her if she would make him a cup of tea.

Mary Knowles began to make the tea but could not help but notice that her guest seemed to be concerned about something. Before she could enquire as to what might be troubling him, Eaton muttered, "Will you phone for the police and ask them to bring a doctor?" Mrs Knowles said yes, of course she would, but what was the matter, was it something serious? Eaton replied, "Yes, I'm afraid so – she's dead."

The first police officers on the scene were Sergeant Charles Warren, who arrived at 8.40am, with Constable Smith. By now, Eaton was sitting in the hotel kitchen and as soon as he saw the two uniformed men, he leapt to his feet and announced, "Follow me, I'll show you." Eaton then led the way as the officers followed him to room two.

The first thing Sergeant Warren noticed was that there were two beds in the room, a double and a single. The single, in the far corner, showed signs of having recently been slept in but in the double bed, Warren saw the head of a woman, the blankets pulled up on to her throat. Despite the fact that most of the woman was hidden from view, Warren could see that there was a great deal of blood around her throat. He turned towards Eaton but even before the sergeant could ask the question, Eaton said, "I did it."

Taking out his pocketbook, Sergeant Warren asked Eaton how he had done this deed, whereupon Eaton replied, "With my hands." Warren continued by asking when this incident had taken place and Eaton thought for a moment before saying, "Last night, about midnight." Finally, Warren asked Eaton who the lady was, to which he replied, "It's a lady I have been going out with. We had some drink, we quarrelled. It's no use anyway. It's over and done with." Satisfied that he had unburdened himself sufficiently, Eaton finally seemed to relax a little, asked Sergeant Warren for a cigarette and then said, "Will you break the news gently to my parents?"

By 9.00am, Detective Inspector Leonard Shipton had arrived at the

Carlton Hotel and waited in the bedroom with the dead woman, Eaton and Sergeant Warren until Dr Walter Milburn arrived. He made an examination of the body, stated that life was extinct and that the woman had died at around midnight. The blankets were then pulled down, so that a more careful examination could be made and it was only now that the full extent of Ivy Warner's injuries could be seen. In addition to the marks on her neck and others which indicated that a pillow lying nearby had been pushed over her face at some stage, the bed was awash with blood. Ivy Warner had, it was later determined, lost something approaching two pints of blood, all through her vagina. Although a more careful examination would show exactly what had taken place, it looked as if Eaton had made a crude attempt at an abortion.

By 3.20pm that same day, Cyril Eaton was being formally interviewed by Detective Inspector Shipton at Full Street police station. Eaton again freely admitted that he was responsible for Ivy's death and said that he wished to make a full statement. This was taken down in the inspector's notebook and read back to Eaton, who then signed it.

The statement read, "About half past eight on Saturday night, I left Ivy in the Green Dragon Hotel while I went down to the Carlton to book the room. I saw one of the maids there, she said she was new there. I asked for a room for two. Another maid came along who knew me and said, 'Give them room two.' I then left and returned to the Green Dragon. Ivy had tea in the town with her daughter, but I had nothing since lunch time. We had been in the Green Dragon since six. I was drinking bitter and Ivy bitter and then gin.

"From the time I returned to the Green Dragon we stopped till ten o'clock, we were still drinking bitter and also gin. We had both had a fairish amount. We returned to the Carlton about half past ten. One of the girls asked if we would like a cup of tea. We refused and went straight to bed. Ivy undressed down to her vest and then got into bed. I also undressed down to my shirt and got into bed with her.

"I knew she had not had her courses [this referred to Ivy's periods] for three months. I had intercourse with her. There was no question of forcing her. We then got angry about something, to be honest it was me, but I won't say what it was. I got hold of her by the throat. I don't know why. She did not struggle. She just lay there silent. I put the pillow over her when I thought she was dead.

"This all happened while I was in bed. When I was getting out I noticed the blood. I then went to my little bed and lay there, thinking of what I was going to do. About half past eight the maid knocked at the door. I went and opened the door and when she asked if I wanted tea, I said 'No' and she went away.

"I had a wash and got dressed and then went downstairs and told Mrs Knowles, 'Something terrible has happened in room two. Will you phone for the police?' She said, 'Have you killed someone.' I said, 'Yes.' I asked for a cup of tea and waited for the police.

The statement continued, "I have been going with her for about 14 months. We have been trying to get a house but each time they have wanted more than we could afford.

"About six weeks ago we were discussing the matter. She has been over most weekends and stayed with me at my home. She stayed in one room and I in another. She said, 'We don't seem to be getting much further and it is worrying me.'

"I was becoming depressed at the way things were going. On Saturday evening she said she was going back home on the quarter past eight train, but I persuaded her to stop, saying we could stay at the Carlton. She agreed.

"When I had finished intercourse with her she said, 'I don't know when I am coming over again.' I said, 'You must have someone else over there,' – meaning Hanley. She said, 'Don't be silly.' I suppose that's when I got jealous and done that. I must have had a temporary blackout. I thought she was dead when I put the pillow over her. I have got a fairly strong grip and I didn't realise I was killing her. I get emotional and erratic but never go to these extremes. I still can't tell you what made me do it."

Despite the fact that Eaton had not gone into any details about how the injuries on the lower part of Ivy's body had been inflicted, he had nevertheless confessed that he was responsible for her death, after they had argued. As a result, he was charged with murder and made his first appearance before Derby magistrates on Monday, December 10th. The proceedings lasted for just ten minutes, during which Ivy was described as a married woman, separated from her husband, and who was living at 126 Eaton Street, Hanley. Cyril Eaton was represented by Mr A.E.H. Sevier who made no objection to a remand of seven days.

It was also on December 10th that the inquest opened before Mr T.H. Bishop. The only witness was William Warner of 8 Marina Drive, Allenton, who stated that he had identified the dead woman as his estranged wife. They had married in April 1931, after which they had lived in Stoke for five years. From there they moved to his present address in Allenton but Ivy left him in October 1950. The inquest was then adjourned until March 1st, 1952, by which time any criminal proceedings should be completed.

On December 17th, a further brief appearance before the magistrates took place but this date was more significant for what took place outside the courtroom. Just after noon, Eaton asked to see Inspector Shipton and admitted that there had been untruths in his first statement. Eaton said that he wished to make a fresh statement, telling the truth this time. This second document began, "After we had intercourse Ivy said to me, 'I am worried because I have not been unwell [referring to her periods] for about three months. Can you help me?' I said, 'I don't know what to do.' She said, 'Put your hand up inside me and try to open up that passage that goes to the entrance to the womb.' I didn't like doing it because I thought it would hurt her. She said, 'I'll tell you if you hurt me.'

"I tried what she asked me. I put my hand inside her private parts and then with my finger I found a passage which I tried to force open. She gave a kind of sigh. I then took my hand away and noticed that it had got blood on it, so with the other hand I shook her. She didn't come to or nothing. I got out of bed, washed my hands. I came back and started slapping her face. It made no difference.

"Then I thought she was probably dead. I walked round the room, I was scared. I thought she was dead then and that I might as well die too. That's when I put my hands round her throat. I wanted to make it look as though I had killed her. I put the pillow over her to cover her face up. I then went and lay on the other bed. By my wristwatch then it was five past 12. It was around half an hour before I put my hands round her."

The statement ended with a small addition in which Eaton clarified which parts of his first statement he did not want to change and restated that he had lied because he wanted to die himself and he had thought that if the police believed he had deliberately killed Ivy after an argument, he would hang.

Further court appearances took place on December 24th, January 2nd, 1952, and January 9th when the evidence was detailed by Mr M.D. Hutchinson and Eaton was consequently sent for trial. That trial opened at Derby on February 20th before Mr Justice Devlin and a jury of nine men and three women. Eaton was represented by Mr Walker Kelly Carter and Mr H.G. Talbot while the Crown's case was led by Mr R.C. Vaughan who was assisted by Mr I. Crutchley. The proceedings lasted for two days.

There could be no disputing the fact that Cyril Eaton was responsible for Ivy Warner's death, but was he guilty of murder? In his first statement, Eaton had said he killed Ivy after an argument, but in his second, her death was the result of a failed attempt to abort her. Which scenario was the truth?

Medical evidence would obviously prove crucial and the prosecution called two important witnesses. The first of these was Dr Milburn who had attended the scene and later performed a post-mortem. He reported multiple abrasions over the front of the neck, slightly to the right of the mid-line. These were a series of small crescent-shaped marks made by means of a thumb and forefingers and were consistent with manual strangulation. This was confirmed by froth in the respiratory tract and a small bite on the tip of the tongue, although Ivy's teeth had not been clenched when she died. Referring to the vaginal injuries, Dr Milburn said that he had found a single tear on the posterior wall of the vagina and this may well have come from a crude attempt at an abortion. This had, though, been entirely a false alarm because Ivy had not been pregnant when she died. The cause of death was given as asphyxia, from manual strangulation and terminal suffocation, the vaginal injuries being inflicted some ten minutes before death.

The second important witness was Jack Alexander Fish, a staff biologist at the Forensic Science Laboratory in Nottingham. He had examined various items from the room, including the pillow found near the body. This showed a small amount of blood which was type 'A' the same as Ivy's. However, whereas Eaton claimed that he had put this over Ivy to hide her face, Mr Fish was able to say that some force had been applied and it had been pushed down on to Ivy Warner's face.

Other witnesses were then heard, including Inspector Shipton who said that after he had been charged with 'wilful murder' Eaton had said, "Couldn't you put killed. I'm guilty of doing it." Then, the time came for Eaton to give testimony on his own behalf.

To begin with, Mr Carter for the defence read extracts from a letter which Ivy had written to Eaton. Dated a few days before her death it began, "Dear Cyril, I have just had my bath as I write you this letter. I am sitting in bed nice and easy. I feel OK but I am getting a little worried now. I wish I could (you know) then I should feel top of the world." This plainly showed that Ivy was worried about the fact that she had still not had a period and was concerned that she might have been pregnant, lending credence to Eaton's second statement. Other extracts showed that they were indeed looking for a house to buy together and were very much in love with each other.

Eaton gave his evidence very quietly and had to be told more than once by Mr Justice Devlin to speak up. He confirmed that his first statement to the police had been wrong when he said that he and Ivy had quarrelled that night. No angry words had passed between them and she had died in the way he had described in his second statement. One point, though, proved crucial. Eaton had said that he believed Ivy to be dead when he put his hands around her throat and strangled her. Asked why he had done this to an apparently dead woman, Eaton replied that he wanted to be found guilty of murder and hanged so that he, too, would die. The point was pressed again and again under cross-examination but Eaton did not sway from his assertion that he had lied so that he would be found guilty of murder.

In his summing up, the trial judge was scrupulously fair, telling the jury that in order to return a guilty verdict they must be satisfied that there was an intent to kill Ivy Warner by the prisoner. At one stage, Mr Justice Devlin told the jury, "He says he laid violent hands on the corpse of the woman he loved, and who had just died in his presence because he wanted to be accused of murder. Was this suicide by a process of judicial execution?"

The jury were out for two hours and 14 minutes in deciding their verdict. As the foreman announced that they had found Eaton guilty, but with a strong recommendation to mercy, the prisoner paled visibly. Asked if he had anything to say before the death sentence was passed, Eaton asked only that his parents should leave the court. No one moved and if Mr and Mrs Eaton were present, they too heard the dread words as Eaton was told he would be hanged by the neck until he was dead.

On February 28th, it was announced that Eaton would appeal against his sentence. That appeal was heard before the Lord Chief Justice, Lord Goddard and Justices Ormerod and Parker on March 17th, and even before it began there was drama. The prisoner had not been brought into court when a man stood up in the public gallery and shouted, "Before you hear this appeal, in the name of justice to God ..." At that point he was restrained by officers of the court but as he was forcibly ejected he cried, "In the name of Jesus Christ, abolish the death penalty."

The grounds of the appeal were that the trial judge had misdirected the jury as to the onus of proof, that he had failed to inform the jury that they must be satisfied that the prisoner had reasonable grounds to believe that the woman was still alive when he throttled her, and that the verdict itself was unreasonable and unsatisfactory. Giving the court's judgement, though, Lord Goddard said that Eaton had admitted his guilt to the first police officer on the scene and it was not until December 17th that he changed his story and claimed that he had put his hands around the throat of a woman he believed to be dead. Lord Goddard went on to describe this as a horrible murder and confirmed that the appeal would be dismissed. Soon afterwards it was announced that a new execution date had been set and Eaton would hang at Leicester at 9.00am on April 2nd 1952. In the event, Cyril Eaton did not face the hangman's noose. On March 28th, just four days before Eaton was due to die, the jury's recommendation and the circumstances of the case led the Home Secretary to recommend the Queen to commute the sentence to one of life imprisonment. The man who claimed he had wanted to commit suicide by having the State execute him, had been saved from just such a fate.

Chapter Twenty Two

Idle Tongues

AT 4.30am on Wednesday, October 15th, 1952, Alfred Osborne went into his son's bedroom at 'Bella Vista', Hill Crescent, Sutton-in-Ashfield, to see why he hadn't got up for his work as a hosiery knitter at George Edward & Sons Limited. Alfred found that his son, also named Alfred, was not too well, claiming that he had a splitting headache and didn't feel like going into work. Alfred took his son a cup of tea and an aspirin and when he left for his own work, at 6.00am, young Alfred Osborne was still in bed.

He stayed in bed all that morning and was not seen by his mother, Beatrice May Osborne, until 1.30pm, when he announced that he felt a little better now and soon afterwards left the house, wearing his raincoat. When he returned home, at around 6.40pm, Alfred Osborne Jnr was without that coat and had a most distressing story to tell. Only Beatrice was home at the time and he began by asking, "Has *(sic)* the police been for me?" Beatrice said that they hadn't and, now worried, asked why they could possibly have needed to. Osborne replied, "I've hit Mrs Bonsall, I've killed Mrs Bonsall."

Beatrice knew that the Mrs Bonsall to whom Osborne was referring was his girlfriend's mother who lived at 70 Somercotes Hill, Somercotes, near Alfreton, but before she could ask her son any further questions, Alfred Snr came home from work. He found his son confused and once again claiming that he had committed some terrible deed. The younger man turned to him and said, "I think I have hit Mrs Bonsall with a poker." Alfred and Beatrice tried to calm their son down, which took some considerable time, but he simply asked his father to take him to the police station. However, as the two men were about to leave the house, there was a sharp rap on the front door.

It was Osborne's father who opened the door to reveal Detective Sergeant Albert Shaw of the Mansfield police. It was 6.40pm as Shaw entered 'Bella Vista', identified himself and cautioned the younger Osborne, adding that he had orders to detain him for an attempted murder at Somercotes. Osborne replied, "I was just coming to the police station. Is she dead? How is she?" Sergeant Shaw did not reply to the questions but took his prisoner to the police station at Mansfield where he was questioned about the attack on Mrs Bonsall.

Osborne seemed only too keen to talk and told Sergeant Shaw, "I hit her with a poker, I think I hit her mother too. I don't know what happened. I have been courting her since I came out of hospital. We have fell (*sic*) out twice. I didn't go to work today. My head was bad. I went down to their house to straighten things out." At 7.35pm that night, Osborne was handed over to the custody of Detective Sergeant McLean and Constable John Reginald Cecil Clarke, who had travelled to Mansfield from Derbyshire. Osborne was told he would be taken to Alfreton in connection with the death of Mrs Bonsall. Upon hearing that the woman he admitted striking had died, Osborne burst into tears.

At 8.35pm, back at Alfreton, Osborne was charged with murder. He made no immediate reply to the charge but after pausing for a good few minutes, said, "I loved her very much, but she did not return it." Asked if he wished to write out his own statement, Osborne said that his hands were shaking too much and asked that it be written out for him. Later the document was read over to him and he signed it, when it was noticed that he still had bloodstains on his hands. The prisoner was then searched and when a key was found, he exclaimed "That's the key from Mrs Bonsall's front door."

There had been two people living at the house at 70 Somercotes Hill. The woman who Osborne was accused of murdering was 57-year-old Lilian Bonsall, a lady who had only been widowed in May, 1951. She had been born at Ripley, moved to Ilkeston for a while and then 25 years ago, had moved to Somercotes, finally settling in the house at Somercotes Hill. Her only child was Doreen May Bonsall, the girl with whom Alfred Osborne had been walking out, and she too had been attacked by Osborne, although she was now in hospital, her injuries were not life threatening.

The next day, Osborne appeared before the magistrates and details of the arrest were given by Constable Clarke. Osborne was then remanded for seven days and was granted legal aid after informing the court that his wages were £17 per week.

On October 20th, the inquest opened at Alfreton before Mr Michael Swanwick. Identification evidence was given by George William Fowkes of 3 Burleigh Street, Ilkeston, the dead woman's nephew, and medical testimony was given by Dr James Mathewson Webster who had performed the post-mortem. Mr Swanwick then adjourned the proceedings 'in view of the police inquiries which are now taking place'. The same day, Lilian Bonsall was buried at Leabrooks cemetery. The service took place at Somercotes parish church and among those attending were some of the police officers investigating the case.

Four days later, on October 24th, Osborne was back in the police court where he was remanded again, this time to October 31st. On that date Mr Max Mather, Osborne's solicitor, was not in court. He had spoken to the police who had confirmed that they were not ready to proceed and would ask for another remand. Since Mr Mather had another court appearance, he was excused and did not hear his client remanded to November 7th. One further remand followed and it was not until November 14th that all the testimony was heard, the case for the Director of Public Prosecutions being presented by Mr J. Michael Evelyn. Doreen Bonsall, who had been released from hospital on October 22nd, gave her evidence sitting down and wore a black diamond-shaped piece of material sewn to her dress as a sign of mourning for her mother. Having been sent for trial, Osborne appeared before Mr Justice Lynskey, at Birmingham, on December 12th. The case lasted for two days during which Mr R.C. Vaughan and Mr M.V. Argyle represented the accused. The Crown's case was led by Mr Walter Kelly Carter who was assisted by Mr Geoffrey Smallwood.

The most important witness was undoubtedly Doreen Bonsall, the dead woman's daughter and Osborne's one-time girlfriend. Doreen

stated that she worked as a clerk at Messrs George Edward & Sons
Limited, the same company which employed Osborne, and that this
was where they first met some two years ago. The friendship between
her and Osborne developed until, in March 1952, they started going out
together. They visited each other's houses and although they did have
one or two quarrels, these were soon made up and on the whole, their
relationship was a happy one.

On Sunday, October 12th, Doreen had seen Osborne at his home, at
about 6.30pm, and they had argued because she refused to have intercourse with him. Osborne said that he thought it best they end their
relationship and when he saw her home, at 10.30pm, he suggested she
get herself another boy because he was going to find himself another
girl.

The next day, Monday, Doreen saw Osborne at work and he passed
her a letter which she destroyed. Later he asked her to meet him that
night but as he was going off duty at 2.15pm he told her that she needn't
bother meeting that night if she didn't want to, as they could always
meet some other time. She told him that she was going out anyway, and
walked away from him.

On Tuesday, October 14th, Doreen again saw Osborne at the factory
but when he muttered to her, "Quarter to seven tonight," she did not
reply. Instead, Doreen asked him if he had found himself another job
and when he asked why, she had told him that it was about time he did.
A few hours later, Osborne again asked Doreen to meet him that night
and threatened that if she didn't, he would 'do something' to himself.
She ignored the remark, carried on with her duties and when she had
finished work, went straight home, arriving at 5.45pm

Doreen's mother was in when she got home, and was still there when
Doreen went out briefly at 6.45pm. However, when Doreen returned at
7.00pm, Lilian was not there. As was usual when she was in the house
alone, Doreen locked and bolted the back door but minutes later she
heard someone trying to get in. Doreen had her suspicions as to who
this might be, so she made no noise and sat by the fire in the dark until
8.30pm. Only then did she switch on the light in the living room, and at
that exact moment she heard Osborne's voice outside shout, "I know
you're in there, Doreen. I want a few words with you."

The noise came from outside the living room window but she did not answer him. Then Doreen heard the sound of footsteps going up the entry at the side of the house. She switched off the light and seconds later, Osborne tapped on the window and said that he was determined to see her if he had to wait all night. He then tried the door and window again, without success. As a result, Doreen sat in the dark until 10.15pm when her mother came home. Osborne was still waiting outside but Lilian spoke to him and he left. There was no more trouble that night.

On October 15th, Osborne was not in work. Doreen saw her mother at lunch time when she went home for her meal and finally returned home from work between 5.40pm and 5.45pm. Doreen walked straight into the living room and was dismayed to find Osborne sitting on the settee by the window. Doreen told him that he had given her a fright but Osborne ignored this and said, "I hope you're satisfied now. I've just killed your mother and I'm going to kill you." So saying, he stood up and began hitting her on the head with something. Doreen tried to escape by running into the kitchen but he followed her and they went back and forth between the two rooms with him constantly raining blows on her. After some time, Doreen shouted that she would go out with Osborne again if only he would stop hitting her. Osborne hesitated for a moment and Doreen seized her chance and dashed out of the back door, running next door to number 71 for help. Doreen was also able to state that the poker produced in court belonged to her mother and was normally kept on the hearth in the living room. She also confirmed that she and Osborne had discussed getting engaged earlier in the year and that Osborne had even been to Nottingham with his father to look at rings but she was not sure that she wanted to get engaged after all, although she had allowed Osborne to buy her things for her 'bottom drawer'.

The house at 71 Somercotes Hill was occupied by 80-year-old Mr May who was rather deaf. Unable to help Doreen himself, Mr May had in turned called Mrs R.H. Curtis who lived at 'Rose Dene', number 72. Mrs Curtis went into Mr May's house and found Doreen, who seemed stunned and had fresh cuts on her head. After hearing what had happened, Mrs Curtis bravely went to number 70 but there were no sound coming from within the house and so she went home and asked her husband to call the police.

Another man who helped Doreen was Ralph Edwin Langton, a

bricklayer who lived almost opposite to 70 Somercotes Hill. He heard the sound of someone running outside and saw the back door of number 71 opened by Doreen whose hair and face were covered in blood. He went across to Mr May's house and tried to calm Doreen down, she being almost hysterical at the time. He saw that the top of her forehead was bleeding heavily and after hearing what had happened, also went to number 70. Langton actually went inside the house and called out for Lilian. There was no reply and upon investigating further, Langton found Mrs Bonsall lying in the front room. There was no sign, however, of Osborne.

Constable Clarke, together with Sergeant Coope, were the first police officers to arrive on the scene. They went into number 70 through the back door and found the bloodstained poker lying on the floor of the back scullery. Going into the living room, they found Lilian Bonsall, lying on her back, a good deal of blood in her hair. After interviewing Doreen, they contacted their colleagues in Mansfield who said that they would send an officer around to Osborne's house and take him into custody.

At 6.10pm, Dr Patrick Colgan had arrived at the house and he confirmed that Lilian Bonsall was dead. Going next door to see Doreen, Dr Colgan found five lacerations on her head, the deepest of which was three-eighths of an inch. There were no fractures to the skull but Dr Colgan still sent her to hospital as the wounds required stitching. In his opinion, only a moderate amount of force would have been needed to inflict the injuries he observed on Doreen's head and they were consistent with the use of the handle of the poker shown to him by the police.

Evidence on the injuries inflicted on Lilian were given by Dr Webster. He had visited 70 Somercotes Hill at 6.25pm on October 15th, at which time the body had not been moved. Although there was blood in the hair, the condition of the neck and eyes suggested asphyxia as the cause of death. Looking around the premises, Dr Webster saw the poker in the back scullery, and a raincoat on the settee in the living room, both of which were bloodstained. There were splashes of blood on the wall and door of the scullery and also on the floor under the left arm of a chair. In addition, Dr Webster found pear-shaped bloodstains on the curtains in the passageway leading from the front room, and accounted for their shape by saying that they were consistent with someone flicking bloody fingers. Lack of any blood on the victim's clothing seemed to indicate that she had been attacked while sitting down and had slumped in the chair with her head over her left arm, and had remained in that position for some time before being dragged to the front room.

At the post-mortem, Dr Webster found bruises on Lilian's hands and wrists, abrasions to her right cheek and others on her nose and neck. Lilian's upper denture was still in place, the lower one having been found on the floor near her body. There were two injuries which had split the scalp, almost certainly caused by the poker. These blows could have rendered Lilian unconscious, but would not have killed her. The actual cause of death appeared to be manual strangulation, due to sustained and quite forceful pressure. In the doctor's opinion, the blood loss showed that there had been quite a passage of time between Lilian being knocked out and her death, suggesting that Osborne waited for some time before strangling her.

On the day of the murder, Osborne had left his home at 1.30pm. From there he had gone to a local billiard hall where he was seen by William Dennis, a friend of his, who had a game of snooker with him. The two men parted at 3.50pm, at which time Osborne seemed to be perfectly normal. Osborne even told Dennis a joke as he pulled his raincoat on.

The last sighting of Lilian had taken place at 4.30pm when Martha Williamson, who ran a grocery shop from 65 Somercotes Hill, served her with some bread and cakes. Lilian was her usual self as she set off towards her home.

Witnesses who had seen Osborne after the attack were now called. Averil Wright lived at 5 Tavistock Square, Alfreton and at 5.20pm on October 15th, she caught the bus at Eastwood which would take her back home. Averil was with a friend, Mrs Dobson, and they both went up to the top deck where Mrs Dobson pointed out a man they had subsequently identified as Osborne. He appeared to be nervous and agitated and when he brushed his hair back with his left hand, the two ladies saw that it was smeared with blood. Averil Wright got off the bus in High Street, Alfreton, but she saw Osborne again a few minutes later. He was standing in a bus queue outside Llewellyn's shop and at 6.00pm, he boarded the Mansfield bus.

Hilda Betty West was a bus conductress on the route from Alfreton to Derby. Although she did not remember seeing Osborne on the day in question, a bus ticket had been found in his possession and from the serial number on it, Hilda was able to say that it had been issued by her on the 4.35pm trip out of Alfreton. This was the route Osborne would have taken to get to Somercotes in the first place, and showed that he had arrived at Lilian's house after this time.

The statement Osborne had made was now read out in court. It began "Me and the girl Doreen had an argument last Sunday and I went down today to try and straighten things out. I apologised to her at work yesterday for the quarrel on Sunday. I went to her house last night at seven o'clock with the same purpose in mind of straightening things out.

"When I got to the house Doreen was in the house, her mother was out. She turned the lights out when the knock came on the door and you know, she pretended not to be in. I sat on the doorstep. Her mother came home just gone ten and she told me to come back another day. I went today at about five o'clock but I'm not sure. She asked me in and we spoke about Doreen. She told me Doreen didn't want to go out with me no more and then she was telling me of all the very unnice *(sic)* stories they were telling about me at work. I told her if they was true why didn't the persons concerned tell me, or why didn't she tell me the names of the persons who had said these things.

"I remarked there was two sides to a story and if they were true they had nothing to worry about. And then if they wasn't true I could make a note of it and see that the persons would get what they were asking for. I mean in the way of scandalising my name. She then remarked that she believed the stories and called me a liar and that's when I hit her.

"She was in the chair when I hit. I picked up a poker or stick or something from the side of the hearth. I just kept hitting her, my mind went blank. I was in a violent temper. Then I dragged her into the front room as I knew Doreen was coming home and I tidied the house up as much as I could. The rug was moved and I straightened that and I knocked the desk over as I was pulling her through to the front room and I put things back in much the same way as I found them. Then Doreen came in and I told her what I had done. No, before I told her what I had done, I asked her if she was satisfied with what she had done breaking us up like this and she replied, 'Yes, I am, it's all your fault you deserve it,' or something like that.

"I told her yesterday that I would take my own life as I had nothing to live for. She then told me she couldn't care less and one thing led to another and I hit her with the poker, I think. She then run out the door. I don't know which way she actually went but I run up the pad and out the gate and there was a bus just pulling up at the stop. I got on the bus to Alfreton and I just managed to catch the bus going to Mansfield. I went straight home and told my father what I had done and I told him I was going straight to the police station. He put his coat on and I put my work coat on as I had left my raincoat at Doreen's home. I was about to open the door when I was met by the police. That's it. The door key you found in my pocket belongs to the front door of Mrs Bonsall's house. When I dragged her into the front room, I tried the door and the key fell out in my hand."

Now, though, as Osborne stepped into the witness box, he gave a slightly different version of these events. After Mrs Bonsall had called him a 'damn nuisance' and told him to leave, she had grabbed for the poker. He pushed her away before she could get to it and picked it up himself but even before he could use it, he received a blow to the back of the neck and remembered nothing more until he saw her unconscious before him. Osborne said he then tried to revive Lilian with a cup of tea but then he panicked and became horrified and frightened at what he had apparently done.

Turning to earlier events, Osborne said that he loved Doreen very much and had wanted them to get engaged on his birthday but she said she wanted to wait. He agreed that they had quarrelled over sex but he had apologised and said he hadn't meant it when he said he would find another girl.

After Doreen refused to see him on the night of October 14th, he slept badly and woke up with a terrible headache. As he lay in bed that morning, he thought of Mrs Bonsall, who he looked upon as a second mother, and made up his mind to visit her in order to ask her to intercede on his behalf. On the way, he even took out an endowment policy as a sign of his good faith, so that Doreen would have her future safeguarded when they married.

Lilian Bonsall was friendly at first but later she said she had heard bad things about him from people that Doreen worked with. Osborne denied all the stories but she said she believed them and was glad that Doreen had come to her senses in time. She went on to say that she knew his parents thought he was an angel but that was only because he told them a pack of lies. It was then that she tried to throw him out, caught him over the right eye and went for the poker.

When Osborne came to, Lilian was unconscious in the armchair. He dragged her to the front room but had never touched her throat at any time. When Doreen came in he was explaining to her what had happened when she screamed and according to Osborne, "Everything just went dizzy to me. I just can't remember anything." He denied ever telling Doreen that he was going to kill her.

In their summing up, the prosecution tried to suggest that Lilian had been strangled accidentally when she was dragged from one room to the other. Despite this, the all-male jury took only 50 minutes to decide that Osborne was guilty of murder. Doreen Bonsall was outside the courtroom as the verdict was announced and after being told the result she left the building in tears.

Alfred Osborne never faced the hangman's noose. On December 28th, the Home Secretary announced that he had recommended a reprieve. At the same time, Imre Kilyen, a Hungarian who had killed his three-month old son, Joseph, also had his death sentence respited.

Chapter Twenty-Three

A Game of Cat And Mouse

AT around 11.00pm on Saturday, June 4th, 1960, a man was found staggering along Boythorpe Road in Chesterfield. At first, people who saw him thought that he might be a drunk but when it was seen that he was bleeding badly from facial injuries, he was taken to hospital for treatment. Here he was interviewed by the police, identified himself as William Atkinson, a married man of 77 Church Lane, North Wingfield, and explained that he was simply walking along Boythorpe Road when a man came up behind him and attacked him for no reason. The police had little else to go on and eventually the case was left on file.

Eight days after this apparently unprovoked attack, Roland England, a university student from Liverpool, was cycling along a thoroughfare known as Clod Hall Lane, near Baslow. It was some time between 12.30pm and 12.45pm on Sunday, June 12th, and as Roland travelled slowly down the lane, something in the ditch caught his eye. The object, whatever it was, could easily have been missed by someone passing in a car but Roland's eye level was higher since he was on a bicycle. Going closer, he saw to his horror that he had found the body of a man. He pedalled furiously to the nearest public telephone box and called the police.

It was 1.30pm by the time Sergeant George Joseph Venables had met Roland England at the call box and been taken back to the ditch on Clod Hall Lane. There was indeed a body and although it was clear that the poor man was already beyond all human aid, Sergeant Venables contacted Dr Sinclair Morris Evans who arrived on the scene an hour later, at 2.30pm. He pronounced life extinct but at the request of the police did not make a full examination of the body because a Home Office pathologist, Dr David Ernest Price had already been summoned.

Dr Price made an initial examination of the scene. There was torn grass around the body as if someone had tried to cover the man, implying that this was not something as simple as a hit and run accident. The victim, whoever he was, was fully clothed except that he had no footwear, headgear or a coat. There were many marks of violence upon the body including horseshoe-shaped marks behind the left ear and across the front of the neck, and geometric patterns on the right side of the face. It looked as if the head had been resting on a hard surface, such as the gravel of a road, when someone had stamped on the man. There were other signs that kicks had been administered and Dr Price determined that there had been at least one, possibly as many as three blows, to the head, causing blackening of the eyes and fractures to the skull. In the victim's mouth, there remained just the top set of dentures, which were themselves heavily bloodstained. Although a full post-mortem would be necessary to confirm it, Dr Price believed that the man had been kicked and beaten to death.

Earlier that same day, a curious incident in Chesterfield, had also been investigated by the police. Fred Victor Clarke was asleep in his front bedroom at 138 Park Road when in the early hours of June 12th he was awoken by a loud crash. Getting out of bed, Clarke glanced at the clock and saw that it was 3.25am. Looking out of the window, Clarke now saw that the cause of the noise had been a bubble car which was now lying on its side in the road. He told his wife what he had seen and both went downstairs to see if anyone in the car had been hurt. The car, though, was empty and the door was closed, although not locked. The police were called and soon Constable William Howe and Constable Gibbs were examining the vehicle.

Constable Howe timed his arrival at Park Road at 3.35am. The car was a yellow bubble car registration 488 KNU. The engine was not running, the lights were not lit and although the door was unlocked, it was difficult to open since it had been badly damaged when the car had hit a nearby lamp post, which bore flecks of yellow paint. Inside the vehicle was a heavily bloodstained Burberry mackintosh, and a pair of shoes which were wedged among the car's controls. There were splashes of blood inside the car and two feet away, on the pavement, Howe found a pair of spectacles and a lower set of dentures.

A registration check on the car showed that it belonged to William Arthur Elliott, a clerk at the teacher's training college at Thornbridge Hill, Great Longstone, who lived with his sister, Sarah Elliott, at 9 Haddon Road, Bakewell. When Miss Elliott was visited by the police she said that her brother had left home, in his car, at sometime around 9.30am on Saturday, June 11th. She was able to identify the mackintosh and shoes as belonging to her brother, and confirmed that he often went into Chesterfield alone, for a drink.

It did not take long for the police to connect the finding of the bubble car in Park Road with the body in Clod Hall Lane. The items of clothing apparently missing from the body had been found in the bubble car and separate dentures had been found at both sites. At 8.15pm on June 12th, Sarah Elliott was taken to the mortuary to view the Clod Hall Lane body. The police assumption had been correct. The corpse was that of 60-year-old William Arthur Elliott.

Since Elliott had told his sister that he was going into Chesterfield, an appeal was made for anyone who might have seen him in any of his regular haunts. This brought forward a number of witnesses who helped police piece together the Elliott's movements in the hours before he died. Thomas Frederick May was a friend of Elliott's and had seen him in a cafe in Chesterfield at 4.30pm. At 9.30pm, he had been spotted window-shopping by Montague Pashley, another friend, and at around 10.15pm, Elliott had been seen leaving a public toilet near the East Midlands bus station. Joseph Henry Hicks was a bus driver and had been on the service from Tideswell on the night of June 11th. His vehicle had arrived at Chesterfield at 9.45pm and was due out again at 10.35pm. Since he had some spare time, Hicks took the opportunity to use the toilets and as he walked in, Elliott was coming out. There could be no mistaking this sighting for the two men knew each other, albeit only slightly, and exchanged polite greetings.

The inquest on Elliott opened on June 15th, before Mr Frederick R.S. Nesbitt, when it was pointed out that William Atkinson, who had been attacked on June 4th, bore a striking resemblance to Elliott and it was suggested that this might have been a mistake, the attacker believing that he might have been striking Elliott, someone he possibly bore a grudge against. William Atkinson described the assault upon himself, although he could speak only with difficulty since he had sustained a broken jaw in the attack and had also lost several teeth. He did say, though, that he would recognise the man's voice again and that he spoke with a Derbyshire accent. Atkinson also testified that he had known the dead man and used to meet him occasionally in the Spread Eagle public house, in Chesterfield. Indeed, he had seen Elliott in the Spread Eagle on June 4th, the very night that he himself had been attacked.

Medical testimony was given by Dr Price who confirmed that Elliott had died from a fractured skull, shock, and intra-cranial haemorrhage. The inquest was then adjourned for four weeks so that the police could continue their investigations, Detective Superintendent E. Stretton having been put in charge of the case.

In fact, the police already knew much more than they had revealed in the newspapers of the day. After the body had been found in Clod Hall Lane, identified as Elliott and his movements traced, William Atkinson was re-interviewed about the attack upon him. He now admitted that he was a practising homosexual and at 10.30pm on June 4th, had visited the public toilets in Markham Road where he met a man who he believed was a soldier on leave. The two men fell into conversation and the 'soldier' agreed to go to the Queen's Park Annexe for sexual purposes. After the act was completed, the man turned on Atkinson, attacked him and left him for dead.

Other information had also come in which seemed to underline the links between the attack upon Atkinson and the murder of Elliott, who by now had also been identified as a homosexual.

Irene Roe Mitchell ran a fish and chip shop from 226 Derby Road and having heard about the murder had come forward to tell the police about one of her customers. After a busy night on June 11th, Irene was just closing her shop, it now actually being 12.25am on June 12th. A man who lived nearby came up to her and asked if she had any fish and chips left. Irene told him she hadn't, whereupon the man walked away, only to return a few minutes later to ask, "Well, have you a match to give me then?" Irene said she had, but asked him to wait until she had finished washing down the step. Once she had done so, she walked into the shop, to be followed by the young man. As she handed over a box of matches, she noticed that the knuckles on one of his hands were bleeding heavily. There was also blood on one side of his face. Irene had known the man for some years and told the police that his name was Michael Copeland, a soldier who had arrived home on leave the very day that William Atkinson had been attacked.

At 9.15am on June 16th, Detective Sergeant Andrew Ingles Wright and Detective Constable Stoneleigh went to Copeland's home at 18 St Augustine's Crescent, Chesterfield, and asked him to account for the blood seen by Mrs Mitchell. Copeland was only too happy to detail his movements on the night of June 11th. He explained that he had left home at 5.00pm and gone to a friend's house at 204 Park Road. He stayed there until 7.00pm when he and the friend, Alan Pickering, went to the Nag's Head together. They had a few drinks, remaining there until 10.30pm when he left Pickering and began the walk home. On the way, Copeland said he was assaulted by two teddy boys and he lashed out at them, hitting one in the face, which accounted for his bleeding knuckles. After that, Copeland said he went home but felt a bit 'fuzzy' and went out for a walk. That was when he had called at the fish and chip shop on Derby Road. For the time being, the police were satisfied with that explanation and left Copeland alone.

That night, though, other information came to the attention of the investigating officers and this also linked Michael Copeland's name to the crime. Carol Brenda Bright had been in Queen's Park with a friend on June 13th when she had first met Copeland. The two got on well together and during the evening, Copeland brought up the subject of the bubble car murder. This was perhaps nothing unusual since this was the main topic of conversation in Chesterfield at the time, but Copeland continued to refer to it over the next few days.

On June 16th, she had met up with Copeland again and he mention-ed that the police had been to see him about the murder. The couple caught a bus to Baslow and it was there that Copeland said he wanted to tell her something. They were standing together on a bridge over a stream and Copeland announced, "I murdered a man in Birdholme." Carol told him 'not to be so silly', although she hadn't thought from his manner that Copeland was joking. When they were standing at a bus stop some time later, Copeland had smiled and said, "You didn't believe me did you? Don't you think I am a good actor?"

When Carol had gone home and reported this conversation to her father, he had immediately contacted the police and made her repeat the story to them. As a result, Copeland was visited again on June 17th when he was asked to come into Chesterfield police station and make a formal statement. While he was there, officers searched Copeland's home, but nothing incriminating was found. There was little other evidence to link Copeland to the crime and after repeating much of what he had said before, he was allowed to go home.

It was about this time that two witnesses came forward and gave information which might help to pinpoint the time of Elliott's death. Brian Ralph Cooper and his wife, Sheila Fay Cooper, lived in Sheffield but on June 11th they were visiting her mother at 534 Chatsworth Road, Chesterfield. The couple left there at 11.20pm and on the way home were driving along Clod Hall Lane. They saw a bubble car which they thought might be yellow, or possibly orange, facing towards Chesterfield, parked on the grass verge. There was a man in front of the car and he turned his back on the Coopers as their car approached him. He was tall and slim, clean shaven and appeared to be fiddling around with the car's door lock. Both Brian and Sheila attended an identification parade in which Copeland appeared, but neither was able to pick him out.

By June 20th, the number of people who had been interviewed was more than 250. Just two days later, this had risen to several thousand and it was stated that anyone who wished to volunteer information would not be visited at their homes by uniformed officers, this being an attempt to get the homosexual community to talk to the police.

By June 29th, house-to-house inquiries had been extended to the whole of Chesterfield and by the time the investigation began to run out of momentum, more than 100,000 people had been spoken to. Eventually the inquest returned a verdict that Elliott had been murdered by a person or persons unknown and for the time being that is where matters rested, although there were senior officers who could not help but believe that Michael Copeland had been responsible. He lived close to where the bubble car had been left, had confessed to a girl that he had committed the murder, sported bloodstains of the night of the crime and his explanation that he had been involved in a fight with two teddy boys was never proved. Nevertheless, the murder of William Arthur Elliott was officially listed as unsolved.

Michael Copeland was a serving soldier and after his leave was over, he returned to his unit at the Caithness barracks in Verden in northern Germany. It was there that later the same year, another murder took place.

Guenther Marchlewski was a civil servant who lived at 4 Karl-Heisse Strasse in Verden and on November 13th, he was walking back into the town along Lindhooper Strasse. Passing the side of the British Army barracks, he could see into the woods across the way and saw a young man and a young girl talking. Marchlewski chose this precise moment to look at his watch. It was 9.47pm.

Further along the pathway, Marchlewski noticed another man standing in the shadow of a large tree. He was some 40 metres away from the young couple but appeared to be studying them intently. Herr Marchlewski walked on and stood at a bus stop. He was still there a few minutes later when three girls came running out of the woods and asked him where they could telephone for a policeman. One of the girls, the one he had seen in the forest just minutes before, said she and her boyfriend had been attacked.

Herr Marchlewski told the girls that the nearest place with a telephone was Glinz the barber's and as they ran there, he dashed back into the forest only to meet two men who were carrying the injured boy out. They all waited with the boy until the police and a doctor arrived.

Police Inspector Heinz Ludwig Burdorf was the first officer to arrive and he was there when Dr Sommerfeld arrived and pronounced the boy dead. Inspector Burdorf then began interviewing all the witnesses. The girl who had been with the dead boy, Inge Alma Ella Hoppe, identified him as Guenther Helmbrecht, and said he was only 15 years old. Inge said that they had gone to the pictures together and the film had ended just before 9.00pm. From there, they had walked through the town forest to a small summer hut known as the Schutzhutte where they had hoped to be alone but were disappointed to find another couple already there. They waited until the others left before going into the hut for a cuddle.

After they had been there for perhaps ten minutes, Inge noticed a man walk past and look into the hut. He then walked on a little way and stood near a large tree, watching them. She became nervous at this and suggested to Guenther that they leave. They walked off together down the pathway but Inge heard footsteps behind them. The man was now following them.

As the man drew near, Inge took hold of Guenther's arm and pulled him to one side to allow the man to pass. The man, though, did not pass but instead attacked Guenther and did something to his neck, with a knife. As Guenther fell, Inge ran into Lindhooper Strasse where she met two men, Herr Varrelmann and Herr Strueuer, at the bus stop. Telling them what had happened, they ran back into the forest to see if they could help while she and the young women who were accompanying the men ran to Herr Marchlewski and asked him for help.

Hans Dieter Varrelmann had been standing at the stop with Analiese Conrad when Inge told him what had happened. He went into the forest with Herr Strueuer, found Guenther and helped to carry him out of the woods. This was confirmed by Adolf Strueuer who had been with Helga Hian. Indeed, it had been Adolf and Helga who had first been in the summer hut when Inge and Guenther arrived.

While all this had been going on, a British soldier had arrived back at the camp, suffering from a stab wound to his thigh. Robert Edward Twisser was the guard commander on November 13th, 1960, when the signalman, Michael Copeland, was brought into the guard room, his trouser leg soggy with blood. The trousers were removed and a wound seen in Copeland's upper leg. It had already stopped bleeding but the regimental orderly officer was called to see what had happened for himself.

Ronald Porter was the RMO and he entered the guardroom some time between 9.00pm and 10.00pm. Copeland was now on the floor, and it could be seen that the cut on his leg was quite severe. He also had a quantity of dried blood on his hands. Copeland said that he had been attacked by two German civilians. Other witnesses also heard this story, including David Flower, a medical orderly, who arrived soon after

Porter, at around 10.00pm. Once news of the murder of the German boy became public, though, it was decided to check out Copeland's story more carefully and to question him more thoroughly.

The deputy assistant Provost Marshall, Robert John Sherville, listened to Copeland's story at 10.30pm and then went outside the camp to where Copeland said the attack had taken place, to search for signs of a struggle. None could be found and the matter was now put in the hands of Captain Hubert Lambert, the officer commanding 70 Section of the Special Investigation Branch of the Royal Military Police.

By the time Captain Lambert saw Copeland, he had already spoken to Sherville. Lambert listened patiently to Copeland's story and then informed him that no signs of the struggle he described had been found. He also informed Copeland that a German youth had been found murdered that same night, to which Copeland replied, "That's right, blame every murder on me. I know you." For the time being, though, the matter was allowed to rest there and Copeland removed to the British Military Hospital at Hanover for treatment on his leg wound.

At the end of November, Captain Lambert interviewed Copeland again and suggested that he was responsible for the murder of Guenther Helmbrecht. He asked Copeland to demonstrate how the man who attacked him had wielded the knife and when Copeland did so, pointed out that the direction of his wound was inconsistent with the scenario he had described. Lambert then said, "Copeland, I now want a straight answer. Did you kill Helmbrecht?" Copeland made no reply.

On December 2nd, Captain Lambert, together with Major John Biddlecombe of the Military Police, interviewed Copeland again and told him he would be placed in an identification parade. Inge Hoppe and Herr Marchlewski were then asked to look at the men in the line-up carefully. Inge failed to pick anyone out but Guenther Marchlewski had no hesitation in picking out Copeland as the man he had seen in the woods, watching the young lovers.

Told that a witness had picked him out, Copeland replied, "The girl didn't, so why should I worry?" He was then asked about a flick knife he had once owned, but claimed that he had lost it some time before the attack on the German boy. Asked to describe the knife, Copeland became arrogant and shouted, "No, if you want the knife badly, then you had better find it." Later he added that if they thought he was involved in Helmbrecht's murder, they had better prove it.

The post-mortem on Guenther Helmbrecht was carried out by Dr Horst Lenz and Dr Adolph Schmidt. They found 27 stab wounds in all: ten in the boy's back, one in his neck, one in the left side of his throat, two in the right side of his chest, six more in the chest, one in the abdomen, two in the upper left arm, one in the lower left arm, one in the upper right arm, one in the thigh itself and one more in the outside of the thigh. The subsequent inquest returned the expected verdict of murder by person or persons unknown and since the murder weapon could not be found, Michael Copeland was not charged with the crime. He continued to serve in the Army until his discharge in January, 1961, when he returned to Chesterfield.

Frank Henry Royal Asker was a lorry driver from Dereham in Norfolk but at 8.15am on March 29th, 1961, he was driving his vehicle along Clod Hall Lane at Baslow when, from the vantage point of his cab, he saw something lying on the grass verge. Finding that it was the body of a man, Asker drove on to Baslow itself where he reported the matter to the police. By 1.05pm, Dr David Price, the same pathologist who had examined the body of William Elliott, was examining this new, as yet unidentified body, and not failing to notice that the man had been dumped very close to the spot where Elliott had lain. Once again, the head and shoulders of the man were covered in grass and, if anything, this attack had been even more severe, since there was some brain tissue lying on the grass nearby. Like Elliott, the man had not been attacked where he was found and also like Elliott, the initial examination showed that he had been beaten and kicked to death.

Even now, the astounding similarities to the Elliott case were continuing. At 12.50pm that same day, Detective Constable Alan Robert Nuttall and Detective Constable Fountain had been called to Park Road in Chesterfield. A car had been reported as being abandoned outside numbers 160 to 162 just yards from where Elliott's bubble car had been found the previous year. The car was a 1930 model Morris Oxford, registration JN 230. The key had been left in the ignition, the lights had been switched off and when the officers checked inside the car they found a grey tweed overcoat, a grey suit jacket and a folded ground sheet, all stained with blood. There were other blood stains on the rear of the seat and smears on the rear passenger window. On the back seat lay a bloodstained walking stick, alongside a buff envelope and a pair of glasses. The registration was checked and the owner revealed as George Gerald Stobbs of 27 Mansfield Road, Newbold, Chesterfield.

The police already had little doubt that they had identified their latest murder victim and a visit to the house in Mansfield Road found Mrs Josephine Cecile Stobbs who reported that her husband had left home the previous night at 8.50pm and never returned. Indeed, Mrs Stobbs had already reported her husband as a missing person. Later that day, she attended the Bakewell mortuary and identified the body found in Clod Hall Lane as her husband. The press immediately dubbed the story the 'Carbon Copy Murder'.

Something of the history of the dead man was published in the local newspapers. Born on January 2nd, 1913, he had been educated at Dulwich College in London. During the war he had served in the Intelligence Corps and on February 19th, 1944, had married Josephine Sorapura. Since then, the family had grown by two boys, the first born on June 6th, 1947 and the second on November 22nd, 1948. Mr Stobbs had worked for some years as a chemist for Robertson & Woodcock Ltd, sweet manufacturers, and had been transferred to their Chesterfield branch on May 16th, 1960. For the first couple of months in Derbyshire, he had lived alone at the Clifton Hotel, subsequently taking a lease on the furnished property in Mansfield Road, where his wife had joined him in July. Both of the boys were at public schools.

As far as the police were concerned, there could only be one suspect in this murder: Michael Copeland. Nevertheless, the investigation did not operate on that simple assumption and a careful reconstruction of Stobbs' movements on March 28th, was made.

Stobbs had gone to work as normal on that day and at 6.30pm had visited a garage owned by Charles Reginald Bradley to pick up his car after it had been serviced. At 6.40pm, Stobbs had driven to the Wheatsheaf Inn at Newbold where he had been served by the landlord, Leslie Heap. As if confirmation of this sighting were required, the rather distinctive old car had been seen parked outside by another customer, Harold Downing.

After having one pint in the Wheatsheaf, Stobbs had driven home where he arrived at 6.45pm, a family friend, Julia Margaret Weekes arriving there at the same time. Julia Weekes was returning some gramophone records she had borrowed and she left as Stobbs settled down to enjoy his dinner. After he had eaten, Stobbs told his wife that he had to go back to work, might call at a pub when he had finished, but would certainly be home by 10.30pm. He left the house at 8.50pm, which was the last time his wife saw him alive.

In fact, Stobbs did not return to his work. Like Elliott the previous year, Stobbs enjoyed the company of men and was well known in homosexual circles. The return to work was an excuse he used to leave the house again.

Between 9.00pm and 10.00pm, Stobbs was in the Three Horseshoes pub in Chesterfield, where he was seen by Fred Haslam, the licensee, Ellen Crow, one of the barmaids, and Joseph Langstaff, the pub pianist. All of these witnesses claimed that Stobbs had been alone when they saw him. Another of the barmaids there was Joyce Mitchell and although she was not on duty that night, she had called into the pub for a drink. She, too, saw Stobbs in the bar and later, at 11.10pm, saw him standing in the Market Place.

Other people also claimed to have seen Stobbs in other public houses that night, but the police treated their statements with some caution since they did not fit in with the times of other sightings. Martha Heathcote claimed to have seen him in the Golden Fleece at 9.40pm to 9.50pm and Stobbs was also supposed to have been in the Crown and Cushion between 9.00pm and 9.30pm. This last sighting, although again doubtful, was of special interest because the landlord's son, Christopher John Feltrup, thought that Stobbs had been in the company of another regular, Michael Copeland. Christopher's sister, Susan Lee Feltrup, agreed that Copeland had definitely been in that night, but she said she had not noticed Stobbs.

By the evening of March 29th, there was another development in the case. Frances Adlington had been walking on the footpath through Gladwyn Wood at Wingerworth, at around 5.15pm, when she found a diary lying on the middle of the path. Frances took the diary home and read that it belonged to one George Gerald Stobbs. Later, when she heard of the discovery of Stobbs' body, she contacted the police and at 7.35pm handed the diary over to Detective Inspector Bradshaw.

It had always been known that neither Elliott nor Stobbs had been murdered where their bodies had been found. Both men had been killed elsewhere and their bodies driven, in their own cars, to Clod Hall Lane. The place where Elliott had been attacked had never been found during the investigation into his death but now that Stobbs' diary had been found in the wood, it seemed reasonable to assume that his murder had taken place somewhere in that area. On March 30th, the police investigation moved to Wingerworth and at Stubbing Court that same day, Constable Nuttall found a penknife and a bunch of keys in a pile of dead leaves at the foot of a stone wall. These were subsequently shown to Mrs Stobbs who confirmed that they had belonged to her husband. It was also on March 30th that Constable Brian Bernard Huntington found a parking permit in Gladwyn Lane near Stubbing Court and this, too, belonged to the dead man.

Other events took place on March 30th. At 3.00pm that day, Detective Sergeant Frank Hulme and Detective Constable Stoneley took Michael Copeland in to the police station for interview. At the same time, other officers, headed by Detective Inspector G.W. Stephen, made a careful search of Copeland's house but as before, nothing was found to link him to this crime. Asked to account for his movements on March 28th, Copeland became aggressive but later said that he had been out alone visiting various pubs but got home well before midnight. Copeland was at the police station from 3.00pm until 8.30pm but he made no admission of guilt and eventually had to be released.

The inquest also opened on March 30th, again before Mr Nesbitt, and after evidence of identification was given, the proceedings were adjourned with no date fixed for their resumption. Medical testimony had already been given by Dr Price who confirmed that death was due to shock following cerebral lacerations as a result of a compound fracture of the skull.

By April 3rd, ten men had been traced, all of whom admitted having homosexual relations with Stobbs but none of the ten had ever heard of Copeland. The facts of Stobbs' double life were announced in the press this same day and any other witnesses asked to come forward. The next day, the police visited all the dry-cleaners in Chesterfield and the surrounding areas to see if anyone had brought in bloodstained or muddy clothing.

On April 5th, witnesses had been found who could narrow down the time that Stobbs' car was abandoned in Park Road. Alan Grainger was a porter for British Rail and late on March 28th, he had been told to fetch Fred Pashley from his house at 16 Summerfield Road. Grainger had cycled to Pashley's house and at one point had passed up Park Road. It was by then 2.15am on March 29th and the old Morris car was not parked in Park Road. However, the car was seen at 3.00am by Frederick James Pashley when he had returned to the rail depot with Grainger, who also noticed the vehicle.

Every attempt was made to apprehend the man responsible for the so-called copycat murders. On April 6th, detectives even sat in the reading room at the Chesterfield public library to see if anyone seemed to be paying particular interest in reports of the crime in the newspapers there. The next day, Alan Priest, another witness, came forward. He had been up in Stubbing Court Woods on his motorbike at 10.15pm on March 28th and had seen a car parked there. While he was watching, a man passed in front of the headlights and the car then drove off. Unfortunately, Alan was unable to give a detailed description of either the man, or the car.

The investigation brought fresh tragedies to light. On April 8th, an inquest opened on John Douglas Robert Mart, a 66-year-old hairdresser of 573 Chatsworth Road, Chesterfield. Another homosexual, he had been interviewed as a matter of routine but this had preyed on his mind and he had killed himself in his gas-filled shop. He had never been a suspect in the crime but had killed himself within three hours of being spoken to by the police.

Once again, the investigation petered out and although the police felt sure that Michael Copeland was responsible, they had little or no chance of proving it at the moment. Only now was it decided that Copeland would be watched constantly in the hope that if he didn't crack and confess to the three murders he was believed to have committed, at least he would be unable to claim a fourth victim.

Over the next few years, the police played a dangerous game of cat and mouse with Copeland. It was made plain that he was being watched and wherever he went, there seemed to be policemen about. Occasionally, this upset Copeland and his frustrations spilled over into violence. On May 22nd, 1961, Copeland assaulted Detective Sergeant Hibbert and Detective Constable Morley, who he had observed watching him, but no further action was taken against him in this matter. The same could not be said for an incident which took place on June 11th, in the Crown and Cushion pub.

Copeland was drinking by himself on the night of June 11th and suddenly seemed to fall ill. Concerned, the landlord called the police and as Sergeant Thorneycroft and another officer arrived, Copeland came round and shouted, "Who's fetched the bloody police?" An assault on Sergeant Thorneycroft followed, for which Copeland was arrested. He appeared in the Chesterfield Borough magistrate's court the following day and received four months' imprisonment.

In fact, this was not the first time that Michael Copeland had been in trouble with the law. Born on April 14th, 1938, he had left school at 15 and started work as a haulage hand in the mines. His first appearance in court came in April 1954 when he was put on probation for 12 months for larceny involving £4. In June of that year he was back in court for burglary and larceny and was sent to an approved school, being released on February 4th, 1956.

In April 1956 he was charged with housebreaking and possessing a firearm for which he appeared at Derbyshire assizes on June 11th, 1956, and was sent back to the approved school. Released at the beginning of 1957, Copeland now did various farm labouring jobs before being arrested, again for housebreaking and larceny. He appeared at Leeds City quarter sessions on April 11th, 1957 when eight other offences were taken into consideration and Copeland was sent to Borstal. In August he absconded and committed further offences before he was arrested at Gloucester in September and sent back to Borstal.

Released from this last sentence, he joined the Royal Corps of Signals on February 5th, 1959 and served until his discharge in January 1961. Now he was back in custody for assault and was also suspected of three murders.

In fact, Copeland had also been suggested as a possible suspect in a fourth murder. On the night of January 16th, 1960, a car had been stolen in Poole, Dorset. At 1.30am on January 17th, Lilian Emily Maud Tharme had been driving home from a dinner when that stolen car collided with her vehicle. Lilian was then abducted by the driver of the other car, taken elsewhere, stripped naked and driven back towards Poole. On the way, the car crashed again and Lilian was dragged from

Inside room 2 at the Carlton Hotel, London Road, Derby. The body of Ivy May Warner can be seen in the bed, having been killed by John Cyril Eaton who mistakenly thought she was pregnant. See Chapter 21. (Public Record Office)

Another view of room 2, this time taken from the bedroom door. The bed in which Eaton slept is to the right. See Chapter 21. (Public Record Office)

The house at 70 Somercotes Hill (right) where Lilian Bonsall was killed by Alfred Osborne. See Chapter 22. (Public Record Office)

The body of Lilian Bonsall in situ. See Chapter 22. (Public Record Office)

DERBY EVENING TELEGRAPh

LATE FINAL

INCORPORATING THE DERBY DAILY EXPRESS

No. 22,241   FRIDAY, DECEMBER 12, 1952   TWOPENCE

'A SIMPLE CASE OF MURDER'

Q.C.'s submission at trial of Osborne

trial of Alfred Osborne (25), hosiery knitter, "Bella Vista," Hill-crescent, Sutton-in-Ash-..for the murder of a 57-year-old Somercotes . Mrs. Lilian Bonsall, opened before Mr. Jus-...nsley at Birmingham Assizes to-day.

...orne is accused of murdering Mrs. Bonsall ... home, 70, Somercotes-hill, on October 15.

. Kelly Carter, Q.C., who prosecuted, submitted that it "plain and simple case of murder," Mrs. Bonsall, he ..having been struck by Osborne with a poker and then ...ed.

...e, who wore the same, ...and black bow tie in ... appeared in Alfreton ...tes' Court, pleaded ...illy" in a clear, firm ...

Carter and Mr. Geoffrey ...ood appeared to prose-d Osborne was defended ... R. C. Vaughan, Q.C., Michael Argyle.

..arter, opening the case ...prosecution, said that woman lived with her ...'d daughter, Doreen ... a junior clerk in the ...n department of ...Edwards, and Sons ...manufacturers, of ...otes.

...ne, a single man, also ...t the firm as a hosiery

...Doreen and ...out to ...house; ...went ...in-...er.

...a qu. ...r. Carte ...made un ...took plac ...

AD QUA ...day, Octo ...hey ...s parents' n ...Ashfield. Tl ...they ...rrel and Mi ...onsall ...that the cau ...of the ...her refusal t ...have ...with him.

...en said he thought ...ip should end.

...work, however, ...xt day Osborne ...n a letter which ...showed to another

...day, October 15, ...to work as usual, ...id not. When his ...d him at 4.30 a.m. ...d a splitting head-

...m. that day Osborne ...ome and went to a ...saloon in Sutton-in-...where he played ...with a man called ...dennis until about 3.50

...nsall was last seen ...30 p.m. that day when ...to a shop at 65, Somer-

...p.m. a conductress on ...elling from Alfreton ...'a Somercotes, issued ...ich was later found ... raincoat.

...p.m. Doreen Bonsall ...me from work and on ...the living-room she saw ...sitting on a settee. She ...sed to see him there. ...Oh, you did frighten

...lied, Mr. Carter alleged, ...you are satisfied now. ...just killed your mother, ...m going to kill you."

'HIT ON HEAD'

...said: "Oh, no," at which ...e got up and started to ...er over the head with a ...er, alleged Mr. Carter. She ...an from one room to another ... avoid the bl...

Osborne was not seen actually leaving the house, but he was seen on a bus returning from Somercotes to Alfreton and later in a bus queue in Alfreton. He got home at 6.40 p.m. and said to his mother: "Have the police been for me?" She replied " No. The police? What-ever for?"

He answered: "I have hit Mrs. Bonsall. I have killed Mrs. Bonsall," alleged Mr. Carter. Later the police arrived and Osborne was arrested.

When the police went ' to Somercotes-hill they found Mrs. Bonsall lying in the front room. In the scullery was a blood-stained poker.

Osborne was taken to Mans-field Police Station. There he was told by P.-c. Clarke what had happened and he began to cry and said: "She is not dead, is she?"

He was cautioned and he said: "I loved her very much, but she did not return it." This clearly referred to Miss Bonsall, said Mr. Carter.

Osborne, in an alleged statement, said that he went to Somercotes-hill and Mrs. Bonsall and he talked about himself and Doreen. Mrs. Bonsall said that Doreen didn't want to go out with Osborne any more and mentioned the "very un-nice stories" that were being told about them at work.

"MIND WENT BLANK"

Osborne replied, went on the statement, that these should have been made to his face and that there were two sides to any story. Mrs. Bonsall then said she believed the stories and called him a liar.

"I picked up a poker or a stick, or something like that, from the side of the hearth, and hit her and just kept hitting her until my mind went blank. I was in a violent temper," Osborne's alleged statement went on.

"I dragged her into the front room, as I knew Doreen was coming home, and tried to tidy things up as much as I could. Then Doreen came in and I told her what I had done. No, before I told her that I asked her if she was satisfied with what she had done with breaking us up.

"She said 'Yes, I am. It is all your fault. You deserved it' or something like that. I told her yesterday I would take my life and she said 'I couldn't care less.' One thing lead to an-other and I hit her with the poker and she ran away."

Mr. Carter said that Professor Webster, the pathologist, was called to the house and found Mrs. Bonsall had wounds on the

Turn to back page

ALFRED OSBORNE

DRIVER OF TRAIN 'TOO HASTY'

AN engine driver was "much too hasty" in jumping to the conclusion that a signal was clear for his own line instead of for an adjoining line.

This is the finding of Brigadier C. A. Langley, a Ministry of Transport Inspect-ing Officer, in his report pub-lished to-day by the Stationery Office, on a derailment on the Southern Region of British Railways at Shawford, near Winchester, on July 20.

Responsibility for the acci-dent rested upon the driver, Mr. W. C. Greenough, who, says the Inspector, "frankly admitted his serious mistake."

DIVERTED

The train, from Southampton to Waterloo, had been diverted to the local line to allow a Southampton - Waterloo boat train to overtake it.

Approaching Shawford, where the "up local" line joins the "up through," the train overran the home signal and went through the points at a speed of 20 to25 m.p.h. to run into a sand-drag.

The engine overturned down a 20-ft. embankment and was followed by the tender and the leading coach, both of which remained upright. There were no casualties.

State 'land grab' suspended

THE Central Land Board announce to-day that they do not intend to make any compulsory purchases of land during the period until the decision of Par-liament on the Town and Country Planning Bill, 1952, is known. The Bill proposes to end develop-ment charges and to abolish the board's powers of buying land.

The board was set up in 1948 to carry into effect the provisions of the Town and Country Plan-ning Act of that year, under which an increase in value of land brought about by its development be-came the property of the State. This meant that land prices were fixed at their existing use values, and, because it was thought this might freeze many deals, the board was given the power of compulsory pur-chase.

The first compulsory pur-chase was of land at Orpington, Kent, and this was confirmed by the Planning Minister in June, 1949.

'With this ring'—Then she fled

THE Victoria State Supreme Court decided in Melbourne to-day that a bride who ran off as the wedding ring was being placed upon her finger was legally married.

Her husband had sought a declaration that the marriage ceremony was invalid. Alter-natively, he wanted a divorce on the grounds of desertion. The couple have never lived together.

The court found that desertion was proved and granted him a decree nisi.

"I CAN'T GO ON"

The evidence was that Mr. David Leslie Quick, a tram driver, and Miss Eileen O'Con-nell, a tram conductress, had agreed at the ceremony— which took place at the home of a Church of England minis-ter—to take each other as man and wife.

As Mr. Quick was placing the ring on the bride's finger she suddenly said she could "not go through with it," threw the ring on the floor, and ran off.

The case had been referred to the Supreme Court because of the unusual legal issues in-volved.

British prizewinner

Alain Villiers, British writer and seaman, has been awarded a £200 prize for the best book of the year in English on a Portuguese theme, says a Lis-bon message. He wrote "The Quest of the Argus" after spending a season on board the codfishing schooner Argus.

Incentives to railmen

Cash rewards to railwaymen and other workers for loading and unloading goods trains ahead of the prescribed time are to be offered in an attempt to overcome East Germany's coal crisis.

Mr. St. Laurent, the Canadian Prime Minister, left London by air to-day for home after attending the Commonwealth Economic Con-ference.

How British ship was boarded

CHINESE Nationalist guer-rillas boarded the 700-ton British-registered ship Rosit off the China coast on December 1 after her master had bee killed by gunfire from China junks, the ship's chief offic told the inquest at Hong Kon to-day.

"I thought they were pirates at first," Chief Officer Eric Shakeshaft (29), of Latchford, Warrington, Lancashire, said in evidence.

"Then I saw soldiers in uni form behind a man in civilian clothes. They gave me the im pression of being a well organised body and that there were people with authorit among them. I would say the were Kuomintang guerrillas."

Mr. Shakeshaft said a board ing party came from two junks one of which had opened fire on the Rosita, killing Captain Robert Adam (55) when Shake shaft was on the bridge beside him. The boarding party carrie Sten guns and some automatic pistols.

The Coroner found that Cap-tain Adam had been murdered by a person or persons unknown.

He said that most of the Chinese boarding party wore cap badges of a white sun on blue sky background (the off cial Chinese Nationalist em blem).

Fowl pest cases confirmed

Seventeen further outbreaks of fowl pest were confirmed yesterday, the Ministry of Agri-culture announced to-day.

Four cases were confirmed in the West Riding of Yorkshire, and two cases each in Derby-shire, Lancashire, Lincolnshire, and Norfolk.

Other outbreaks were in Kent, Hertfordshire, Gloucester-shire, Cambridgeshire, and Bed-fordshire. There have now been 130 outbreaks since the begin-ning of the month.

70,000 see "Carmen"

A performance of "Carmen" at the Metropolitan Opera House in New York was seen last night by about 70,000 people — 3,000 in the Opera House itself, and audiences in 31 cinemas watching it on tele-vision screens.

Former Essex bowler

Mr. C. J. Kortright, former Essex fast bowler, died at his home at Brentwood early to-day. He would have been 82 on January 9.

Judge 'uses' cosh: Woman juror gasps

A WOMAN juror at the Old Bailey, to-day, uttered a horrified "Oh" when the Lord Chief Justice, ...his ...dence as a cosh.

Lord Goddard as... cosh, which was ... the case, and ... closely. He ... hand and ...

...examine...

Alfred Osborne who killed his girlfriend's mother and then attacked her, pictured on the front page of the *Derby Evening Telegraph*. See Chapter 22. (Derby Evening Telegraph)

Clod Hall Lane, where Michael Copeland dumped the bodies of William Arthur Elliott and George Gerald Stobbs. See Chapter 23. (Public Record Office)

The body of William Arthur Elliott, lying beside a dry stone wall in Clod Hall Lane. See Chapter 23. (Public Record Office)

(Below: Michael Copeland, who was an early suspect in the murder of William Elliott and who would, years later, be found guilty of that, and two further murders. See Chapter 23.

(Above): William Elliott's damaged bubble car found in Park Road. The lamp post to the right clearly shows flecks of paint from the impact. See Chapter 23. (Public Record Office)

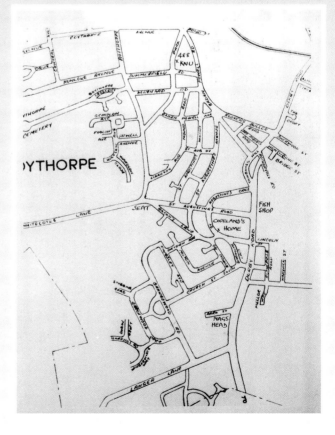

(Right): A map from a contemporary police report on the extensive inquiries into William Elliott's death. At the top of the map, a cross marks the point where the bubble car was found and almost in the centre of the map, a second cross marks Copeland's home. See Chapter 23. (Public Record Office)

The body of George Gerald Stobbs, also found in a ditch in Clod Hall Lane. See Chapter 23. (Public Record Office)

The Morris Oxford, JN 230, belonging to Stobbs and also abandoned in Park Road. See Chapter 23. (Public Record Office)

The *Derby Evening Telegraph* reports that Michael Copeland is sentenced to death. Of course, changes in the law meant that he would not face the ultimate penalty.

The house at 113 Town Street, Pinxton, where Frank Gordon Pockett murdered Frank Bernard Mycroft. See Chapter 24. (Public Record Office)

A rear view of the house at Town Street, showing its' use as a scrapyard. See Chapter 24. (Public Record Office)

The kitchen at Town Street, where Mycroft's body was found. See Chapter 24. (Public Record Office)

The chair to which Frank Mycroft was tied. The string used can be seen quite clearly. See Chapter 24. (Public Record Office)

the car by the driver, raped and left where she lay. Lilian Tharme died from the injuries she received which included marks on her face which could have been caused by someone stamping on her head. Copeland was on leave at the time but it had been impossible to show if he was anywhere near Dorset, and so although he was questioned, he was never charged.

Michael Copeland was released from prison on September 1st, 1961 and immediately the police watch was started again. By now, he had decided that if he was a suspect in three murders, he might as well cash in on that fact. He contacted the *News of the World* and his story appeared on October 1st. Copeland claimed that his involvement in the three murder investigations was purely coincidental and he was not responsible for any of the deaths. He received £20 for his story.

The police presence continued to annoy Copeland and he again turned to crime. On January 18th, 1962, he was found inside Boots Chemists in Market Place, Chesterfield, long after the shop had shut. Copeland appeared at the quarter sessions on April 4th and was sentenced to nine months' imprisonment which he served at Leicester, being released on August 28th. Further offences followed. On July 26th, 1963, he appeared in court at Derby charged with two offences of storebreaking and received two consecutive terms of one month, being released on September 5th. For a time, Copeland then moved to Leeds but soon he was back at Chesterfield and on December 2nd, 1963, was arrested for actual bodily harm and damage to a shop window. For that he was given 18 months, again to be served at Leicester.

However, between being arrested and appearing in court, Copeland had made an astonishing admission. During his various troubles with the police he had come to trust one officer in particular, Chief Inspector Ernest Stephen Bradshaw. On Sunday, November 17th, 1963, Copeland had telephoned Bradshaw at his home and asked to meet him. Although this was at 10.15pm, Bradshaw agreed and met Copeland at the police station at 10.40pm. A conversation then took place at which no other officer was present. Copeland had not been cautioned and the only record of what was said was Chief Inspector Bradshaw's notebook which he wrote up afterwards. According to that notebook, though, Copeland finally confessed that he had killed Elliott, the German boy and Stobbs. At his own request, Copeland was allowed to sleep in the cells that night and the following morning told Bradshaw that what he had said was true, although he refused to repeat it in front of other officers or to make a statement. Since there was no corroboration, the police had no alternative but to release Copeland once more.

On December 12th, by which time Copeland was in prison, Bradshaw saw him again and Copeland remarked, "I am wondering whether I ought to tell you anything else." The two men spoke from 11.35am until 1.10pm and met again that afternoon. Once again Copeland referred to the murder in Verden.

Actually, Copeland had already confessed to all three murders to another officer, Superintendent Thomas Henry Peat, to whom he had spoken in May 1961. On that occasion, too, there was no other officer present and no written statement from the suspect and this was further complicated by the fact that Superintendent Peat had died on April 2nd, 1964.

Shortly before this, on March 25th, 1964, Copeland had been visited at Leicester by a civil servant named William Allen. Copeland appeared to be distressed and said, "I have a lot on my mind and I would like to discuss it with somebody." Allen took Copeland to a private office where Copeland continued, "I have a lot on my mind but if the truth was known, I would be put away for a long time ... The shock of this would kill my father ... I know that I have homicidal tendencies and a hatred of homosexuals ... I was wrong to have judged them myself, they, like me, needed treatment."

The police now considered all the evidence carefully, taking into account what had been said to the late Superintendent Peat and to Chief Inspector Bradshaw, and the other evidence linking Copeland to the crimes, until eventually, on Friday, December 11th, 1964, Copeland was charged with three murders.

Michael Copeland, who had by now announced that he had changed his name to Michael Crowther, although he had not done so legally, made his first appearance before the magistrates at Chesterfield on Tuesday, December 15th. The three charges were put to Copeland separately but he made no reply of any kind. Brief details of the three crimes were then given by Chief Inspector Bradshaw, after which Copeland was remanded to the following Wednesday. At the end of the proceedings, which had lasted just five minutes, Copeland was again asked if he had anything to say and replied, "I would like legal aid and suggest you give some legal aid to the police as well because they will need it."

Copeland was back in court on December 23rd and again on December 30th when a further remand to January 6th, 1965 was made. On that date, the hearing was again very brief and it was stated that the evidence would start to be heard on Monday, January 11th. At this stage, the committal proceedings concerned only the two Derbyshire murders, details of the German crime being held over until the witnesses could be brought over to England. In the event, the witnesses in the Elliott and Stobbs cases took until January 19th to give all their testimony and the Helmbrecht case opened on January 21st and concluded on January 28th by which time Copeland had been committed to the assizes on all three charges.

The trial of Michael Copeland opened at Birmingham on March 16th, 1965, before Mr Justice Ashworth. The proceedings lasted until April 2nd, during which time Copeland was defended by Mr Rudolph Lyons while the case for the Crown lay in the hands of Mr Graham R. Swanwick.

After the long opening speeches, the early witnesses all related to the second murder, that of Guenther Helmbrecht, on November 15th, 1960. One of those witnesses was Hubert Lambert who by now had left the Army and was living in Benfleet, Essex. He recalled his interviews with Copeland who seemed to be fully aware of the fact that if he did not confess, there could not be enough evidence to charge him with the boy's murder. Mr Lambert also reported a conversation with Copeland during which he had referred to the significance of the 11th of the month for him. Copeland said that his first dog had to be put to sleep on the 11th, as did his second and that his mother had also died on the 11th. It did not escape notice that the first murder, that of William Elliott, had taken place on June 11th, but this was hardly proof of Copeland's involvement in that crime.

The trial continued with the witnesses in the other cases giving their testimony. On Thursday, March 25th, the prosecution case was seriously damaged by a letter which was read out in court. This had been received by the Chesterfield police on September 24th, 1963 and contained a torn letter dated that same day. The letter read, "Dear Anne,

I am sorry for not turning up for our last date. I got a bit scared of what you got to know about me. I am very frattened *(sic)* now because I was hoping it was going to be forgotten. I did not want anyone else to get to know about it. It has been hard to keep it quiet so long then all of a sudden start to come to life again. I had to kill it ..." The next part of the letter was torn but later it continued, "His car was the only thing I could use to get away, although I have never drove *(sic)* a bubble car before. Luck got me as far as it did. You will understand why I have stopped seeing you. It was not far to ..." The rest too was indecipherable but for the words "Husband" and "Goodbye for now."

This letter had been sent to the police anonymously and handwriting experts had examined it and confirmed that it could not possibly have been written by Copeland. This suggested, of course, that someone else knew a good deal about the crime and was confessing that he had done it, possibly to an estranged wife named Anne.

An important part of the case against Copeland was his alleged confessions to Superintendent Peat and Chief Inspector Bradshaw. Peat was, of course, dead but Sergeant Trevor Arthur Evans had worked with him and had been present in the police station when Copeland was interviewed.

According to Evans, he was at the Chesterfield police station at 11.00pm on Thursday, May 4th, 1961 and saw Peat, who was then a chief inspector, with Copeland. Peat left the office and Copeland remarked to Evans, "What do you think about this job then?" Sergeant Evans asked Copeland what he was referring to but he did not elaborate. Chief Inspector Peat then returned to the office and Evans left them alone.

At 11.13pm, Evans returned and saw that Peat was still there with Copeland who asked for a cup of tea. Sergeant Evans left to fetch one and when he returned, he heard Copeland say, "How's the murder going Mr Peat?" The chief inspector replied, "What about this theory you told me about on Saturday?" According to what was said next, Copeland had claimed that the crime was the 'vengeance of the killer' and the 'violence of the devil'. He continued, "When the devil rises inside the killer he can't control it. I can't control it. When the devil tells me to use violence I've got to use it."

In an attempt to draw him out, Chief Inspector Peat asked him to tell him more but Copeland said, "I want to talk to you Mr Peat but I can't talk in front of an audience." Taking the hint, Sergeant Evans then left the two men alone together and did not go back into the office until 11.40pm. At that time, Copeland was sitting at the desk with his arms folded in front of him and his head resting on his arms. The floor of the office was littered with loose matches, a book, a tea cup and other debris which had apparently been swept from the desk top. As Evans entered the room, Chief Inspector Peat said, "Do you feel any better for that Michael?" Later Copeland said, "I am glad I met you tonight Mr Peat. Goodness knows what I would have done." He then asked for another cup of tea and again Evans went to fetch it.

When Sergeant Evans walked back into the room, the chief inspector was saying, "You've told me you killed Elliott and Stobbs, Michael, now let's have the rest of the story." Copeland refused to be drawn and at one stage said, "If I make a statement, I will be signing my death warrant."

Although there was further conversation, Copeland said nothing else of significance in front of Sergeant Evans except for the phrase, "I hope you catch him before the next one Mr Peat because the next one will be a mess. I don't think the killer will pick on a middle-aged man next time. I think he will pick on someone about his own build and nearer his own age to prove to the police that he just didn't pick on older men. It might even be a detective." To this, the chief inspector replied, "There mustn't be another one, Mick."

At 2.00am, Copeland was still in the office and demanded to know whether he was going to be arrested or not. Peat said that he didn't know if he could let him go as he had confessed to killing Elliott and Stobbs. At this, Copeland walked over to Sergeant Evans and asked, "Did you hear me say that?" Copeland was later taken home and later that day both Peat and Evans wrote up their pocket books, detailing what they had heard and witnessed.

The other confession had been made to Chief Inspector Bradshaw. He had first interviewed Copeland on September 27th, 1961, when Copeland admitted to him that he had associated with homosexuals but said that he wasn't one himself. He added that he did think he was a psychopath and had a personality which would allow him to commit murder. The next day he was seen again and denied having anything to do with the murders.

The next incident of significance took place on November 17th when Copeland telephoned Bradshaw at home and asked to see him. They met at 10.40pm and the interview lasted until 11.50pm after which Bradshaw wrote up his notes. As soon as the interview began, Copeland admitted that he had killed Elliott and Stobbs. He was cautioned but said that he still wished to tell his story. Copeland continued, "I killed them because it was something I hated. Elliott wanted to suck me." He claimed that this had taken place in Elliott's car at the opposite end of Clod Hall Lane from where the body was found and Copeland had struck him with his fist before finishing him off with a stone from the wall.

At 2.30am, Copeland was seen again but steadfastly refused to make a written statement, but he continued to give details about the murder of Elliott including the fact that his shoes had come off when he pulled him from the vehicle. That night, Copeland slept in the cells, at his own request, and he was seen there at 8.30am on November 18th. Copeland admitted that what he had said the night before was true but again refused to put it in writing.

On December 12th, 1963, Copeland was back at the police station, talking to Bradshaw again. Although the discussion took place with the two men alone, a loudspeaker transmitted the conversation to another room where Detective Sergeant Dowling and Detective Constable Nuttall listened. The interview began at 11.35am when Copeland said that he wanted some advice and added that he wanted to talk about the murders. He then referred to his previous conversation and admitted that it had all been true and said that he had also killed Stobbs and said that in both cases he had gone out looking for a 'homo to rob'.

Copeland said that he had met Elliott in the Markham Road toilets and at the time he had no intention of killing the man. It was only after Elliott had tried to perform oral sex on him that Copeland attacked him. After dumping the body, Copeland claimed that he had driven the bubble car back to his own home and parked it outside, later driving it to the chip shop where the bloodstains he still bore were spotted by Mrs Mitchell. After that he moved the car to Park Road so that it wouldn't be connected to him, and crashed it deliberately.

In his summing up for the defence, Mr Lyons said that his client had been subjected to nothing less than a refined form of torture by the police. He had been hounded, followed and pressurised until he had made some sort of confession when in reality there was little or no hard evidence against him. Copeland himself had been in the witness box for a total of 17 hours and had never once wavered from his claim that he was not guilty of any of the murders he was charged with. The jury were out for nearly three hours and when they finally returned, Copeland had been adjudged to be guilty on all three counts, whereupon he was sentenced to death.

On April 3rd, 1965, Copeland's solicitor, Mr Colin Eagle, announced that an appeal was unlikely. By April 8th, though, Copeland's legal advisors were saying that although they still did not consider there were sufficient grounds for an appeal, Copeland had stated that he wished to enter one and the appropriate forms had been submitted.

The appeal was due to be heard by the Lord Chief Justice, Lord Parker and Justices Sachs and Browne on Monday May 3rd but just two days before this, on May 1st, notice of abandonment was lodged. Copeland had withdrawn his application, preferring instead to rely on a commutation of the death sentence. Just nine days after the appeal was to have been heard, on May 12th, the Home Secretary, Sir Frank Soskice, announced that he had advised Her Majesty to respite the sentence to one of life imprisonment. The game of cat and mouse was over.

Chapter Twenty-Four

Unpaid Work

SIDNEY Chappell simply couldn't understand it. It was 8.40am on Friday, March 19th, 1965, and still Frank Bernard Mycroft, known to all as Barney, wasn't up and about. Chappell had been a friend of Mycroft's for many years and often visited the house at 113 Town Street, Pinxton, from which Mycroft ran his scrap metal business. Indeed, he had been there only the previous evening and when Chappell returned to his own home at 26 Slade Lane, Mycroft was his usual self. Now the curtains were still drawn, the back door was locked and there was no answer to Chappell's urgent knocking. The curtains at one of the windows at the back of the house were slightly open, though, and through them Chappell had seen Mycroft's pyjamas strewn on a chair. This indicated that Mycroft was up and about, but when there was still no reply when he tapped on the window, Chappell thought that Mycroft had gone out for something and decided to call back a little later.

It was 9.00am when Sidney Chappell made his second attempt to rouse Frank Mycroft but again without success. Now he was becoming concerned that there might be something wrong with his friend, who was after all 69 years old. Chappell thought it best to take his worries to Mycroft's nephew, Harry Baggaley.

Harry Baggaley lived at 59 West End, Pinxton, and on March 19th was delivering milk around the town. After speaking to Chappell,

Baggaley said that when he was in Town Street, he would call at his uncle's house and see what was wrong. By the time he arrived it was 10.30am and after talking to a neighbour, Mr Monks, who confirmed that no one had seen Frank Mycroft all morning, Baggaley decided that he would have to break into the house, so he went to the rear of the premises, forced open the middle window and climbed inside.

It was when Harry Baggaley entered the front room that he saw why his uncle had failed to answer when Sidney Chappell had knocked. Mycroft was lying on the floor in a pool of blood with one of his wrists still tied to a chair. Quickly Baggaley opened the front door to admit Mr Monks who cut the string with a knife before rushing to fetch Dr Johnston. By the time Sidney Chappell returned a few minutes later, the front door was wide open and Dr Johnston was attending to the badly injured man who had to be rushed to Mansfield General Hospital, but so severe were his injuries that he was transferred that same day to the Derbyshire Royal Infirmary.

Frank Mycroft was found to be suffering from a compound depressed fracture of the left side of the head and at the infirmary, Dr Reginald Harry Shephard performed an emergency operation to remove some of the fragments of bone from the brain. He also observed signs of damage to the brain itself and the fact that a blood clot had formed. Meanwhile, the police were trying to determine who was responsible for this vicious attack.

Sidney Chappell told the police of his visit to Mycroft on March 18th. He left the premises at 5.45pm and at that time there was a young man there. Chappell didn't know the man's name but did say that he had been a frequent visitor and had even been known to stay at the house for two or three days at a time.

This young man had also been seen by Sarah Hilda Marriott, a woman who had known Mycroft ever since they were both children. Sarah was in the habit of collecting Mycroft's pension for him and on March 18th, she had gone to the house in Town Street and handed Mycroft two one-pound notes, two ten-shilling notes and three half-crowns, a total of £3 7s 6d. As she watched, Mycroft took a large roll of banknotes out of his pocket and added the four notes to it. Sarah estimated that there might have been as much as £200 in that roll and since it was now missing, the motive for the attack seemed to be obvious. Sarah, though, was also able to tell the investigating officers that during the half hour or so she spent at 113 Town Street, there was a young man there, sitting on a motor scooter.

This same young man was also seen by a number of other witnesses and they were able to finally put a name to him. Leslie Abbott lived at Pye Bridge but had done business with Frank Mycroft for many years. At 6.30pm on Thursday, March 18th, Abbott had driven his van into Mycroft's yard. About half an hour later, Derek Wright, who lived nearby at 104 Town Street, drove his lorry into Mycroft's yard. Wright had an arrangement whereby he was allowed to park the vehicle in the yard and he recalled Leslie Abbott being there at the time. Both men left within minutes of each other, at around 7.00pm, and both saw a young man who had been there many times before. This man was 27-year-old Frank Gordon Pockett, who remained behind when Abbott and Wright left.

Roger Atherton of 6 Arthur Street, Pinxton, was another visitor to the yard on the evening of Thursday, March 18th. He had known Mycroft for many years and sometimes did odd jobs for him. It was 7.30pm when he arrived at the yard and although he only stayed for three or four minutes, he saw Pockett there. All these three men said that it was common knowledge that Mycroft kept a roll of banknotes, usually inside a small bag, and that Pockett would also have known about them. It became vital for the police to talk to Pockett, especially when they discovered that he was an escaped prisoner.

Frank Gordon Pockett had been born in Castleford on June 29th, 1937. Leaving school at 15, he had gone into the mines until he joined the armed forces on August 7th, 1955. Serving for three years he had been released into the reserves on August 7th, 1958 and less than a year later, on July 11th, 1959, had married. Taking various jobs around the Castleford area, Pockett and his wife moved to Leeds in 1963 and it was soon after that he began to get into trouble with the police. On July 31st, 1963, he was summonsed on two charges of obtaining £10 by virtue of a forged instrument and two others of obtaining £10 by false pretences. Pockett failed to appear in court to answer those charges and travelled to France under a false name.

Returning to England shortly afterwards, Pockett was dealt with for those offences on November 20th and fined £40, plus costs and compensation, a total of £63 4s 6d, or three months' imprisonment in default. There then followed another period during which he did various jobs in Hull and Grimsby before, on October 1st, 1964, he was arrested again for not paying the fines and costs imposed on him earlier. Pockett was sent to prison for three months but had escaped on October 21st. It was known that he had returned to his parents' home, briefly, in December 1964, but since then, his whereabouts had not been known.

Initial police investigations revealed other witnesses who could give details of Pockett's movements after he had last been seen at Mycroft's house. Maggie Ward worked part-time at the Greyhound Inn and knew Pockett as a regular there since the beginning of 1965. She said that he had come into the bar at around 7.40pm on March 18th and after having one drink, left at 8.00pm.

The next sighting was made by William James Palfreeman who lived at 36 Portland Road, Selston in Nottinghamshire. Palfreeman was visiting his mother at 35 King Street, Pinxton, on March 18th and left her house at 8.35pm to catch the 8.45pm bus back home. As he stood at the corner of Slade Lane and Victoria Street, a man he had since identified as Pockett came up, rather breathlessly and asked, "Is there a C2 due?" Palfreeman said that there was one due at 9.05pm and at that moment, his bus appeared from around the corner. Pockett had then asked him where this bus went to and when Palfreeman told him that it was Nottingham, Pockett had retorted, "That's better than ever because I want to get to Grantham tonight." Palfreeman saw Pockett go upstairs on the bus and noticed that he was carrying a bag which was tied up with string, and wore a leather cap. Pockett was smoking a cigarette at the time and Palfreeman thought he was puffing at it in a rather nervous fashion.

Two other people saw Pockett on that bus. Raymond Mayfield was the conductor and he told the police that he recalled picking up four people at Victoria Road in Pinxton. He was unable to state positively that Pockett was one of them, but did recall the rather distinctive leather cap which Palfreeman had said Pockett was wearing. At the Underwood garage, just after 9.00pm, Mayfield was relieved by another conductor, Neil Henderson. He could not identify Pockett either but did recall a man with a shiny black leather cap getting off at Bentinck Road in Nottingham.

A description of Pockett was now circulated: "Five feet eight or nine inches tall, slim build, fair hair going bald at the front, thin faced, pale complexion and is believed to be wearing an olive green coloured combat jacket, a leather cap with peak and ear flaps, and possibly grey flannel trousers."

On a previous occasion, Pockett had fled to France and it was reasonable to assume that he might do the same again. Officers at the southern ports were told to keep a particular watch for a man fitting Pockett's description and it was this, on Wednesday March 24th, which led to him being arrested at Dover on leaving a ship which had just docked from Belgium. The next day he appeared at the magistrate's court at Alfreton where he faced a charge of robbery with violence. In reply to the charge, Pockett had said that he 'got worked up and hit him in the head with the little hammer'. Evidence of arrest having been given, he was then remanded to Monday, March 29th.

Back in the hospital, Frank Mycroft had not responded to treatment. After his operation he had developed pneumonia and it was this which claimed his life at 9.30am on March 26th. As a result, Pockett was seen by Detective Inspector G.W. Stephen who told him that he would now be charged with murder. Pockett replied, "Oh Christ!" He subsequently appeared in court that same afternoon, when he was remanded to April 3rd.

By April 3rd, Pockett had obtained legal representation and his solicitor, Mr Wesley Sumner, made no objection to a further remand to April 9th. Two days before this date, on April 7th, the inquest on Frank Mycroft opened at Derby before the assistant deputy coroner, Mr A.J. Moors. Once identification details had been given by Howard Bernard Mycroft, the dead man's son, and Dr Alan Usher, the pathologist, had confirmed that the cause of death had been hypostatic pneumonia, due to the head injuries, the inquest was adjourned sine die.

Other magistrate court appearances followed on April 9th, April 17th, April 25th, May 2nd and May 7th when the committal proceedings finally opened. During these hearings it emerged that Pockett's father was a good friend of Mycroft and had introduced his son to the victim. The case for the Director of Public Prosecutions was given by Mr Dorian Williams and Pockett was now represented by a barrister, Mr T.T. Dineen. There were a total of 27 prosecution witnesses, meaning that the hearing lasted all day before Pockett was sent for trial.

Since Pockett had been charged with murder and this crime had been committed in the furtherance of theft, the charge was a capital one. This meant that when Frank Pockett appeared before Mr Justice Paull, at Birmingham, on June 28th 1965, he was on trial for his life. Throughout the two-day hearing, Pockett was defended by Mr Dennis Cowley and Mr Dineen while the prosecution case was led by Mr Graham R. Swanwick who was assisted by Mr J.F. Kingham.

As the trial opened, Pockett began by pleading not guilty to murder, but on the second day he changed this to one of guilty to murder but not guilty of murder in the furtherance of theft, which was the capital crime. The prosecution now not only had to show that Pockett had taken Mycroft's life, but that he had also killed him with the intention of stealing money from him.

Details of the events leading up the Pockett's arrest were then given. After arriving in Nottingham, Pockett sought to go on to London and boarded a train for that reason. The train was not a direct one, though, and Pockett had to change at Leicester where he had a three-hour wait for his connection. At one stage he was at a coffee stall there and upon leaving, was seen to thrown something away. Police had later recovered a small bag identical to the one in which Mycroft was known to keep his money.

Arriving in London, Pockett had deposited various articles at the left luggage office at King's Cross station. After he had been arrested at Dover, Detective Constable John Arthur Herrett had travelled down from Pinxton and informed Pockett that he was being taken back to Alfreton. On the way, they paused in London where Pockett was left at the Caledonian Road police station while Constable Herrett went to King's Cross and retrieved the deposited items. These included a duffel bag, a rubber torch, a knife in a sheath and a plastic cap which looked like leather and fitted the description of the one Pockett had been wearing on the Nottingham-bound bus.

Continuing the details of Pockett's initial flight it was shown that in London he had obtained a visitor's passport, in a false name, and then taken a plane to Ostend. Eventually, though, he reported to the Consul and said that he had no money left. He was given passage back to

England on a ship leaving Ostend and was arrested at Dover as he arrived.

When he was interviewed at Alfreton, Pockett had asked, "How is old Barney?" He was told that the injuries were serious and replied, "Look here, can I tell you all about it? It's the only way," whereupon he made a full statement which began, "I worked hard there and never got any money. You know I am on the run from prison and not having any money preyed on me and I got worked up.

"I hit him on the head with that little hammer while he was sitting in the chair. I don't know how much money was supposed to be missing. I was told he had £2,000 in the house but all I got was £56 from his pocket. It was a lousy trick."

Later still, Pockett made a written statement in which he said, "While we were reading I started thinking about the work he said we were going to do next day and about what I had already done and never been paid for.

"I felt really mad inside at him looking so smug in the chair. I knew he had a lot of money in the bank and presumed he had some in the house. Previously he had told me that he had about £100 in the house.

"Something seemed to snap inside my head. I was just mad about it and I picked up the hammer, spun round and hit Barney with it, right on top of the head. He slumped further down in the chair. He looked round and said 'What's up?' sloppy like. His face was brick red, like a child just starting to cry. I said, 'You,' and hit him again. He then slumped right over. I put my hand in his waistcoat and pulled out a green cord money bag." The statement continued to describe the escape to Nottingham and the admission that in London he bought some new clothes for himself, leaving the old ones in the left luggage. He paid £33 for his ticket to Ostend, where he had stayed at the Hotel Moderne, but by the Tuesday the money had all gone and he was forced to go to the British Consul.

The concluding part of the trial was taken up with the medical evidence. Dr Usher was a Home Office pathologist and a lecturer in forensic science at the University of Sheffield. He had performed the post-mortem on Mycroft and said that he found two curved wounds on the head. The larger of these ran from the left temporal region, from two inches behind the eye for some eight inches to a point close to the crown of the head, causing fractures and much bruising of the brain. There was no evidence of defence wounds, suggesting that the attack was sudden and unexpected.

Jack Lawrence Fish was the principle scientific officer at the East Midlands Forensic Science laboratory at Nottingham and he had visited the scene of the crime on March 19th. He observed a large pool of blood on the kitchen floor and smears of blood on the walls. On the back of the armchair was a bloodstained cap, a navy blue donkey jacket and a khaki overcoat. The left arm of the chair still had a piece of white nylon cord attached to it. Ten days later, Dr Fish received a hammer from Constable Hobster. There was a small stain on the head of this hammer, which proved to be human blood. The two wounds on the victim's head could have been caused by a violent assault with the curved end of this same hammer.

In his summing up, Mr Swanwick suggested that Pockett had attacked Mycroft with the intention of stealing from him and, since Mycroft had died from the injuries he had received, this was murder and murder in the furtherance of theft. For the defence, Mr Cowley suggested that taking the money had come as an afterthought after Mycroft had been attacked in anger. Referring to the tying up of his victim after the attack, Mr Cowley said that this was surely not a cold-blooded act but simply one of self-preservation. Pockett had not believed Mycroft to be badly injured and had tied him merely to prevent him raising the alarm before he could get away.

The jury took 45 minutes to decide that Pockett was guilty of capital murder and the prisoner was then sentenced to death. An appeal was heard on Monday, July 19th, before the Lord Chief Justice, Lord Parker, and Justices Ashworth and Waller. Here it was admitted by the defence that there was no doubt that Pockett had killed Mycroft but it was not a murder in the furtherance of theft. The theft had been incidental to the crime and had taken place afterwards but giving the court's verdict, Lord Parker said that there was no way that the judge's summing up could be criticised and there was ample evidence to support the verdict as it stood. The last executions in England had taken place on August 13th, 1964 when Peter Anthony Allen and Gwynne Owen Evans were hanged for a murder at Workington. Capital punishment was under much discussion and in November 1965, the death penalty would be abolished for a trial period of five years. While all these debates were continuing, all death sentences were commuted as a matter of course and it was never seriously thought that Pockett would face the ultimate sanction of the law. It came as no real surprise, then, when on July 30th Frank Gordon Pockett received notification that his sentence had been respited to one of penal servitude for life.

Appendix

There have been just four executions at Derby this century, and all four stories are covered in the main body of this book. A list of all the executions at Derby since 1868, when public executions ceased, is as follows:-

Benjamin Hudson, 4th August, 1873
John Wakefield, 16th August, 1880
Albert Robinson, 28th March, 1881
Alfred Gough, 21st November, 1881
Arthur Thomas Delaney, 10th August, 1888
George Horton, 21st August, 1889
William Pugh, 5th August, 1896
John Cotton, 4th December, 1898
John Bedford, 30th July, 1902
John Silk, 29th December, 1905
Walter Marsh, 27th December, 1906
William Edward Slack, 16th July, 1907

The following executions have taken place at Leicester prison this century:-

Thomas Porter and Thomas Preston, 21st July, 1903
William Henry Palmer, 19th July, 1911
Arnold Warren, 12th November, 1914
Thomas William Thorpe, 23rd December, 1941
William Alfred Cowle, 8th August, 1944
William Frederick George Meffen, 8th August, 1944
John Christopher Reynolds, 17th November, 1953

Finally, there were eight executions at Bagthorpe jail, Nottingham:-

John Hutchinson, 29th March, 1905
Edward Glynn, 7th August, 1906
Samuel Atherley, 14th December, 1909
Percy James Atkin, 7th April, 1922
Albert Edward Burrows, 6th August, 1923
Arthur Simms, 17th December, 1924
William Knighton, 27th April, 1927
George Frederick Walter Hayward, 10th April, 1928

Bibliography

Newspapers
Ashbourne News and Dove Valley Record
Ashbourne News Telegraph
Belper News
Buxton Advertiser and Herald
Buxton Advertiser and Weekly List of Visitors
Derby Daily Telegraph
Derby Daily Telegraph and Derby Daily Express
Derby Evening Telegraph and Derby Daily Express
Derby Evening Telegraph
Derbyshire Times
Derbyshire Times and Chesterfield Herald
Glossop Chronicle and Advertiser
Glossop Chronicle, North Derbyshire and North Cheshire Reporter
Glossopdale Chronicle and North Derbyshire Reporter
Matlock Mercury
The Times

Assizes Documents
ASSI 13 31 Hobbs and Harrison
ASSI 13 32 Bedford
ASSI 13 33 Redfern
ASSI 13 35 Silk
ASSI 13 36 Smith and Marsh
ASSI 13 37 Slack
ASSI 13 42 Mowbray
ASSI 13 52 Atkin
ASSI 13 53 Burrows
ASSI 13 57 Knighton
ASSI 13 58 Hayward

ASSI 52 440 Rowland
ASSI 13 66 Batty
ASSI 13 67 Smedley and Brunt
ASSI 13 70 Myatt
ASSI 13 71 Prince
ASSI 13 230 Eaton
ASSI 13 264 Osborne
ASSI 13 707 Copeland
ASSI 13 721 Pockett

Index